D0935027

Tales from
the 1980
Louisville
Cardinals

JIM TERHUNE

www.SportsPublishingLLC.com

ISBN: 1-58261-658-2

Publishers: Peter L. Bannon and Joseph J. Bannon Sr.
Senior managing editor: Susan M. Moyer
Acquisitions editor: Mike Pearson
Developmental editor: Doug Hoepker
Dust jacket/photo spread design, imaging: Dustin Hubbart
Project manager: Greg Hickman
Copy editor: Cynthia L. McNew
Photo editor: Erin Linden-Levy
Vice president of sales and marketing: Kevin King
Media and promotions managers: Monica Heckman (regional),
Randy Fouts (national), Maurey Williamson (print)

Printed in the United States of America

Sports Publishing L.L.C.
804 North Neil Street
Champaign, IL 61820

Phone: 1-877-424-2665
Fax: 217-363-2073
Web site: www.SportsPublishingLLC.com

To the players, coaches and support troops of the 1979-80 Louisville Cardinals, who made a six-month portion of my life a joy to behold.

To Kara and Krista, a couple of daughters who, at ages 13 and 8, did their share of fawning over tall men in short pants, and who made the last four decades of my life a joy to behold in even more wondrous ways.

To South Bend Tribune *sports editor emeritus Joe Doyle, who taught me the difference between "since" and "because," that "win" should never be used as a noun and a few thousand other things.*

And to Lou Younkin, sports director of the late, lamented Louisville Times, *who filled the 6 a.m. desk jockey duties and creative writing challenges with enough balanced helpings of goofiness, seriousness and skill that we could relax, have fun and hopefully make ourselves better reporters and writers.*

Contents

Foreword vi
Preface viii
Acknowledgments ix
Introduction xi

CHAPTER ONE
The Personnel *1*

CHAPTER TWO
Striking the Match *9*

CHAPTER THREE
Lighting the Fire *18*

CHAPTER FOUR
The Season Begins *34*

CHAPTER FIVE
Spark-less in Hawaii *45*

CHAPTER SIX
Stirring the Embers and Fanning the Flames *59*

CHAPTER SEVEN
Scattering Demons and Fanning More Flames *76*

CHAPTER EIGHT
A Fat-Cat Infestation, Quickly Treated *92*

CHAPTER NINE
Mates Flame Up to Sustain Their Smoldering Leader *107*

CHAPTER TEN
The Ville Really Is in the Nap, and It's Wide Awake *137*

CHAPTER ELEVEN
The Aftermath *168*

CHAPTER TWELVE
The Season in 3-D *191*

CHAPTER THIRTEEN
Where and Who Are They Now *204*

CHAPTER FOURTEEN
The 1979-80 Louisville Cardinals' Season *217*

Epilogue ....*.233*

Foreword

Any coach can look back at a season and accurately analyze why that year was successful or not. After a highly successful season, he would probably mention factors such as senior leadership, especially at the guard position. Depth is also usually a contributing factor, including an inspirational sixth man. Strong post play, consistent defense, and fierce rebounding are all essential for a good season.

There are also factors beyond a coach's control. Sometimes it's a pivotal win or loss that coalesces the team and drives it to overachieve. And of course there's always luck, because every team has its share of good and bad bounces, even if we play with a round ball.

While hindsight is always 20/20, a coach never knows for sure what a season holds in store. Certainly, as I prepared for the Cardinals' 1979-80 campaign, I had every reason to be optimistic, but almost as many reasons to be nervous. Darrell Griffith resisted the temptation to turn pro, and with Griff and fellow senior guard Tony Branch—as well as Scooter McCray, Derek Smith, Wiley Brown, Roger Burkman, and Scooter's promising younger brother Rodney as a freshman—we had the talent on paper to be successful.

As I mentioned, however, luck can turn in an instant. Only three games into the '79-80 season, Scooter McCray injured his knee and was lost for the year. That put added pressure on a lot of young frontline players, especially the rookie, Rodney.

Early in the season our play was spotty. We got an impressive win over Ohio State, but then stumbled twice in December. We were inspired at times, but we were inconsistent as we piled up a lot of wins over a schedule that was not as difficult as many we had played. As talented as Darrell Griffith was, he had never been in the position of having to take over games, and while he sometimes did, he also failed to fire on several occasions.

Late in the season we reached one of those watershed moments, when a team can go one way or the other. Jim Valvano's Iona team, behind a dominant performance by their center Jeff Ruland, just flatout embarrassed us on national television. And that's when the true championship character of that Cardinal squad really showed itself. Pride became the great motivator, which is a situation every coach dreams of.

My job for the rest of the year became pretty easy. All the players not only understood their roles, they relished them. From Griff to Rodney to the mercurial Poncho Wright, from Tony Branch's quiet leadership to Derek Smith's and Wiley Brown's joint commitment to success and comedy, we were truly a team in every respect.

Still, there were those lucky bounces that could have gone the wrong way. Obviously, two overtime wins in the tournament against Kansas State and Texas A&M could have gone either way. And then against UCLA there was the hustle play by Jerry Eaves that distracted Kiki Vandeweghe just enough to miss a wide-open layup and give us a chance to come back in the championship game.

No, it wasn't until Rodney hit that last free throw that I was confident we would win U of L's first national championship. Then again, I never counted us out, either.

I have never identified one of my 30 Cardinal teams as my favorite, but if you asked me to pick the most interesting story, I would point to the 1980 national champions and say, "This is it!" I'm glad Jim Terhune wanted to tell it.

—Denny Crum

Preface

The thought of writing again—anything at all—was as abhorrent four years into retirement as it was the day I walked away from journalism. Thirty-five years of never being able to basically satisfy myself on my choice of words, choice of sentences, structure of paragraphs and sometimes approach to subject matter will do that to a person.

So when this project was proposed to me in the late summer of 2002, my gut reaction was, "Don't think so." A daughter and I had just returned from running a portion of the Colorado River in the Grand Canyon in paddle boats, which further triggered the desire to experience hundreds of other places, and I didn't see the need to rediscover frustration and aggravation.

Except that there wasn't nearly as much stress in 1979-80 as there had been before or would be after.

One reason was that money from the sports operations of Louisville's two newspapers was made available to allow each beat writer to travel to practically all road games instead of making them alternate trips as had been the rule in the past.

Another was access. The press conference formality and "us vs. them" journalist-athlete mentality was on the verge of taking over, but not in the 1970s. Then you stayed in the same hotels, rode on the same planes and in the same buses, vans and rental cars and leaned against a wall in a locker room or hallway to have a conversation with someone, not sit before a podium for a ritualistic interview.

At least that's how it was at the University of Louisville. And as much as you might come to connect with many of the personalities, it didn't seem to be hard to maintain objectivity when it came to trying to bring the season to life on newsprint.

It was a time of warmth and respect for the people who played the game, more so than how they played the game. Of course, it turned out that they played it pretty well, and the combination made it the best year in the business for me.

It led to a commitment to another hunt for decent nouns and adjectives, but hopefully not to a commitment to a funny farm down the road.

Acknowledgments

To those who were kind enough to give up the time and make the effort to allow me to revisit the season with them:

Coaches: Denny Crum, Wade Houston, Jerry Jones, Bill Olsen.

Players: Tony Branch, Wiley Brown, Roger Burkman, Steve Clark, Daryl Cleveland, Greg Deuser, Jerry Eaves, Darrell Griffith, Rodney McCray, Scooter McCray, Marty Pulliam, Poncho Wright and a special thank you to Monica Smith.

Former player: Bobby Turner.

Support team: Don Belcher, Steve Bing, Randy Bufford, John Crawley, Steve Donohue, Norbert "Knobby" Elbert, Rob Hickerson, Tim Hynes, Betty Jackson, Jack Lengyel, Jerry May, Robert "Bosey" Thrasher, Kathy Tronzo, Debbie Young, Joe Yates.

Opposing coaches: Dale Brown, Larry Brown, Lute Olson.

Opposing players: Kenny Arnold, Rolando Blackman, Bob Hansen, Clark Kellogg, Ronnie Lester, Durand "Rudy" Macklin, Jeff Ruland, Jeff Schneider, Willie Sims, Kiki Vandeweghe.

An additional thumbs up to current Louisville sports information director Kenny Klein and to Tronzo, Louisville's sports information administration/program honcho who went out of her way to search out magazines, yearbooks and regular books involving the '79-80 Cardinals, besides taking my intermittent phone calls and answering more questions.

Also to Crawley, the assistant SID from that era, who on his own loaned me his book of clippings from that season that enhanced certain items and originated others. And to Gary Tuell, author of the definitive book on U of L basketball histroy.

Also a hearty "thank you" to the intrepid reporters and columnists from the Louisville papers who were along for large to medium portions of the journey, and from whom I reached into their work after they had left the building and pirated some quotes and anecdotes:

Most especially the labor and skill of the late Mike Sullivan, my main adversary with the *Courier-Journal*, plus *Times* sports columnist Dick Fenlon, *CJ* sports columnists Billy Reed and Earl Cox, *Times* news columnist Bob Hill, *Times* sports director Lou Younkin, *CJ* sports writer Russ Brown, *CJ* news columnist John Filiatreau and a few others.

Then there is the deep bow that must go to Doug Hoepker, the developmental editor at Sports Publishing who was sent on a forced march through the entire manuscript. Another bow to the photo suppliers: Host Communications, for permission to recreate art from a book it published shortly after the championship; U of L's sports information photo library and archives; Bill Straus; and the Associated Press.

Introduction

For 100 years, Louisville had two newspapers, *The Courier-Journal* and *The Louisville Times*, owned from 1918 on by the Bingham family.

While the papers were serviced by separate staffs, the sports department couldn't clearly define itself. It also had two staffs, but they came together for one Sunday edition. Each of the major beats—Louisville, Kentucky and Indiana college sports, Kentucky and Indiana high schools, horse racing—had a writer assigned to them by each paper's sports director. But to save money, reporters alternated on road trips, one writing stories for each publication every day out of town and usually not traveling at the same time as the team.

That changed drastically in 1979. For the first time, the *Courier* and the *Times* split into completely separate sports operations, with the *Times* being eliminated from the Sunday offering. If either paper wanted a staff-written story on the football-basketball exploits of one of its colleges, it had to send its guy.

I was the beat writer for the *Times*, the afternoon publication, the late Mike Sullivan for the morning paper, the *Courier*. I missed one game. Sully missed three, being denied the Hawaii trip because the games wouldn't end until after the *Courier*'s deadline (it took Mike months to get over that).

At the same time, both of us quickly found out just how welcoming University of Louisville basketball coach Denny Crum was and how accessible he allowed his program to be, surpassing probably 80 to 90 percent of the top of the line Division I operations.

And, again at the same time, a bunch of guys began to reveal themselves as one of the most stimulating, goofy, determined, expressive, classy teams a reporter could ever hope to stumble upon.

Mostly for convenience, Sully and I booked onto the same flights as the Cardinals. Because of Crum's beneficence, we stole rides in their vans, rental cars and buses, whether they broke down or not. We stayed in the same hotels, hung out in their rooms as they would sometimes hang out in ours and generally blended into the scene for over six months.

It was a wonderful opportunity to attempt to do what I always believed was my mission, to bring a team to life through words. But there's a lot of pressure to the writing-well aspect of that, and a lot of work.

And there is a thin wire a reporter must constantly walk. I was employed by a newspaper, not a college. I couldn't afford to care whether a team won or lost games, because then emotions destroy objectivity.

If I was rooting for anyone, it was for me to beat the other beat writer in the writing, reporting, and scooping phases of the job. Because the other beat guy was Sully, it was a formidable (and often failing) task.

Yet it seemed like it was okay to take the handcuffs off whatever feelings began to surface about the quality of the people I was covering. Maybe that was wrong, too. But as the season progressed I realized that these guys were on the higher rungs of the human ladder.

I can't give someone a higher compliment than to call them a human being. It's such a hard thing to achieve every day. That, however, was what I discovered inside the 1979-80 Cardinals.

Sully and I ambled in, around and through the journey. I was a foot away from Derek Smith when Daryl Cleveland coerced him into dipping his head into the Pacific Ocean's salt water, which was followed by a panic attack. Sully spent a day watching Smith in class and speaking to kids.

When the two inky wretches performed our heavy-breathing jogging ritual before road practices, the players jeered and assistant Jerry Jones named us "Hustle" and "Muscle." Thankfully, we never knew who was which or what the coach's definition of those aliases really was.

It was a shame the fans, who had wrapped their arms around this team so tightly they turned Freedom Hall into a throbbing sound machine, couldn't get more up close and personal with the Cardinals. They deserved to.

They knew Darrell Griffith as a high-rise who could leave the floor on an angle and straighten himself out in mid-air.

I saw his extraordinary patience with a dozen different tape-recorded interviews at Madison Square Garden and at every NCAA Tournament stop. I sat next to him as the bus pulled away from Utah's arena and saw how upset he was, mumbling a choice word or two as he glanced at the flashing "U" on a hill signaling victory and U of L's first loss.

I remember him laughing and yelling, arms outstretched, in the front position of a Hawaiian canoe crashing through the waves off Waikiki, as usual leading his band of merry young'uns but at once being one of them.

I felt a hand on my shoulder and heard Griff's voice say he was going to get my dilapidated self into a three-piece suit, and me saying I'd wait a couple of months until he could buy me one. I was sitting on a load of lumber for a backyard project, riding down a busy street in the back of a pickup truck in the late '80s, when I heard someone in a car say, "Hune-y?" It was Griff. Big smile. Big sideways shake of the head.

And I remember the hug he gave me as we ended the interview for this project, having spent nearly two hours when I probably could have used two days.

Fans saw a rebounding acrobat with monstrous hands in Derek Smith. I saw an 18-year-old who shook my hand whenever I entered the gym, whose non-stop mouth couldn't be muted with a pile of towels and the light that glowed from his eyes when assistant coach Bill Olsen's young son, David, walked up to him, palms up for a hand-slap, and plaintively muttered, "Deh-wick?"

Fans knew Wiley Brown as the fake-thumbed hard-banging power forward who was always hurting a body part. I knew him as a kid who liked to wear his Metro Conference cap sideways, who called me "Ta-hoon," who blocked my unstoppable hook shot with a grin and without leaving his feet, who sat on me once on a bus because it seemed like the thing to do and who threatened to do much more bodily harm to the geezer because that also seemed like the thing to do.

Wiley and I sat for an hour and a half in a new locker room in a new building in 2003 and laughed at the old lunacy until tears nearly came—and until tears nearly came at the thought of Derek not being able to make it a threesome.

By the time Louisville reached Houston and the NCAA Midwest Regional proper, I had been asked to make predictions by the *Times* managing editor. I chose top-seed Louisiana State. Sully and I by now were firmly entrenched in the team operations, so I instantly became Benedict Hune.

Rodney McCray and Roger Burkman were really angry, felt betrayed, and Burkman told me to take the knife out of his back. They wouldn't answer questions for the first day and a half, and after U of L's second-half blitz of LSU in an 86-66 rout I found myself hoisted into the showers.

In succeeding years Burkman and I had a couple of semi-heated debates about the ethics of newspapering and beat coverage, neither of us making much of a dent. But when I started on this book, Burkman, the guru of reunion organizing, was one of the first calls I made. I left a message with my intentions. Twenty minutes later the phone rang. The first words I heard were, "What, you want to take another shower?"

My daughters, 13-year-old Kara and nine-year-old Krista, wrote a good-luck letter to Greg Deuser before the 1980 Final Four. I passed it along and showed him pictures. "Your daughters are cute," he said. "What happened?"

Before the championship game, Steve Clark asked who *Times* columnist Dick Fenlon and I were picking. I told him that after much deep thought we came up with Louisville by maybe seven.

"You really picked us?" asked Burkman, listening in. "Well, well."

"You picked us?" asked assistant coach Bill Olsen, also listening in. "Oh, no."

When the big one was over and I was busy hunting interviews, a figure moved slowly toward me. It was Rodney McCray. I could count on maybe two hands the number of times I'd seen him smile all season. He had that menacing glare working as usual.

I figured this would be his ultimate revenge, that he had something especially painful or sharply critical in mind. Instead, he stuck out his hand. He sort of nearly smiled. "Believe in us now, Terhune?" he asked.

I did. And I do.

CHAPTER ONE

The Personnel:

Where It Came From, How It Got Here

A Uniformity in Diversity

Denny Crum's recruiting goals were similar every year:

Find a guy between six feet four and six feet eight, with a vertical jump of 30 inches or higher, with speed and quickness within shouting distance of world-class sprinter range, who can play four or five positions on a basketball floor.

Crum's early teams quickly became notable for their big and interchangeable backcourts, none more prototypical and efficient than the 1972-75 combo of 6-5 Junior Bridgeman (guard on offense, forward on defense) and 6-5 Allen Murphy (guard on defense, wingman on offense).

So it was, generally, in 1979-80. Ten of the 13 players landed within the height boundaries, all but a couple qualified in the leaping category, three-fourths (including six-foot guards Tony Branch and Greg Deuser) brought end-to-end speed or the "quicks" (the latter perhaps a more valuable asset) to the club and eight could be considered multiple position guys.

When Scooter McCray suffered a blown knee in the third game of the season, Louisville lost a forward who had been a center who could back out to midcourt and run delay games because he was a remarkable passer. Wiley Brown, perhaps the squad's fastest straight-ahead runner, moved from center to power forward. Rodney McCray, at 6-7, took over the middle but would be a small forward during his 10-year NBA career. Forward Derek Smith, the leading rebounder at 6-6, was a shooting guard in the pros. Darrell Griffith (6-4) and Poncho Wright (6-6) could get shots off no matter how big the traffic jam in the lane. Point guard Jerry Eaves (6-4) supplied spurts of offense and ball-handling without many flaws. Roger Burkman (6-5) was a guard who drove men of all sizes bonkers with his defense.

Crum licked his lips and delightfully squeezed his rolled-up program at the rich variety of choices. No big man. No worries.

"Not having a seven-foot center was probably the best thing to happen to us," Burkman said. "He would have slowed us down."

Yet this uniformity of skills was all but equaled by the diversity of geography.

Daryl Cleveland, Derek Smith and Wiley Brown were rural Georgians from, respectively, Thomasville, Hogansville and Sylvester.

Four represented the entire jump-shooting length of Indiana – Branch from the northern border town of Michigan City, Burkman and Wright from the mid-state capitol of Indianapolis and Deuser from the southern river borough of New Albany.

The McCray brothers brought deep-voiced swagger from the biggest of cities—New York.

Two, Griffith and Eaves, were the local reps, solemnly carrying exorbitant expectations and added pressure from fans who had watched them perform for years. Another, Steve Clark, was from Louisville, too, but he had been allowed to join the team without a scholarship and wasn't shouldering the burdens of his fellow hometowners.

And, near the bottom in playing time but near the top in popularity and pranks was 6-9 Marty Pulliam of Harrodsburg, representing rural Kentucky.

There was also a diversity of personality. One day Smith said he was from Jupiter, the next from Gilligan's Island.

"Wiley and Derek had such southern drawls," Burkman said. "Derek would ask for an 'ernge.' I'd say, 'What the heck is an ernge?' He wanted an orange."

Griffith and Branch were the only seniors. Four starters and one key reserve were sophomores or a freshman. Smith was 16 years old the first three months he was in college. Yet this diversity of locales and traits and ages melted into a uniformity of values.

"Wiley and I were like kids in a candy store, trying to outdo each other in craziness," Smith said in 1990. "Rod had his New York 'yo' talk. But there was no backstabbing, finger-pointing and putting each other down."

The laughter and warmth poured out of Griffith as he thought back. "Derek and Wiley were so funny," he said. "…We had a great time. Nothing came close to the bonding. The college experience was the ultimate."

"I know we came from different backgrounds, some a little more challenged economically, but as far as the way people treated each other, everybody was pretty much the same," Wright said recently. "I grew up with guys like Derek, Wiley, Rod and Scooter. It was like being on my high school team as far as how guys acted and were respected. A little more competitive, though."

Their Paths to U of L

Darrell Griffith

U of L wanted Darrell Griffith as badly as every other NCAA Division I school in the country. Luckily for Louisville, Griffith generally felt just as strongly about U of L. He checked out Maryland for a few hours one day in May of 1976, canceled a visit to Michigan and a few days later announced his decision to attend Louisville at a downtown hotel press conference his parents had arranged.

"I grew up watching this team," he said, looking back, "and they got so far in 1975 (a 75-74 overtime loss to UCLA in the national semifinals). Seeing that, being a basketball fan, loving the game, I thought it'd be nice when I got to the university to win a championship. I thought I could add a heck of a thing to get us over the hump."

Derek Smith

Furman and Gardner-Webb had showed some interest in Derek Smith when he was a mid-sized junior playing center for tiny Hogansville (Georgia) High School. But certainly not the big-time Division One schools. Certainly not Louisville.

Then, in the fall of 1977, a wide receiver from Hogansville on U of L's football team named Kenny Robinson walked into assistant head basketball coach Bill Olsen's office and introduced himself. As Olsen best recollects, the conversation went like this:

Robinson: I have a friend who plays high school ball in Georgia and I think you ought to consider him.
Olsen: How tall?
Robinson: 6-4 or 6-5.

Olsen: Does he play guard?

Robinson: No, center.

Olsen: Kenny, have you ever seen us play or watched practice—are you aware of the level of talent?

Robinson: Yessir.

Olsen: You think he can play here?

Robinson: Yessir.

Olsen: We can recruit 6-4, 6-5 guards all over the place.

Robinson: Sir, I played basketball and played with Derek. I know he can play.

Olsen: Would you bring me some information?

The next week Robinson showed up with a nice, neat manilla folder brimming with newspaper articles and pictures—"like a term paper," Olsen said. In it was a picture of the 15-year-old dunking the ball with a grasp reminiscent of a claw on the end of a 100-foot crane.

"His hand was all around the ball so that it looked like it was reduced in size," Olsen said.

Olsen: Kenny, did you have a photographer do this?

Robinson: Nosir. It came from the paper.

"I was a little more excited," Olsen said. "I flew down to see him before we played at Georgia Tech (in February of '78). He was the best player I had seen in two years. He actually lived seven miles out of Hogansville (2000 population: 2,774) in a little community called Corinth—the 'suburbs'—in a row home with an outhouse (and four brothers, a sister and his mom, Maybell Blackman)."

Smith was a sleeper when Olsen first encountered him, but not by the end of his senior season. Hugh Durham had left Florida State, signed on to coach the University of Georgia and went after Smith with both hands and the help of Smith's high school coach. Auburn also became interested.

"But Derek had committed to us earlier in the season," Olsen said, "and he didn't back down."

Carlton "Scooter" McCray and Rodney McCray

Scooter McCray, the elder of the McCray brothers by nearly 19 months, could pretty much name his college. He was Player of the Year in New York state, most valuable player of the state tournament and joined

Rodney, a junior, to gun Mt. Vernon High School to a 26-0 season and the 1978 New York state title.

Rodney followed with a 27-2 campaign and the New York State Public School crown in 1979. Name an All-America team, and they were on it, more often than not among the first five.

Wade Houston, Louisville's Northeast recruiter, was dumbfounded by their skills and approach to the game.

"They played all over the floor," Houston recalled. "They could pass, they could shoot—Rodney was not great but adequate from outside—they'd bring the ball up the floor if they felt like it. I'd never seen two guys as big and versatile as Rodney and Scooter in all my years of coaching and playing. And consummate team players. They were amazing."

And they probably would have been playing for Al McGuire. Except that the late McGuire, in a series of wonderful ironies, announced his retirement as Marquette's coach on the eve of a game with U of L (which the Cardinals won) in December of 1976, went on and won the '77 national title, stuck to his decision and found himself, as an NBC-TV analyst, emptying his deep bag of mystical phraseologies on Louisville's swooping birds of 1980.

"Al had gotten almost every player he wanted out of the Mt. Vernon-Yonkers area," Houston said. "He had a stronghold not only there, but on New York City as a whole. If Al had still been there, I think Scooter would have been at Marquette."

"I was going to Marquette," Scooter said, "but Al retired, and it opened the door for everyone."

Scooter visited hometown St. John's and Kentucky before attending U of L's 1978 basketball banquet and meeting Jerry Eaves, Wiley Brown, Derek Smith and Poncho Wright. After that day, Scooter was sold on Louisville.

"I liked the honesty I got from Alice (Houston's wife) and Wade," Scooter said.

"I think he developed a good relationship with the guys in for the visit," Houston added.

As the lithe six-foot-eight Scooter was climbing on board, Houston was already at work on his thick 6-7 brother.

"Scooter was hiding from recruiters and didn't want to talk on the phone—they were bugging the heck out of him," Houston said. "Rodney always answered and would tell me who called that day, who was coming in, all the inside info. ...I developed a real good relationship with him."

Rodney took hard looks at Wichita State and Purdue. He listened to people saying the McCrays would never go to the same school because they'd be competing against each other for the same position.

"It was an issue that had to be dealt with in his mind," Houston said. "I didn't think it was that big an issue. He and Scooter were so close growing up—no animosity, loved playing together, loved being together as brothers. It was pretty intense with Wichita (where Scooter and Rodney's high school coach had taken an assistant's job) and Purdue, but it ended up being a no-brainer."

The late Jim Valvano, coach of Iona College in New Rochelle, N.Y., practically within walking distance of Mt. Vernon, said he recruited the McCrays "quite heavily. You can see how well we did. I knew I was in trouble with Rodney on his campus visit. He sat down in our cafeteria and ordered french fries, a hamburger and a mint julep."

Rodney wanted to go to a place where he'd get at least some immediate minutes. He knew what skill level existed at U of L.

"Even with young and talented guys I thought I'd be able to come there and still be able to play," he said.

He had no idea how much, or how soon.

Wiley Brown

Two Georgia newspapers named Wiley Brown the state's player of the year in both football and basketball in 1978. The 6-8, 220-pounder planned to make use of both skills at Florida State.

Then, Larry Gay, who recruited him for basketball, and head coach Hugh Durham pulled up stakes and hired on at, hmmmm, Georgia.

"I was thinking Florida State, Alabama, Auburn and maybe Georgia and I was going to play one if not two years of football at those schools, but it was mainly going to be basketball," Brown remembered. "I didn't really want to go to Georgia. Louisville got in late on me."

An acquaintance of U of L assistant Jerry Jones recommended Brown to the Cardinals staff. Jones scheduled a visit. Lo and behold ...

"I knew about Darrell Griffith," Brown said. "What really got me was Daryl Cleveland was here. We played against each other in high school. I couldn't believe it. He took me around and I loved it."

Sylvester (Brown's home) and Thomasville (Cleveland's) are 53 miles apart on Georgia state road 33. Cleveland insists his Central High School team never lost to Brown's Worth County Club. "They always went down to the wire," Cleveland said, "and every time I see Wiley I remind him, 'You guys never could beat us. '"

Jerry Eaves

Much like Griffith, Jerry Eaves grew up enamored with U of L basketball, although he followed the Cardinals from a fairly new high school in Louisville's east end, Ballard, rather than Griff's established downtown power, Male.

If Eaves felt he was good enough to play for his local institution, and said local institution felt the same way, and family and friends could follow his career on a regular basis, well, bring it on.

The 6-4 guard helped Ballard shock Male and seniors Griffith and Bobby Turner as a sophomore in 1976, was part of a triple star power show as a junior when the Bruins won the state championship in 1977, then averaged 24.8 points and 9.1 rebounds for a Ballard team stripped of two all-state front-liners in 1978.

"We had it down to four guards, and Jerry made the first commitment to us," U of L assistant Bill Olsen said. "He became a salesman for us, encouraging Scooter, Wiley and Derek."

All four, of course, signed, easily forming with Poncho Wright the deepest and most talented single class in Denny Crum's first seven seasons.

Roger Burkman

Assistant Bill Olsen had a friend and U of L graduate in Indianapolis who was constantly feeding him names of prospects from middle Indiana. Olsen wouldn't recruit one of the offerings because he was "too short." His miffed buddy didn't like it, but in a later letter to Olsen said, "I found you one of those tall guys."

That was 6-5 Roger Burkman, who was ignored by Indiana University, not at home for a one-time phone call from UCLA's Gene Bartow, and only seriously recruited by Evansville, Ball State and Wyoming.

Olsen went to see him play.

"He was very aggressive, all over the place," Olsen recalled. "He reminded me of a Globetrotter—bringing it behind his back and between his legs on the break. His shooting was flawed, but I remember thinking we'd probably offer him a scholarship. I remember telling him we'd correct his free throw technique 'when you come to U of L.'"

Burkman's scoring wasn't flawed at Franklin Central High, a school just outside of Indianapolis. He averaged 27.2 points and 12.5 rebounds as a senior, 21.3 and 13 as a junior. But, as Olsen indicated, he became a player who seemed to clone himself in the heat of battle. Relishing the role of

first guard off the bench, he was a one-man S.W.A.T. team on defense, one
of the most annoying, destructive forces a Cardinal opponent had ever
seen, before 1979 or since.

David "Poncho" Wright

It was going to be Purdue or Louisville for Poncho Wright, a 6-5 forward with Griffithesque jumping ability from Indianapolis Marshall High.
Wright had relatives in Louisville's west end, making the decision a difficult
one. Then, Purdue coach Fred Schaus retired.

"I couldn't lean one way more than the other until that happened," he
said, "but when they brought in a new coach that made it a definite.
Having relatives in Louisville kind of sold me [on U of L], too."

Plus, so much talk had filtered north about Griff the myth, he wanted
to experience the man for himself.

"I remember hearing things about this guy when he was 16 years old, see-
ing things in *Sports Illustrated* when he was still in high school," Wright said.
"I wanted to play with him. Purdue didn't have any legends [apologies to Joe
Barry Carroll] on their team. If I had gone there, I'd have been the legend."

Wright averaged 24.2 points and 13.4 rebounds as a Marshall senior.
He didn't qualify academically to play as a freshman at U of L but was on
board the next three years. As the first front-line sub, he became "Instant
Offense" to Burkman's "Instant Defense" in '80 and the team's best pure
long-range jump-shooter.

Tony Branch

Ohio State was one of the schools on Tony Branch's mind when the six-
foot guard took his official visit to Louisville in 1976. But Branch had links
to U of L, too, even though Branch was from Michigan City, Indiana, a
town on Lake Michigan a full state away from Cardinal land. One of those
links was a bit bigger than a bouncing ball.

"I followed Louisville because Ike Whitfield (also a Michigan City player) went there," Branch said, "and I liked their style and was a Louisville
fan. But before that I was an Ali fan [that would be three-time heavyweight
champ and Louisville-born Muhammad Ali]. I knew about Central High
School, the Louisville Lip. I idolized Ali."

Branch visited campus the same weekend U of L had Male High teammates Darrell Griffith and Bobby Turner in. Academics forced Turner, a two-
year starter, to miss his fourth season. Griffith and Branch, in roles 180 degrees
apart from each other, would become masterful senior leaders in '79-80.

CHAPTER TWO

Striking the Match:
March 15, 1979, to October 15, 1979

A Glimmer of Grit

Darrell Griffith stared grimly out onto the Riverfront Coliseum court on March 15, 1979, publicly cheering on his University of Louisville teammates and privately gnashing his teeth.

Double-teamed by Arkansas and off his game anyway during the NCAA Midwest Regional semifinals in Cincinnati, the junior had been jerked from the lineup by coach Denny Crum after being called for his fourth foul.

The Cardinals were at an embarrassing crossroads. They were down 17 points with 12:38 to play, pointing fingers at each other, playing little defense, crying for the ball on offense and heading toward their worst loss in a decade.

Tony Branch and Roger Burkman were subbed for Griffith and Derek Smith. Crum ordered an all-out full-court press denying the in-bounds pass. Stunningly, with Burkman diving and Branch sprinting, a desperate U of L began to rally.

Griffith watched from courtside, his request to go back into the game denied.

"It didn't really bother me," Griffith said afterwards. "With everybody playing so good, why take them out? You just watch them and encourage them."

But one had to wonder what thoughts were really swimming through his mind. He was at the end of his third season. Unless a miracle came to pass in the next few minutes, all three would end depressingly.

In 1976 he promised fans who turned out for his signing announcement "several" national titles. Now he was about to go 0 for 3. If he finally took one of the pro offers that had tempted him every year since his last at Male High School, he would leave school with zero NCAA crowns and under increasing criticism for his defense and ball-handling deficiencies.

Certainly, this was not what he or anybody else had envisioned.

Adding to the distress was the fact that this 1978-79 Louisville team, at one time 21-3, had lost four of its last seven games. It barely squeaked past South Alabama in the opening round of the NCAA Tournament. Crum was upset with his team's performance—and apparently with the journalists assigned to cover his team. In a unique move the day before taking on Arkansas, Crum closed practice to people with pens and cameras, refused to say why he wasn't starting Bobby Turner and sarcastically blamed Louisville's stretch-run troubles on his local scribes.

Arkansas' domination over the first three-quarters of the semifinal game completed the circle of negativity.

But the Cardinals' comeback intensified. A reenergized Branch, Burkman, Scooter McCray, Larry Williams and Turner began to claw at the Razorbacks. A 14-0 Louisville run closed the gap to 51-48. Branch's two free throws gave U of L a 56-55 lead, its first in 27 minutes.

Branch went to the line for a one-and-one with 5:06 to play. A three-point lead here might give Louisville just enough impetus to take it all the way.

But Branch missed.

"It was right on line but hit the back of the iron," he said. "I won't forget that for a long time."

The exhausted Cardinals had fired their last bullet. Griffith got back into the game, but Arkansas regained the lead, went to a 1-4 alignment with star Sidney Moncrief working out top against Branch and steadied the Razorbacks for a 73-62 victory.

"Moncrief was too much," Branch recalled. "When they threw it to him in the middle, you felt very alone."

A similar feeling must have wafted over Griffith—the way he sullenly bit off quick answers to questions afterwards made one suspect that this man still had lots to prove to himself and others—not that he would ever admit it. He hit five of 14 shots, scored 12 points and sat during the six-minute, 15-second rally in which Louisville outscored Arkansas 22-4.

Today, Griffith will shrug at the thought of critics and pressure.

"I throw all that out," he said. "You have to understand I was in the public eye ever since I started to dunk a basketball, and that was in the seventh grade. I'm 12 or 13 years old and hearing comments from the public I wasn't used to. My father told me, 'Son, one thing you can't control is what other people say. Don't let it worry you. Do your thing, keep your head up.' That always stuck with me."

Griffith stayed for his senior season. Did unfulfilled promises and discombobulated teams factor into his decision?

"What bothered me most about not getting to the championship game the previous three years was sitting back and watching it," he said. "The excitement of those people who were still there playing, I had a problem with that. I said, 'I'm going to do whatever I can to fix that problem.'"

Griffith found some helpful aides. And, against Arkansas, Crum and his staff got an interesting look at a defensive octopus. Maybe the 1979-80 Cardinals could embrace both a Griffith upgrade and a full-court press, and get their program righted again.

The Declaration

In May of 1976, Darrell Griffith stood at a podium in a Louisville hotel to announce his college choice. He had led the city's Male High School to one state title, been named an All-American and was just about the most sought-after kid in the U.S. by colleges and—even in those ancient days when prep celebrities actually went on to places of higher learning—the pros.

He picked the University of Louisville over Maryland and Michigan (both barely in the running), and as his announcement was winding down, added this gem: "I plan on bringing several NCAA championships to Louisville."

Minutes later, off stage, he softened the promise. "I don't want to be greedy," he said, "but I'm definitely thinking about one."

This wasn't some foolish spew of words from an excitable 17-year-old. He was serious. But, of course, the gathering of about 40 fans heard only the word "several." Hence, Griffith would be elevated to Zeus-like stature and held accountable for his proclamation.

"In my heart, when I made that statement, I didn't say it for political reasons or for the press," Griffith recalled. "I meant it."

Three years later, how much did the load weigh after a trio of late-season stumbles left only one more shot?

"I'm not the type of person who lets a monkey stay on his back," he said in 2003. "I worked harder and sacrificed parts of my summer to fulfill a dream. What you do off the court is a reflection of what you do on the court. I wanted to go out a champion. I was hoping. I was extremely focused."

Several Titles? Why Not?

What credentials would allow anyone to stand up and soberly assert a UCLA-type run of championships?

If you're Darrell Griffith, soon to be known as "Dr. Dunkenstein," "Stein," "His Griffness" or, more commonly, "Griff," three early career examples may suffice:

Liftoff: In 1976 Griffith was the only high school player asked to try out for the U.S. Olympic team. Height and weight for all the contenders were checked, as was their reach and vertical jump. Griffith's vertical was certified at an even four feet—48 inches.

"We didn't even get a full step (before the jump)," Griffith remembered. "Just a 'lean back.'"

Griffith didn't make the Olympic team, but certainly not because he couldn't jump high enough. Age and experience were the determining factors.

In the spring of 1980, when Griffith went to Los Angeles to receive the Wooden Award as Player of the Year, columnist Jim Murray of the L.A. Times summed up Griffith in Murray's typically mesmerizing way:

"UCLA players showed up (at the ceremony) in fascination. They wanted to get a look at Darrell Griffith at ground level. . . . Like the Abominable Snowman and California condor, Griffith is rarely found at low altitudes . . . He's not a guard, he's a satellite."

No fear: In one of Griffith's early 1976 summer pickup games in Crawford Gym, U of L's steamy practice quarters, the rookie was in the nightly mix of clashes with pros, former Cardinals and current team members. Tony Branch, also a freshman, was there.

"Pros like Wes Unseld, Artis Gilmore and Junior Bridgeman were playing," Branch said. "Artis (the seven-foot-two center for the ABA Kentucky Colonels) was standing in front of the basket. Darrell goes in and dunks on him. He didn't beat Artis to the basket. Artis was standing there, waiting on him. Darrell goes up and throws one down anyway. I knew then Darrell had reckless abandon.

"Fans watching from the bleachers just about fell out of their seats and started laughing. Artis was mad. Real mad. He said, 'Gimme the ball!' Ricky Gallon (a Cardinal seven-footer from the mid-'70s) was guarding Artis. He cleared Ricky away with one arm and dunked with the other. Three times in a row. I thought the basket was coming down. Ricky goes over and tells Griff afterwards, using words I won't repeat, 'Don't you ever dunk on him again.'"

Griffith smiled at the memory.

"I had no fear," he said. "I got a thrill out of cuting a big man down to my size."

Take a charge? Doubt it: Griffith has always insisted that his air shows were the product of instinct and focus, not clever planning. So it was at the World University Games in Sofia, Bulgaria, in 1977, the summer between his freshman and sophomore seasons, during the moment when he leaped over a tall person with a single bound.

The U.S. team was playing Poland. Griffith got a Larry Bird outlet pass and began a two-on-one break with Freeman Williams. A 6-5 defender from Poland backpedaled. As Griffith approached the free throw line, he shot a glance toward where Williams was supposed to be so he could give the ball up. For some reason Williams had slowed. The wily opponent faked a move and stepped back into Griffith's path, in a semi-crouch but ready to take a charge just inside the free throw line.

Griffith had a split-second to decide what to do next.

"I just went up," Griffith said. "I was focusing on the rim. When you do things, you don't plan them. It's natural."

Easy for Dunkenstein to say. Legs splayed, feet aimed perfectly over each shoulder, he leapfrogged directly over the guy and laid the ball in, "nice and soft off the glass," remembered Denny Crum, coach of the U.S. team. Fans did double-takes, then began hollering. A timeout was called. Griffith headed to the bench where he was met by wide-eyed teammate Ricky Gallon.

"I can't believe you, man," Gallon said.

"What are you talking about?" Griffith asked.

"You just jumped over that guy's head," Gallon said.

Later on the bus, people were still buzzing and Griffith was still not believing.

"But the next day a guy was selling pictures of me," he said. "I'm seeing it for the first time and I'm like, 'I guess I did.' The picture's hanging up in my basement."

Plenty of Work to Do

Darrell Griffith couldn't palm the ball.

"Because he didn't have big hands," coach Denny Crum said, "his ball-handling and dribbling were more difficult than they were for a lot of people. It was one of the reasons that late in games I'd use Tony Branch. He had bigger hands."

Tiny hands didn't mean tiny dunks, though.

"He could jump so high he'd just cup it or dunk with both hands," Branch said.

But his feathery jumper and levitating gift brought other problems. He ruled the high school ranks simply because he was playing a couple feet higher than the other guys. He didn't have to worry much about losing his dribble, being beaten on defense or being beaten to a rebounding spot. He'd just jump over somebody's back without touching him and get the job done anyway.

Sometimes that worked in college, too. But not nearly as often.

"Darrell didn't have to be a good passer," assistant Jerry Jones said. "In high school he was the guy who did the scoring. And he didn't have to play defense."

"When he was a freshman," said Branch, in his first year, too, "I could time Griffith and pick him (steal his dribble) about 30 percent of the time."

Griffith was a 6-3 forward at Male High before adding an inch in college. As a high schooler, he could have played any of the front-line positions. In college (or beyond), however, he would be a guard.

"My first year it was [a rough transition], but those are the adjustments you've got to make," Griffith said.

He made them, but not at nearly the speed fans and news people demanded. During his first three years, on teams abundantly talented but susceptible to playing down to an inferior opponent and falling into potholes at season's end, Griffith was a magnet for the oncoming scrutiny.

"Things that worked in high school didn't in college," Griffith said. "Each year the competition level increased. I welcomed it. I wasn't a ballhandler, and you've got to accept constructive criticism. I was not the perfect player coming out of high school or the most well-rounded. I listened when Coach Crum said I needed to work on ball-handling and defense because he knew what he was talking about."

No to the Pros

The train leaving for the National Basketball Association had a seat with Darrell Griffith's name on it every year from the moment his high school squad lost in the regional finals of the 1976 State Tournament.

He could have signed with the hometown Kentucky Colonels at the age of 17 in April of '76. Others came calling with particularly strong overtures after his junior season at U of L. He refused to climb aboard, even though an apparently substantial stipend awaited him in an era when going hardship was a rare occurrence.

"I was flattered, but my first thought was that I wasn't ready," he said. "I knew I needed more grooming."

Plus, hardship wasn't part of Griffith's upbringing.

"My mother and father (Maxine and Monroe) kept me grounded," he said, "and I wasn't stressed from a financial standpoint. They explained the real world to me. And after my junior year, there was something in my soul about unfinished business."

Folding Chairs and Volleyball Poles

Pickup games and youth camps in Louisville's practice facility, Crawford Gym, were an annual summer rite. The same could not be said of the raid that Darrell Griffith made on the equipment room. That became a rite of passage.

After the steamy, often bruising, games in the July-August Crawford hotbox—and once in a while before them—Griffith would pull out volleyball stanchions, pretend they were really tall defenders and work on his jump shot. Then he'd push those aside, set up folding chairs in an obstacle course and work on his ball-handling.

Assistant head coach Bill Olsen, not allowed to observe officially, sneaked peeks and marveled.

"Something made him go in the gym and work harder than I've ever seen a player work," Olsen recalled. "He set up the poles and chairs with nobody telling him, 'Here are the drills you need to work on.' He worked one to two hours. A long time. Even after we started practice October 15, he did it.

"He would challenge the pole, go right up to it, jump high enough and put more arc on the ball. The chairs would be defenders all over the floor. He'd do crossover dribbles and reverse pivots and work on his left (off) hand, because we felt at times he dribbled too high."

Said Griffith at the time: "It was the first time I worked on specific parts of my game. Then I'd run a half-mile to a mile four nights a week. If you want to make something of yourself, you've got to be dedicated."

Of course, not all were enamored with the clutter.

"[The chairs and poles] would be sitting there when I'd come in the next morning," assistant Jerry Jones said, "and I'd have to roll them off to the side."

But the results would be, in the eyes of Olsen and several thousand others, spectacular.

"For three years Darrell was one of the most gifted athletes who ever played at U of L," Olsen said, "but I don't think anyone would have evaluated him any higher than being a good to very good basketball player. Of all the things that qualify you to be a great player—ability to handle the ball, run a team, play good defense—Darrell only qualified in his athleticism and ability to shoot and score.

"He could make plays no one else could make. But then he made a commitment, and I don't think at Louisville or anywhere a player as talented as Darrell Griffith made as much improvement from the end of one year to the beginning of the next. He was a great shooter. After that he was unstoppable, able to shoot the jump shot off the dribble with no one being able to get high enough to defend. There's so little margin for improvement, but I think he became between 10 to 25 percent better."

Hide the Key...

A key to Crawford Gym, U of L's practice facility, mysteriously found its way under a bush to the left of the main double doors. It remained there throughout the summer and into the season, an invitation to those seeking pickup games, extra work and equipment aids.

Apparently only the '79-80 team members were privy to knowledge of the bush. How did that come to be?

"Those of us who were involved have to have sealed lips," assistant Bill Olsen said. A small chuckle crept into his voice as he added, "Well, we always left a key there in case we came in to work late and had forgotten ours." Sure.

Night after night through the summer of 1979, a darkened Crawford awakened from 7 or 8 p.m. to 1 or 2 a.m. with the sounds of squeaky sneakers, pounding basketballs and rough language. Only custodian Alma Robinson stood in the way of the intruders. She was no barrier at all.

"Miss Alma," as she was known, was U of L's unofficial lead recruiter. Olsen said that when a prospect first entered Crawford, he was initially introduced to Miss Alma. She would then sit him down for an interrogation, make him feel important and report back to a coach whether he should be recruited or not.

Miss Alma was the "surrogate mother" to all players, Olsen said. She made sure Crawford was presentable in the mornings and evenings, yet she would never bar the way to those seeking extra time on the court.

"If anything, she would have provided another key to those guys," Olsen said.

...Start the Combat

The players didn't just trickle into Crawford Gym for light exercise and ego massage during the summer of '79, like they might have at some public park. Led by Darrell Griffith, they strode in with a purpose to undo past shortcomings.

These weren't games—they were collisions. Depending on whom you talked to, there were fights, square-offs, constant verbal harangues and not many smiles.

"I couldn't tell you the number of times guys would fight or there would be physical and verbal confrontations," Griffith said. "But that was cool. We wanted to win that much even in pickup games."

Word got out that the heat of the engagements matched the draining humidity of Louisville's mid-summers. Crawford had two courts, side by side, with a double row of bleachers along the back of the second floor. Those seats soon filled, then people had to stand, then they grew into a crowd, groaning with delight at airborne maneuvers and needle-threading no-look passes, and finally the nondescript place became a pulsating, rock-on nightly attraction.

"[Fans] packed little Crawford, and it carried over to scrimmages and the high school gyms we went to (for intrasquad games)," said Scooter McCray. "By the time we got to Freedom Hall (the home arena), the buzz had been created that these guys play hard."

CHAPTER THREE

Lighting the Fire:

October 16, 1979,
to November 23, 1979

The Cloying, Annoying 2-2-1

Denny Crum had used bits and pieces of full-court presses in each of his first eight seasons at Louisville, but never as a standard defense for an entire season.

He said he never quite had the personnel to run it long term and had trouble watching it cough up easy baskets. But if the stars were properly aligned, he was certainly a believer. Crum's guru, John Wooden, employed the 2-2-1 zone press in the mid-1960s to jump-start UCLA's unfathomable string of 10 titles in 12 years.

Seeing what it delivered in the Arkansas NCAA loss a few months earlier, and thinking he had the right guys at the right moment, Crum went for it in '79-80.

"I don't think the zone press will ever again be the factor it was when UCLA teams won with it in 1964 and '65," he told *Louisville Courier-Journal* reporter Mike Sullivan. "Then [an opponents'] idea of 'attacking' [the zone] was to fight their way upcourt, hold the ball and set up the offense. So you could gamble and gamble and gamble and never pay for it. Nowadays, their idea is to get a two-on-one or three-on-two and burn you. But our current personnel is as good as we've had for this kind of defense."

Crum didn't mean his players should force 50 five-second counts or steal every in-bounds pass. He was mulling over the drain game – physical and mental fatigue. It was another problem for an enemy to think about with, perhaps, a 12-2 point burst as a reward every so often.

In the 2-2-1, the Cardinals would align according to how the previous offensive trip ended. They might deny the in-bounds pass; they might trap the player who caught it. They might put a hard two-man trap on two or three times upcourt; they might fake backing away and then pin a dribbler to the sideline, or slap on a vise in the corner the moment he crossed the 10-second line.

Louisville would have to get very serious about conditioning, but the press could energize the team and the crowd plus demoralize the enemy.

Scooter McCray, a 6-8 sophomore with arms that unfolded like an erector set, was key. He generally was aligned in the second two-man level of the press. Crum considered him the best anticipator and ball thief, but just minutes into the third game of the season, McCray went down for the remainder of the season with a knee injury.

There were momentary doubts about the 2-2-1's ability to go on effectively in his absence, as alignment changes would include McCray's reluctant, unproven brother, freshman Rodney. But the press hardly missed a beat, Rodney became a formidable, sometimes terrifying, force at the "1," and if an anticipator award had been given out—Scooter or no Scooter—Roger Burkman would have received it.

Bobby Dotson became a Louisville assistant in 1980-81, coming from Florida State. U of L played (and whipped) the Seminoles three times in '79-80. Crum remembers a conversation with Dotson.

"Bobby told me they knew they'd have trouble stopping (Darrell) Griffith from scoring," Crum said, "but they hated it when Burkman came in the game. He got his hands on more balls, got in the passing lanes, made more deflections and created problems because of his aptitude to be a good defender and his knowledge of what was going on. Roger was always in the way."

Burkman was the first sub at guard. By the end of the first week in February he was sixth in minutes played but the leader in assists and second in steals. He preferred coming off the bench. He loved his role.

"I did my scoring in high school," Burkman recalled. "I could sit over there and know who I was going to guard, whether the guard liked to go to his right or left, whether he had a quick or slow (shot) release. I felt I could be a pickpocket, that I could anticipate a reverse dribble, step over and take a charge. A lot of it is anticipation."

Uprooting a team's offense became more of a badge of honor for the '79-80 Cardinals than a dunk or a long jumper. And if U of L got the steal, well, see ya.

"On a break [the opposing team was] pretty much at our mercy," said Poncho Wright, the first forward off the bench. "All you had to do was throw it up at the rim and anybody from a point guard to a center would go get it. That was pretty much the most talented nine or 10 guys I had ever seen on one team."

Heads Up, Basketball Iron

The rims on the basketball goals in Crawford Gym had already undergone a great deal of suffering during the summer of 1979, but October 15—the first day of formal practice—brought an official warning shot from the most unlikely of sources.

Steve Clark, a freshman and lone survivor of a six-man non-scholarship tryout to give the Cardinals a 13th man, fired home a dunk that first day, hung on the rim—and bent it.

"They didn't have breakaway rims then," Clark recalled. "They had to go get another one. Being the new kid, I was torn up over it. Denny (Crum) had a famous line that went, 'If you can't dunk, lay it in,' but he didn't say that to me. I guess I didn't make a big-enough impact to where he thought I'd be a problem to the team.

"But the next day the *Courier-Journal* had it in the paper under a headline that read, 'Louisville player bends rim, delays practice first day.' That was me."

Thumbthing's Different

The above catch phrase was the headline *Louisville Times* sports editor Lou Younkin slapped on an October 31 story that first revealed publicly the work being done on forward Wiley Brown's right hand.

When the 6-8 forward-center was four years old, he cut his right thumb with a knife. The cut wasn't taken care of properly and became infected, causing gangrene to set in. The thumb eventually had to be amputated above the first joint.

Brown compensated by becoming left-handed. He grew into such a gifted southpaw in Georgia that he was named Player of the Year in both football and basketball as a senior and turned down football offers in order to go to Louisville to play basketball.

He was living quite nicely with a stub for a thumb. But Denny Crum, ever the technician, ever the detail man, thought Brown's ability to control the ball, rebound and shoot free throws could be enhanced, perhaps greatly, with two good thumbs. And Crum had Drs. Joseph Kutz and Harold Kleinert, world-renowned Louisville hand surgeons, available for consultation.

Brown was hardly enthusiastic. He had been operating without a right thumb for 15 years. He was used to nothing being there.

"Crum noticed that when I'd catch passes the ball would roll off my right hand," Brown said. "I never noticed it being a problem, but you know Denny. If you fumble one pass …"

At the doctors' office, an orthoplast with a rubber base was cast from Brown's left thumb and molded to fit on the right. U of L trainer Jerry May mixed up a rubbery liquid solution to apply to the knob, slipped the prosthesis on and held it in place with two surgical gloves, one with the fingers cut out.

Kutz and Kleinert were thinking that if the prosthesis held up for Brown's sophomore season, they might do a toe-to-hand transfer before his junior year. "We haven't done that on athletes before," Dr. Kutz said, "but we've performed the surgery before."

Wait a minute, Brown thought.

"I didn't want to do that," he recalled. "Then I talked to Dr. Ellis (late team doctor Rudy Ellis) and he said, 'I don't care what they're going to do, they're not going to do that.'"

May identified with Brown's reticence.

"He'd been without the thumb his whole life and had learned how to adapt," May said. "Control of the ball was the main thing, He wouldn't catch it, he would palm it and pat it back to the other hand. He didn't like to wear the prosthesis, and we didn't like the idea of toe surgery."

The artificial thumb may have helped. Brown's free throw percentage rose from 51 to 61 percent. But he also lost 23 pounds and had an operation to clean out a knee filled with bone chips. A leaner, more chiseled Wiley Brown started 36 games to none as a freshman, went from an average of 13 minutes a game to 30, 3.7 to 10.4 points and 2.6 rebounds to 5.6. Who's to say how much was thumb and how much was conditioning and determination?

Brown tried not to wear the thumb at the start of his senior season in 1981-82.

"I didn't feel I needed it, but the coach did, and he's the coach," Brown said. And after that?

"That was it for the thumb."

One Prosthetic Adjustment

Considering the battering a front-line rebounder's hands undergo during a season, Wiley Brown's fake thumb stood up amazingly well.

The consensus was it may have popped off four or five times from December through March, including during practice. But that was after some unsavory moments in November and a major change in adhesives.

In an intrasquad scrimmage at Charlestown (Indiana) High School on November 2, four days after the device was attached, guard Jerry Eaves accidentally hit the thumb, hard. It tore through the outer glove and skidded to a stop in front of a fan.

The thumb was quickly retrieved and handed back to an irate Brown, who ripped off the surgical gloves, threw the apparatus at the bench, slam-dunked on his next offensive trip and went on to finish the night with 34 points (16 of 22 field goals) and 13 rebounds.

"The thing would be like a slingshot and take off across the floor," remembered then-student trainer Steve Donohue. "The ref would call a timeout and we'd have to go get it."

Head trainer Jerry May saw an even uglier scene.

"When it flew off, people screamed and Wiley really got mad," May said. "It was like his hand flew off. He thought it made him look like a freak. We had to find something else, because he wasn't going to wear it. Too embarrassing."

May, Donohue and manager Randy Bufford found epoxy.

"With one part glue and one part hardener, we'd mix them together, stick it on the thumb, then stick the gloves on," Donohue said.

The latex gloves held up. The thumb, for the most part, stayed on. But at game's end, how hard was it to get off?

"Not hard," Donohue said. "Between the sweating and the shower he could just twist it a little bit and it would pop right off."

Precision Passing Redefined

Denny Crum was adamant that Wiley Brown's new thumb was going to be a success.

This adamant. Brown's teammates were instructed to pass to Brown's left hand—not his enhanced right hand.

It was true the Louisville coaches had assembled perhaps as fine an array of passers as the Cardinals have had before or since. But, hey, c'mon.

"Coach Crum believed in our ability so much that he would say, 'Don't pass it to that hand in traffic,'" recalled Scooter McCray, one of the best package-deliverers. "And I'm like, 'Coach, this is a game of acting and reacting (as opposed to perfection).' But he was insistent. Pass it to the good hand, not the bad hand.

"Now, Wiley didn't want to wear the thumb because he was getting more notoriety for it than his playing ability. So—and these were the type of jokes we'd shoot at each other—we'd grab Wiley and start to slap him 'five,' then suddenly stop and say, 'Give me your other hand, I can't give you 'five' on the bad hand.'

"We'd laugh (as Brown grimaced and shook his head). But, actually, what Coach Crum said was the ultimate compliment he could pay you as a passer."

The 'Ville? The 'Nap?

The personalities, accents and slang from such a variety of locations east of the Mississippi often made conversations difficult to follow and sometimes to fathom.

Such was the case with one of the newcomers, David "Poncho" Wright, a 6-5 sophomore from Indianapolis who had to sit out his freshman year to become eligible. But it was important to listen closely to Wright, because one never knew when something prophetic might roll off his tongue.

Like after the Charlestown scrimmage, when he hit 10 of 14 shots, most extremely long-distance jumpers, then interrupted *Courier-Journal* columnist Billy Reed's interview with Wiley Brown to blurt out, "The 'Ville is going to the 'Nap."

The who is going to the what? The natives called their town "Luh-vul" and "Lou-a-vul" and had to endure "Lou-ee-ville" and "Lou-is-ville." Now it had become "The Ville?"

Truth was, Wright played for LouisVILLE and the NCAA Tournament's Final Four was going to be in IndiaNAPolis, Wright's hometown.

Memories of his prophecy were a bit cloudy as Wright looked back in 2003.

"I vaguely remember saying it," he said. "I hadn't played with these guys the year before and remember thinking how tough, how dominating we looked. It just came out like that. Some people were like, 'Yeah, they're going to the 'Nap all right, they're going to take a nap.' And I thought, 'Well, we'll see.'"

Rodney in the Raw

Rodney McCray showed up on Louisville's campus late in the summer of 1979 with a trunk full of high school championship hardware, a somewhat less than buff physique, an impassive face, a deep voice that spoke about once a week, no idea what the phrase "work ethic" meant and an attitude that said, "Get out of my face, because I'm going to destroy you when they tip it off."

The entire Rodney package was so spectacularly different in style and build from his older brother Scooter that the coaching staff was bewildered. After a few weeks, they secretly wished they had put the recruiting hammer down on Sidney Green of Brooklyn (signed by Nevada-Las Vegas) instead of this guy from Mt. Vernon, N.Y.

He was always last in the twice-a-week mile runs after workouts, lagged in the postpractice sprints, and trotted on the fast breaks.

"In high school I pretty much got by just going through the motions," Rodney recalled. "I thought I was mentally and physically ready to play, and my train of thought was, 'Do you want it in a game or in practice? I can give it to you [during] one or the other.' Looking back now and talking to my ex-teammates, they remember saying when I first walked into the gym, 'This is the guy we signed? He looks like a little chubby kid.' Which I was."

What McCray really walked into was a swarm of angry athletes seeking atonement. He hardly fit into that picture of determination.

"When you've got 11 or 12 guys busting their tail, he sticks out like a sore thumb," said Jerry Jones, who coached the second team in practice. "We used to go five-on-five full-court. I would tell him, 'You should never get tired because you only get from one free throw line to the other, You meet the other guys. They're going one way, you're going the other.'"

Exasperation spilled over to other staffers. Assistant head coach Bill Olsen felt like he was talking to a mummy when addressing the younger McCray.

"I thought we'd made a mistake after two or three weeks of practice," Olsen recalled. "He didn't work and didn't respond when you said something. You couldn't see any athleticism. He'd show up … go through the motions and go home. You couldn't get him upset. I know. I tried."

Olsen had a couple of motivational ideas. First, when cones were being set up for the mile run after practice, Olsen went up to McCray and said, 'I'll run backwards and outrun you.'"

Did that make Rodney mad? Naw. "I said, 'I bet you can, too,'" McCray remembered. Olsen, of course, did.

Then there was the broom. Colleges had freshman/reserve teams in the early 1970s and every so often Olsen, a former Marine, would have his units play "brutal ball"—everybody had to dive for every loose ball. Olsen, now the "big-man coach," retained a branch from his old sadistic tree. He took a broom and swatted rebounders as they neared the goal.

"He beat the crap out of Rodney," said student trainer Steve Donohue, "and after practice Rodney would say, 'He's just killin' me, this (expletive) guy.' Rodney was mad, but he wouldn't let people beat him when it came to the boards."

That was a rare burst of words and emotions. But McCray mostly remained McStoic, even as disgusted teammates tried to give him a jump-start.

"We were down on Rodney," Wiley Brown said. "He was last in everything. We'd say, 'Rod, you got to put out, man. You got this big name, you ain't doing anything.' All he'd say was, 'I'm all right.' It got so that we didn't want to say anything to this guy any more."

Brother Scooter was hardly an impartial observer.

"He wouldn't push himself, and then he'd tell the guys he was better than they were anyway," Scooter said. "'I'll show it in the game,' he'd say. 'I'm a gamer. I can play.'"

The person who seemed less concerned than anyone was the head man, Denny Crum.

"I thought that subconsciously he had the feeling he didn't want to compete against his older brother (and take away some of his minutes)," Crum said. "In my mind I kept going back to watching Rodney play in the Dapper Dan (a high school all-star game in Pittsburgh). He wasn't as big as those guys, but coming down the stretch he got every key rebound and dominated the boards. It was an indication of what kind of heart he had."

But where was the heart, the soul and the effort now, in late November? Oh, well. Maybe the rookie wouldn't be needed in 1979-80.

Not Shorts, Wides

Before we momentarily leave Rodney McCray, there's one other small item. Okay, not that small.

To go with derisive descriptions such as pudgy, chubby, plump and amply-hipped, there was the matter of Rodney and U of L's practice shorts.

The 220 pounds McCray carried on his six-foot-seven frame was about right. The tone of the weight, however, was all wrong. Thus McCray needed size-40 duds.

"Size 38 was the largest we had at the time," manager Randy Bufford said. "We had to make a special request for 40s, then I had to go get them. I also clipped the size marker out of them so the guys wouldn't get on him."

McCray agreed.

"Oh, yeah, that's true," he said. "After practice Wiley would be like, 'Get on those scales.' I'd be like, 'Oh no, man, I'm not getting on those scales.' After everybody left I'd get on. They had me at 220, but it was flab. I put my uniform on and the other guys put theirs on, and I came out looking a whole lot different in mine."

All But the Grand Finale

Three players from 1978-79 chose not to be around for 1979-80, or had a choice made for them.

Bob Albertson, who averaged 4.1 minutes in 18 games, decided to transfer after two seasons. Steve Bugg, a non-scholarship guard who received a total of 20 minutes in nine games, decided to concentrate on baseball.

The most lamentable case belonged to Bobby Turner. Turner and Darrell Griffith had been running mates—and enemy-destroying mates— for over a decade. They had been bookend forwards for Male High's state champion and regional final teams in the mid-'70s and key components at U of L for three years, the last two as starters. As a junior Turner had averaged 13.6 points and five rebounds, shooting 54 percent from the field and 74 percent from the free throw line.

But he lived in Griffith's shadow.

"People always said that, but I always thought we played side by side," Turner said. "We played together and hung together, since the fourth grade."

Both were 6-4. Griffith had the body and skills to make an early conversion to guard. Turner, although he had spring-loaded legs similar to his buddy and looked 6-7 in his afro, was destined to live athletically as a "tweener"—not big enough for an NBA forward, perhaps not good enough for a pro backcourt.

More problematic was schoolwork. Turner had struggled with the books for three seasons, always needing summer school to remain eligible. Then, in February of '79, the court and classroom battles were compounded. He injured a finger on his shooting hand and went into a slump. His father, a single parent, developed legal troubles, and Bobby had to become temporary head of a four-person household.

It all left Turner overwhelmed academically, and he flunked out.

But the university and coach Denny Crum gave him another shot in '79-80. He was allowed to re-enroll. He couldn't play in games, but he could practice. Crum let him back as a guard, his best pro chance.

"Coach Crum is doing me a favor, but the main thing is the studies," Turner said then. "The professors know my problem and say they'll give me all the help they can. I appreciate that. I know I can do it."

But Bobby Turner didn't. He stayed a few more weeks, had more grade troubles and dropped out. As U of L mounted a surge and sustained it, the sidelined Turner ran through a laundry list of emotions.

"It was the most difficult thing I ever had to go through," Turner recalled. "I was praying for those guys, happy and sad at the same time. I just felt so bad not being a part of it after playing all those years. It was truly devastating to watch, and sometimes I even cried about it. I knew I should have been there.

"But I can't blame anybody but Bobby Turner. I had the opportunity and let it slide. Sometimes, though, you go through things and they make you a better person. I think that's what it did for me."

In the spring of 1980, Turner was drafted in the middle rounds by the NBA's New York Knicks, then was the second to last player cut, he said. He went to the Philippines, where he played a season and a half before food poisoning, of all things, ended his career.

"I averaged 37 points a game my one full season, playing a bit of both forward and guard," he said. Then he chuckled. "I got a chance to shoot the ball all the time. Playing with Griff, he took most of the shots. It felt good."

Bombing Bobby

Bobby Turner was also one of the early victims of a season-long rampage of pranks that may have set records for their durability. A major instigator was center Marty Pulliam. A willing accomplice was walk-on guard Steve Clark. There would be others down the road, but these two would do for now.

One of the therapy treatments for the team was a spray bomb for sore muscles. It was sprayed on and rubbed into the affected area.

"It smelled awful and instantly turned hot," Clark recalled. "They used to just have an ointment, but then came out with this spray that would deep-heat your muscles."

Turner forgot to lock his locker the first days of practice in '79-80.

"We'd spray his underwear down, he'd come in, take a shower, put his pants on and it would light him up," Clark said.

"I was on fire," Turner said. "I figured somebody had my locker combination. I told myself if I ever catch somebody ..."

The next time he made sure he snapped that dude closed, but Pulliam was already a step ahead.

"Marty and I had lockers close to Bobby's," Clark said. "Bobby put his lock on the bench when he sat down. When he wasn't looking, Marty took his own lock and swapped it with Bobby's. Bobby put [Marty's] on, checked it three or four times, and said, 'You (without knowing whom "you" was) aren't going to get me today.' He thought he had all bases covered.

"Marty and I are just dying. Marty acts like he sticks his lock—really Bobby's—on his locker and pretends to lock it. With Bobby out of the room, Marty takes his own lock off, sprays his underwear down again, then locks it back up with Bobby's real lock. Same deal. Bobby had to take his clothes off, run back and take another shower, all the while still swearing somebody knew his combination.

"Marty would always get things going, then back out and let others take over. Nobody ever 'fessed up to the spray. I don't think Bobby ever had a clue."

Turner didn't, until 24 years later. "I had no idea who or how," he said.

Sawing off a Branch, Regrettably

Tony Branch had earned his spurs. And his boots and saddle and probably a horse.

Although at six feet he was not of the stature of Denny Crum's prototypical 6-5 backcourt-sidecourt swing men, the senior from Michigan City, Indiana, had an abundance of quicks, the best free throw stroke on Louisville's team and the smarts and passing skills to run the Cardinals nicely from the point guard spot.

He had started 22 of 32 games in '78-79. He averaged a fifth-best 21 minutes, 5.3 points, a third-best 79 assists and shot 47 percent on field goals and 80 percent from the line. He was one of catalysts who nearly brought U of L back from the grave in the NCAA regional semis against Arkansas a half a year earlier. And he was studying pre-law.

So 1979-80 was to be his season. The team featured Darrell Griffith for star power but was designed and implemented by point guard Tony Branch. Except ...

Jerry Eaves could play. Roger Burkman could play. Greg Deuser could play. And they all wanted to play. Badly. Plus, Derek Smith and Poncho Wright were indirectly in Branch's way as guard-forward possibilities.

Branch knew he was in for major combat by the number of competitive backcourt shellbursts going off in Crawford Gym during the summer. But he could also tell himself, "Hey, it's my turn."

The conflict intensified as practice began in mid-October. As Louisville labored through November with five intrasquad scrimmages, mostly at area high schools, Crum refused to be pinned down. After the last scrimmage on November 20, Crum said: "One scrimmage it's one guy, the next it's someone else. Guess I'll flip a coin."

But he knew. On November 24, with Louisville about to play its lone exhibition against Marathon AAU, Griffith was a given at shooting guard, Smith and Scooter McCray had taken up residence on the wings, and Wiley Brown had locked down the pivot spot. The point went to sophomore Eaves.

"It's never easy when you have a kid who's played so hard, done everything you've asked him to do and is such a wonderful person as well," Crum said 24 years later. "But you have to do what's in the best interest of the team."

Assistant Jerry Jones recalled how the decision came down.

"Denny was a stat guy," Jones said. "He kept all of them from practices and scrimmages. He asked each of us who we would start there, but what he really wanted was [for] you to agree with him. I told him Tony had been around here four years and might have earned his shot. Bill (Olsen) and Wade (Houston) kind of felt like that.

"Then Denny said, 'If two kids are equal, I think you probably ought to play the younger one. He's going to be here two or three more years and has a chance to improve.' Then he threw out the real reason. 'Plus, I think Tony can handle [a demotion], where I don't think Eaves can.'"

Eaves had made no secret of how badly he wanted the job—and how much pain he would feel if he didn't get it. Looking back from a playing career that included two full NBA seasons and coaching stops at three colleges and three pro clubs, the current coach at North Carolina A&T said:

"That's probably the most competitive thing I've ever done. We were all very close in ability. I think I had a pretty good career, played professionally and coach made the correct decision. But it's a tough business we're in. You have to play the young kids so you can get better the following year, and Tony got dinged because he was a senior. Roger got the most backup minutes because he found his (defensive) niche early with us pressing and him having those long arms and great anticipation. Tony Branch sacrificed himself, then made it easy for me to flourish."

A Smoldering Branch Flames Back Up

About a week into practice, Tony Branch got an unwelcome message.

"[Coach Crum] divided up the team (to establish first and second units for practice)," Branch said. "We all knew who would be four-fifths of the starting team. I was waiting for my name and he called Eaves. I knew I was in trouble, and that's a horrible feeling for a guy trying to break into the lineup his senior year. I don't think I was any good the rest of that practice."

Branch can see the reasons more clearly now from the perspective of assistant and head coaching jobs in college and as the current basketball boss at Louisville Seneca High School.

"I think what Denny had in mind was that 'we were going to be decent this year but not win a national championship, so I'm going to play these young guys,'" Branch said. "Now years later in coaching I can see how he's thinking: 'I've got this sophomore who's maybe more talented than Branch, certainly taller (6-4 to 6-0) and fits better probably into my UCLA system.'"

But that didn't make the ache any more bearable when Crum gaveled the competition to an official conclusion in late November.

"Naturally I was crushed," Branch said. "I think anybody who started (over) half the games the year before, led the team in free throw shooting, was [third] in assists and was one of your better defensive players thought he'd have a shot.

"The first week I was hurt, the second week angry, the third bitter and then after about a month I was able to get myself back together. In that period I'd thought about quitting. I loved my teammates but thought mentally I'd be so negative I would hurt them."

A year ago in his office, Crum gazed into the distance and smiled wistfully. To a degree, it had been an ordeal for him, too.

"Tony made it easy," Crum said. "He never griped or complained—he just accepted it. As seniors, not a lot of kids have the character to accept that kind of situation. …Not only did his attitude never waver, he was such a great ambassador for our team."

Branch lost more than a starting slot. He became essentially the eighth guy, a utility man called on to shoot key free throws or handle the ball. He bit his lip, set his jaw and gave himself a pep talk.

"I felt I could outplay some guys on the team and play better under pressure," he said. "And when you win a national championship you can't fault the coach. But when some people ask me if the coach made the right decision about me with us 33-3, I tell them if he'd started me we'd have been 36-0."

Maybe so. But without him at all, the Cardinals might very well have not even hit the 30-win mark, as we shall see.

Is That Crawford Gym or Parris Island?

Once the first unit was named, the Crawford practice facility came alive with the sounds of kung fu fighting.

Tony Branch, of course, was determined to show some folks he could play. Same with Greg Deuser. Poncho Wright and Roger Burkman had some skills and aggravating gamesmanship ready for the regulars. Daryl Cleveland and Steve Clark were happy to stick out a forearm to stop driving wingmen. Marty Pulliam didn't mind hip-checking somebody out of rebounding position. And Rodney McCray was available to do all the above and more, should he feel like it.

In short, the second unit gave the marquee people more grief from three to six in the afternoons than the No. 1s generally had to deal with from eight to 10 on game nights.

Events would dictate that McCray be a member of the second team only the first seven weeks. He remembered being one of the muggees, not muggers, after he joined the first unit.

"How good were they?" he said of the second unit, repeating a question. "I'm glad there weren't cameras in there some days, because you'd look and say, 'Which one is the first team?' Those guys were competitive and knew what we were running. It was like another Division I team. I never looked at it like first team-second team."

How did Denny Crum and the coaches see the conflict?

"Coach Crum was like, 'Don't hurt yourselves. We've got a game to play tomorrow—tone it down a bit,'" McCray said.

Sometimes tempers flared.

"Wiley (Brown) hurt his hand in one game," McCray remembered. "In practice, Tony Branch threw the ball to him real hard and hit his hurt hand. Wiley looked at Tony and said, 'Didn't I tell you my hand is bothering me? I ought to kick your butt.' Tony (6-0, 175 to Brown's 6-8, 220) just looked at him and said, 'Go ahead. I'll hit you 10 times before you hit me one time.' Everybody just busted out laughing."

There were many of those. None became truly serious, but defusing them wasn't always quite as easy as the Branch-Brown dustup.

Guys like Cleveland, a 6-7 junior, and Deuser, a six-foot redshirt soph, created their own shining moments in the Crawford sweatbox to counter their frustrations with the minimal minutes they were handed when it counted. The moments weren't always pretty, but they were remembered fondly.

"We beat up on [the first unit]," Cleveland recalled . "We made them good. Real good. Practice was my time. Rodney and Wiley hated us because they said we fouled them all the time. We did. We could get away with it. Derek wanted to hurt me. He'd elbow. I'd elbow back. A lot of times it would get out of hand, but we'd hang together afterwards. I know we made them better. If they could overcome practice they'd be okay in games."

"I decided that [practice] was going to be my gametime," Deuser said. "We'd do our darndest to beat them and they'd do their best not to let that happen. Everybody was exhausted from giving their best effort, then we could just be friends again. To me, that was the best kind of competition."

And true preps for the campaigns to come.

Beginnings of a Spiritual Uplink

The daily engagements rolled on. Elbows were thrown. Forearms were delivered. Blood appeared. Guys stopped and looked at each other and exchanged unprintable words.

Derek Smith had his testy moments with coaches and mates. Wiley Brown bared a mean streak every so often. Rodney McCray was still sullen and mostly silent. Before the phrase "trash talk" came into vogue, these people were dishing it out by the shovelful whenever they'd spy a teammate on campus or in the gym.

The makings of bad karma, right? The start of a negative current that would become a disease, infecting a team's connection and driving it into an ugly, dismal and disturbing season.

That could have been what outsiders sensed, but looks were deceiving. If one word could describe the constant harangues, it was that none of them were personal. They were the by-products of one quest.

There was as much positive talk and help as elbows, blood, square-offs and anger. This bunch wanted to get better. It wanted to have success for the name of the school on their jerseys, not the name of a guy in the box score unless—if you were one of the young admiring helpmates—his name was Darrell Griffith.

It was never about "I" or "me," and if one looked and listened closely, the early weeks of practice provided the first inklings of spokes being screwed tightly into the hub of one wheel. The athletic cliché for this is "chemistry." At U of L it was more like epoxy, fusing Brown's thumb and 13 men together.

No one was better equipped to observe this uplink than trainer Jerry May, who was assistant trainer from 1975 to 1977, head trainer for basketball from '77 to 2000 and the designated mother hen for the chicks on the road.

"I was the one who checked them in their rooms at night and took them to eat," May said. "I never left the hotel, ever, because I guess I always thought it was my fault if we had a kid get in trouble. I never went out to eat, never left the floor other than to feed them, and I did that my whole career.

"The thing about this team more than any we ever had was how people acted. They treated each other like family. Being with them was never a chore. [In other years] it was a hell of a chore. But this year it was fun, always enjoyable. They'd come sit in your room and talk. It was easy to leave your door open because you wanted them to stop by. And they were that way with each other."

But why now? Why this season?

"I think the new blood were tremendous competitors," recalled Tony Branch, the other senior. "Wiley Brown, Derek Smith, Jerry Eaves—you want them in a foxhole in Vietnam with you. Warriors. They'd protect your back."

"We were so determined to make things work," Brown said. "They recruited two guys from Georgia (Smith and himself) used to living as low as you could possibly go to guys from New York (the McCrays) who had experienced the world. Yet we all knew our roles and accepted them. Darrell was such a great leader. Get him the ball as much as possible and we'll do the dirty work."

Said Crum: "I thought it was the best collection of talent we had (in his first nine seasons). What we didn't have was a lot of experience. But they were all good players with good attitudes, coachable and they had a senior leader. Young teams without leadership have a lot harder time."

CHAPTER FOUR

The Season Begins:
November 24, 1979,
to December 19, 1979

Start Your Engines:
Marathon, South Alabama, Chattanooga

The Louisville lineup was set—6-8 Wiley Brown in the middle, 6-8 Scooter McCray and 6-6 Derek Smith on the wings, 6-4 Darrell Griffith and 6-4 Jerry Eaves in the backcourt. Not big, but quick, fairly fast and populated with terrific passers and pogo-stick-like jumpers. Roger Burkman (6-5) would be the first guard off the bench to be a defensive irritant and Poncho Wright (6-5) the first front-liner in to provide long-distance shooting.

The press, mostly a 2-2-1 full-court and 1-3-1 half-court trap, had been pounded into place over six weeks, and the Cardinals looked like they had inhaled an accelerant in comparison to past Cardinal teams.

Now it was time to prove it.

All systems looked to be go in a 111-72 splattering of Marathon AAU in an exhibition game on November 24.

But there were coughs and sputters aplenty when U of L opened for real against South Alabama on December 1 at Freedom Hall. Scoring 20 second-half points and benefiting from a technical foul and controversial traveling call down the stretch, the Cardinals escaped the school it nudged in its first game of the 1979 NCAA Tournament by the score of 75-73.

"I told you we'd be exciting," coach Denny Crum said. "I never told you we'd be perfect."

Louisville didn't have to breathe hard on December 5 to beat Tennessee-Chattanooga 87-63, but committed 23 turnovers and shot just 45 percent from the field.

The real Tennessee—University of—was coming up three days later in Knoxville. U of L needed to sharpen some rough edges in a hurry.

A Different PhD

In the mid-1970s, shortly after Lew Alcindor (Kareem Abdul-Jabbar) departed and the NCAA restored the dunk, a columnist asked Louisville's Phil Bond about the roster-full of Cardinal throw-downers. "We have excellent dunkers," Bond said. "We're the Doctors of Dunk."

The nickname caught on across the college basketball land, but in late November, 1979, Wiley Brown asked for an alteration.

"It's time we changed our name from the Doctors of Dunk to the Doctors of Hustle," Brown said.

Whenever people refer to a team identifier, such as Houston's Phi Slamma Jamma squads in the '80s, Doctors of Dunk is still the one that rings a bell at U of L. But Brown's point was more than well taken. It was the truth.

Could a Brother Get Some Props?

As Louisville tried to work out kinks after squeaking by South Alabama in their first game of the season, the saga of non-responsive soft-working Rodney McCray took a small but memorable turn.

After the South Alabama game he was sitting next to brother Scooter in the locker room. Rodney played six minutes and scored a couple of points; he was an afterthought, in other words.

"I thought, 'Oh, my goodness, what's going on here?'" he recalled. "I played well in the scrimmages. I thought it would lead to some playing time. In the locker room everybody's all happy. Not me."

Scooter: "What's wrong?"
Rodney: "I can't believe it. I didn't get no playing time, man."
Scooter: "You thought you were going to play?"
Rodney: "Heck yeah, thought I would."
Scooter: "You don't even practice hard. I told you, practicing hard is what will get you playing time."

"I'm thinking, this is my brother, my sibling," Rodney said. "He's supposed to be telling me I should have played, consoling me, telling me I'm this and I'm that. Instead he's rough on me, and real, saying, 'You don't deserve to play because you don't give it all in practice.'

"The first game was an eye-opener. Then my brother was an eye-opener."

Louisville—the Father of the High-Five?

Daryl Cleveland may have been shuffled toward the lower portion of the bench, but he had inventive ways of making himself seen and heard.

Through the late 1970s, college athletes came up with various forms of greeting each other and celebrating success, although it was usually tastefully understated and nothing even remotely like the chest-pounding, point-to-the-heavens stuff perpetrated these days.

In the seasons before '79-80, basketball players started slapping hands, sideways across their chests or from a low arc down around their knees.

For the opener against South Alabama, Cleveland had another idea. After the lineup was announced, the whole team rushed together for the usual group huddle and sendoff. "We went to center court and everybody was jumping up and down and acting crazy," Cleveland remembers. "I said, 'Let's put 'em up high.'"

In short order introduced players were slapping high-fives on their way to the court and on the way back to the bench. The infection spread across the college hoops landscape.

"By the end of the season everybody had it, and here it still is now," Cleveland said, beaming.

But the reserve forward has always had to be ready to speak up and defend his Thomas Edison moment. Fellow Georgians Wiley Brown and Derek Smith and the other regulars were the noticeable high-fivers.

"Cleve, Wiley and Derek started it, " Scooter McCray said. "Before it was low-fives or a pat on the butt as you ran out."

"Derek, Wiley and Cleve," Darrell Griffith said. "I can still see them doing it in practice, and they made it a ritual during games."

Game 3: Tennessee, December 8

If someone was looking for the definition of a coming-of-age game, this was the place to look.

Tennessee had just beaten ninth-ranked St. John's by 17 points. The Volunteers were playing at home, and having lost at Louisville a year earlier were anxious to make amends. Tennessee had won nine in a row near the end of the previous season and then won its first game ever in the NCAAs. The team was primed.

Tennessee threatened a blowout early (leading 11-4, 16-10 and 28-22) and a pullout late (cutting a 10-point U of L lead to a field goal three times). The Vols shot 56 percent. The Cardinals' Wiley Brown got in early foul trouble. Louisville gave up two points on a technical foul and missed the front end of three one-and-ones in the final minute. And Louisville lost Scooter McCray, its best passer with 15 assists in the first two games, to a knee injury after 3½ minutes.

Yet Louisville held on to win 77-75.

The Cardinals won because Darrell Griffith had perhaps the finest all-around game of his starburst career—32 points, seven assists and four steals. One play may have revealed more about Griffith in '79-80, and thus U of L in '79-80, than any other.

At the 11-minute mark of the second half, Griffith stole a ball at midcourt and attacked two retreating defenders. In past seasons he might have tried to step between them and perform an acrobatic combination of moves the Wallendas would have applauded. The result might have been (1) a dunk, (2) a charge or (3) a ball flying out of his hands and out of bounds. This time he stopped and shoveled a pass to an unnoticed Brown cutting for a layup, taking a sure team thing over spectacular personal uncertainty.

Griffith hit 13 of 22 shots, nearly all of them jumpers, not dunks. "It's hard to guard a guy when his knees are in your face," Vol guard Gary Carter said.

The Cardinals won because Rodney McCray—yep, the same Rodney who had set a new low for practice habits—stepped off the pines with Louisville desperate for a big-man presence and grabbed a team-high seven rebounds, added three assists and two steals and twice blocked star Tennessee forward Reggie Johnson's shots.

The Cardinals won because they fired at a jaw-dropping 67.3 percent pace from the field, because Derek Smith hit seven of eight shots and scored 16 points, because Brown kept himself in the game despite four fouls for 29 minutes and 12 points.

And the Cardinals won because the team kept itself under control at key moments in stressful adverse conditions on an enemy floor.

"We held our poise better than I thought we would," coach Denny Crum said.

"We were more under control and together," Griffith said, "and we didn't let the threat of a comeback shake us up."

Rodney's Epiphany

Most remarkable, most utterly astonishing given the previous seven weeks of aggravation, was Rodney McCray's grand entrance onto the Division I stage at Tennessee.

It was paid scant notice at the time, considering the import of what Louisville was doing to fight off the Volunteers. But, when the guys looked back at the event, they could scarcely believe it a quarter-century later.

Rodney went from a crusty, recalcitrant 18-year-old "Baby Huey" (the nickname his new teammates quickly gave him after the roly-poly Bill Cosby character) to a man in a matter of minutes.

Sadly, it came at the expense of his brother, Scooter. Yet had not Scoot been injured, Rodney might not have been able to reconstruct his work habits. Would coach Denny Crum have ever given him more than token minutes?

Some players have even wondered if the Cardinals would have been able to accomplish what they did if Rodney had not emerged. For the next 33 games, Rodney was the "1" in the 2-2-1 press, an eraser, an intimidator to guys three inches taller, a man who sacrificed when he had to, who stepped up when he had to, who cared not about numbers but only about the fabric of the game.

"I always felt like the game came easier for me than for Rodney, but he had the better body," Scooter said. "We complemented each other so well. Plus we both had the attitude that it wasn't about scoring, it was about winning, and as long as you had the confidence you could play with people, then winning should be the bottom line. If the team won, everybody won."

Within weeks his nickname changed from "Baby Huey" to "Hard."

Scooter was a huge loss because of exquisite fundamental skills that went with an attitude about the sport that matched his brother's. Had Scooter been able to have his damaged knee fixed and return in a few weeks, the Cardinals' run would have been even more devastating than it was. Had Rodney never gotten a real shot, well ...

Just 3:27 into the Tennessee game, teammate Darrell Griffith got into a rebound battle, stumbled and fell backward into Scooter. McCray was helped off the floor, and even though team doctor Rudy Ellis was hoping for maybe a sprained ligament, Scooter was certainly done for the night.

"I'm sitting there, the game's tight, they've got Reggie Johnson and Dale Ellis, and although I've got confidence, I'm wondering, 'Can I really play with these guys?'" Rodney remembered. "When Scooter went down, my first concern was, is he going to be all right? He's in a lot of pain. Coach Crum says, 'He'll be all right. Now we've got to get our focus back on what we're here for, and that's to win this game.'

"I'm thinking he's going to put Poncho (Wright) or somebody like that in. He says, 'Rod, come on.' I go out, first road game, a little nervous playing against Johnson, their main man. We start banging bodies. Griff had a great game, and all I had to do was play defense and rebound. It was a confidence builder, an opportunity to play against one of the best players in the Southeastern Conference on the road. And we win the game. I was happy and excited. But worried about Scooter."

Three days later Scooter was declared out for the season. That afternoon Crum called Rodney into his office.

Rodney remembered Crum's words almost verbatim: "He said, 'I need you to give it to me in practice. I need you to work like you worked in the game. I guarantee you the game will be a whole lot easier.' He was absolutely right. When he told me those words I never forgot them. From the day I walked out of his office I practiced hard the rest of the year and the next 13 (3 U of L and 10 NBA) seasons."

"After that [talk] he busted his butt every single day," the coach said. "He was night-to-day different. He worked really hard, got himself in shape and just got better and better."

Said Scooter: "I'd been telling the coaching staff [Rodney] could play, that because of his body he'd be able to withstand a lot more than I could. To see him get the opportunity and live up to the expectations he had of himself was a glorious thing."

The Sculpting Begins

Wiley Brown, Derek Smith, the rest of the Louisville Cardinals and the coaches were dealt a double culture shock by the rookie from the City.

Brown spoke eloquently about the Rodney McCray he saw in the weeks leading to December 8 and the emerging action hero of the months leading to March 24.

"Worst practice player I'd ever seen," Brown said. "We couldn't be more down on Rodney. Scooter got hurt and he took the chip off his shoulder. We're like, 'Who's this guy?' He stepped it up like this is my time to shine—rebounding, blocking shots, running up and down the court, talking, cheering us on, encouraging every day from that day on. Ooohhh, man. Great. Unbelievable."

Assistant head coach Bill Olsen, the man who swatted McCray with a broom and tried to embarrass him by running a mile backwards, echoed Brown.

"I'm saying to myself, 'Where did this guy come from?'" Olsen said. "I wondered if this was a fluke. But from then on he was the most consistent player on the team, probably the unsung hero. I'd never seen anything like it. Yet it kind of speaks to the kind of team this was."

For McCray, any new practice ethic would have to be mind over matter. Sometimes mind over painful matter.

"Before, I was never in condition," he said. "I'd reach a point where I'd tell myself if I go any harder something (injurious) could happen. I'd reach that point and back off, not understanding that if you reach that pain and go through it, on the other side [you will get] into condition and over the hump.

"After Tennessee, once I felt pain in practice and kept pushing myself … it was a whole lot easier. I'd start looking forward to the end of practice where I'd say to Coach (Jerry) Jones, 'Gotta run that mile today,' or 'We gotta run those sprints.'"

Brown was the fastest straight-line guy on the squad.

Said Rodney: "It reached a point where me and Wiley ran sprints, with me telling him, 'I'm going to get you this time.' We'd come neck and neck and I'd say, 'Uh-oh, kind of tight, I'm going to have to dive across this line.' We'd push ourselves to the limit."

"Rodney was smart, he knew how to get position, how to get a rebound, how to score," Jerry Jones recalled. "He had something inside him that let him enjoy winning over everything. …He was not the greatest athletic talent to come down the pike, but he was one of the best players ever to play at U of L."

Setting Your Jaw and Carrying On

"Damn it, we're going to have to open it up."

Scooter McCray had been asleep on a hospital operating table nearly three hours on December 11 when team physician Rudy Ellis turned to his partners, doctors Raymond Shea and Walter Badenhausen, and spoke the words that put Louisville's forward on the shelf for the rest of the season.

Through an arthroscope, all three had tried to remove a floating cartilage fragment and repair three cracks in attached cartilage in McCray's right knee. They couldn't, so they had to open the knee up and fix it with full-blown surgery.

It was, seemingly, a staggering punch to the midsection of a team full of promise. Gone was the Cardinals' most versatile player. Coach Denny Crum had to choose among (1) moving Darrell Griffith to forward and starting a backup guard; (2) losing bench spark by putting Poncho Wright at McCray's spot, or (3) switching Wiley Brown from center to forward and starting Rodney McCray in the pivot, thus making a young team even younger.

Only two of Crum's top nine players stood taller than 6-6. Privately, Crum said his club would be lucky to win 15 games. None of his first eight won fewer than 20.

But instead of gloom and doom, the roster paid proper homage to a tough loss, then gritted its teeth.

"Each of us will just have to work harder," Burkman said. "We will."

"I still think we'll be a great team," Brown said.

Crum chose option three—Brown to forward, the mostly unproven Rodney to the middle. But the Rodney performance at Tennessee made skeptical teammates sudden believers.

"He's young, but he can handle it," said Brown, himself all of 19. "He won't get pushed around. And me and Derek are going to have to work harder on the boards."

"He'll bring as much or more to the lineup than Scooter," Derek Smith said, "and that's not taking anything away from Scooter."

Crum, publicly at least, joined the chorus.

"Scooter gave us depth, size, experience and a great court sense," the coach said. "What hurts most is that he always knows what's going on, that he's a tremendous team player who makes everybody else better. But you can't live in the past. It's always tough to make adjustments, but we're going to do it right and we're going to do it well."

Accelerated Rehab

By all accounts, Scooter McCray was a remarkable rehabilitation patient.

He was back on the floor by mid-February, 1980, cutting a month off his expected return to mobility. As Greg Deuser, one of the second-team practice maniacs, said, "When we got Scooter, all of a sudden we got a whole lot better."

And McCray would come to mean a whole lot more to the team in nonphysical ways.

"We were devastated when he was hurt," trainer Jerry May said, "and you just can't take a talent like his—handle the basketball, pass on a dime—and not feel something for awhile. He healed quickly, built the knee back up quickly and rehabbed quickly because he'd do anything you'd ask him to and be anywhere you'd ask him to be.

"And, boy, we had people step up and play that much harder, his brother being one. But a lot of that was Scooter. He was a coach while he was hurt—staying on the bench, hollering, screaming, getting people in line, doing things that needed to be done for us to be good. If he stays in a corner and accepts defeat, we would not have been half the ball club we were."

Games 4 and 5: Holiday Classic, December 13-14, North Carolina Charlotte, Western Kentucky

For a half during the opener of its own four-team tournament against Charlotte, Louisville missed Scooter McCray desperately. It was passive, lethargic and ahead by a slim five points at the break.

Appearances were deceiving. In a riveting 6:41 stretch after intermission, the Cardinals laid down a blanket of suppressing fire that produced a 26-4 thunderclap, a 70-41 lead and eventually a 93-76 victory. The run alerted future foes that, Scooter or no Scooter, Louisville would always be carrying dynamite sticks and fuses in its gym bags.

"It was like a prizefighter who keeps hitting you in the nose," UNCC coach Mike Pratt said.

The next night against Western Kentucky, the onslaught picked up where it left off. Louisville started 14-0, led 48-31 at halftime and won 96-74 as Rodney McCray, easing the loss of his brother, went seven for seven from the field, scored 17 points and grabbed eight rebounds.

Twelfth-ranked U of L was now 5-0, but there was a sobering thought: No. 3 Ohio State, tall, thick and talented, was due in town in five days. Not too sobering for a couple of Cardinals, though.

"The crowd will be berserk," Jerry Eaves said after a career-high 19 points against Western. "We'll be ready to do some killing."

Derek Smith was heard talking about "eating his Kellogg's corn flakes for dinner," a typical Smithian mix of verbs and nouns referencing freshman Clark Kellogg, Ohio State's once and future star forward.

Whoa. Might it not be better to hold the euphoria and gulp down a mouthful of intensity?

No Pass? No Problem

In the midst of the flash flood of points Louisville used to drown Charlotte, a subtle incident was a reminder of how this team had found the missing link. Darrell Griffith grabbed a loose ball in backcourt. He took a quick glance toward his basket. Roger Burkman was down there, alone. Griffith drove it for a two-handed jam.

"I should have passed to Roger but I ... well, I didn't," he said, a bit taken aback by his hoggishness. "It hurt me that I did that."

How upset was Burkman? Not very.

"It was just one of those things," Burkman said. "He gives it up to me (usually), I give it up to him. I thought he was going to do a 360 and everybody would get crazy."

Game 6: Ohio State, December 19

Tennessee was a large test for Louisville because it was on the road against a name school on a roll, and because of the events surrounding the McCrays.

Ohio State was a much different deal: An entrenched Big Ten power that had ripped Louisville 85-69 on its own floor a year earlier, it had four returning starters, went 6-8, 6-9, 6-10 across the front line, had a 5-0 record and was now ranked No. 2.

But for U of L, also 5-0 and up to No. 11 in the rankings, it was the first big chance to show its sold-out Freedom Hall homies that it, too, was good enough even sans Scooter McCray to be pounding on the national door.

Pounding was right. The Buckeyes opened with three slams, three blocked shots and stomped off to leads of 18-8 and 22-13 in the first eight minutes. Then coach Eldon Miller subbed out three of his starters—later defending the move by saying he wasn't going to win with five guys going 40 minutes. Louisville caught up at 25-25. The three returned. Louisville's motor warmed by then, the Cardinals scored the next nine points, nursed the advantage to 59-48, went to a delay game, watched Ohio State cut it to 59-57, then used poise, layups, steals and free throws to upend the Bucks 75-65.

The visitors noticed an abrupt change from one year to the next.

"They were patient on offense, really got what they wanted and dictated the whole game," guard Carter Scott told *Louisville Times* columnist Dick Fenlon. And center Herb Williams added: "They play with a lot more intensity and seem a lot closer."

Darrell Griffith scored 19 points, Derek Smith 18. Smith and Rodney McCray each grabbed nine rebounds and U of L hit 57 percent from the field.

Asked what he remembered from the game, Kellogg, now a CBS television in-season analyst and NCAA Tournament studio host, said, "I've got selective amnesia."

What he could recall would suffice.

"The thing that stands out most was the great atmosphere, as it always is, in Freedom Hall," said Kellogg, who had 12 points and eight boards. "I didn't look at them as a national championship-caliber team, but certainly one that was going to be formidable that night and into the rest of the season. We got off to a pretty good start, then momentum shifted and they were able to get away with a pretty impressive win."

Louisville's style of play seemed to offset Ohio State's size.

"Exactly," Kellogg said. "They had good quickness and a good scheme in terms of how they would defend you and try to speed you up a little bit. Certainly we thought we could play that way, and at first we did. We just didn't do it long enough. I think you have to give Louisville credit for that."

Louisville coach Denny Crum agreed.

"It was a perfect example of our press keeping them off-kilter the whole game," he recalled. "That showed me we could be competitive with anybody even with the young kids we had."

Now 6-0, maybe a touch full of themselves, the Cardinals headed west, into adventures unknown.

CHAPTER FIVE

Spark-less in Hawaii:

December 22, 1979, to January 1, 1980

Game 7: Utah, December 22

Utah was 5-4. The school had been to the last three NCAAs, had an All-America named Danny Vranes and a future All-America and NBA star named Tom Chambers, and had lost to, among others, an NAIA team at home. And Vranes was going to have to sit out the Louisville game because of a correspondence school transcript controversy.

It was all a deception, as Louisville would soon learn.

The thoroughbreds that had buzzed past Ohio State were off their feed against the Utes. They didn't motor hard or play a lot of defense the first half, which ended with Utah up 40-32. They rallied for ties at 65 and 69 in the second half, but with 3:04 left Utah had the ball and an eye on a stall.

It wasted away nearly three minutes, then ran a play U of L was ready to handle. Dan Larson, double-teamed down low, fired a pass to Karl Bankowski in the dead left corner with two seconds left. Roger Burkman, arms flailing, soared at him—and on past him. One second. Rise and fire. Perfect. Utah 71-69.

Derek Smith scored a career-best 25 points and hit a frightening 12 of 13 field goals, Darrell Griffith scored 23, and the Cardinals shot 58 percent. But it was not good enough. Utah shot 64.6, and the Louisville team that outrebounded big, bad Ohio State 30-26 was reamed on the boards 28-19.

"We're not going to beat anybody when we don't hustle," coach Denny Crum said. "You've got to play 40 minutes, not 15 or 20."

If Crum was right, and this turned out to be more than a one-time deal, it was a major worry. The one thing this squad promised to never become was the Doctors of Non-Hustle.

Looking back, then-assistant Jerry Jones thought it was the Salt Lake City locale. "Altitude," he said. "A concrete game. It looked like we were playing in stone."

Jerry Eaves disagreed, saying, "We just didn't have it that night. We were ready to play. We just didn't play well."

One man wasn't about to bow to altitudes. The lights on a big "U" sitting on a hilltop on the Utah campus flash after a victory. As U of L's chartered bus pulled away from the arena to return to the hotel, Griffith looked up at the blinking letter and bitterly snapped off a curse word. He was mad. The Cardinals had lost one. They had better not lose (m)any more.

Black or White? No, Black and White

The unhappy Cardinals trooped back into their hotel's restaurant after the Utah loss to grab a bite to eat before hitting the sack for an early flight to San Francisco and connection to Hawaii the next morning.

Coach Denny Crum's table was served promptly. But another table of five Cardinals—Cleveland, Griffith, Brown, Smith, and Wright—waited and waited for someone to take their order. Eventually an irate Crum made certain the group got something to eat.

"I remember saying, 'I'm never coming back to this city again,' and I haven't," Cleveland said. "Griff said the same thing. Then he played 10 years here (in the NBA)."

If there was a racial tinge to the incident (the five at the table were black), that wasn't part of Griffith's thinking.

"I don't remember that part of it," Griffith said. "I was just upset at the loss."

But racism, as we know, was a large and despicable part of American culture in the 1970s. Louisville was hardly immune to it, and the city's university wasn't an oasis, either.

But on the 1979-80 Louisville basketball team, race without the "ism" was an open invitation to comic relief, stupidity and insanity. The politically correct cops of the 2000s would have been appalled at the utter disregard these guys had for throwing out lightning-rod words and phrases and staging dueling putdowns. Today, some of that stuff would call for a month of angry keep-it-alive blasts in the press, probably followed by an infection that would hound a team the rest of the season. Then, however, everybody laughed, rolled their eyes or shook their heads and went about their business.

There was Scooter McCray coming to the season opener with his head shaved and calling himself the "black Moses" just as Greg Deuser was cultivating his "Harpo Marx Afro" and saying, "I'm trying to look like Scooter and look what he does."

Roger Burkman dunked on Chattanooga, his first dunk in two years, and said, "It's been a long time since a white boy dunked around here." Then the 6-5 guard beat a black Tennessee big man to a tip the next game, prompting McCray to say, "No more White Man's Disease," referring to the old adage that white men can't jump. "I told him he was over it, that he just didn't have it any more."

When the late Jim Valvano was asked how high his 6-10, 260-pound Iona center Jeff Ruland could jump, he said, "There's no reason to measure the vertical jump of a 6-10 white kid. All my kids have the white man's disease. In fact, I'm the only coach in the country who has black kids who can't jump."

In a feature on Deuser, Mike Sullivan of the *Courier-Journal* spent several paragraphs discussing the entry of a six-foot rural-area white (Floyds Knobs, Indiana) onto a mostly-black squad. "I came to U of L not knowing how to act toward blacks or how they would act toward me," Deuser told Sullivan. "With all the joking we do, it's not a big thing. It's not even any kind of thing."

Local newspapermen had few qualms about addressing black-white issues and rumors, but not in an attack mode.

Marty Pulliam, a slow-footed, low-jumping 6-9 center from rural Harrodsburg, Kentucky, was part of a four-white, one-black recruiting class in 1977. It was said coach Denny Crum was forced by powerful backers to get some white faces on the club. Crum has denied that, angrily, to this day.

Pulliam, a pragmatist then and now, talked about coming to a "city" situation and encountering people with different styles, personalities and cultures. After three or four years "you see things in a broader view," he said then, "and it has to change you, some for the better, some for worse. You're exposed to things you might not want to be, but I think I'm a more complete person."

Pulliam, a prankster then and now, also became just about the most popular member of the team.

"We formed the WPA or WBA—White Players Association or White Boys Association," he said. "We had a motto: 'On my honor I'll do my best to take what they give me and steal the rest.'" The "steal" part referred to how many pairs of sneakers the guys could secretly pry away from the equipment folks.

"Now it's not politically correct," Pulliam said. "You got to watch what you say. You're going to offend somebody. People take more out of it than what you mean."

The guys on U of L's planes and buses in '79-80 were all trying to be more complete people. It just didn't have anything to do with skin tone. They took things that often generated hatred and rage, turned them into absurdity, dumped them into their comedic trash can and went on with the biggest task we all had (and have) – improving as human beings.

Hearts (and Other Stuff) in Their Mouths

The morning following the team's loss to Utah, December 23, the Louisville Cardinals left the flashing "U" behind and began their trek to the Rainbow Classic on Hawaii's main island of Oahu.

The first leg would take the team and several family members from Salt Lake City to San Francisco, then on to exotica. The flight went fine until the plane hit a vicious air pocket as it flew over the Sierra Nevada mountain range.

"It was awful," recalled guard Roger Burkman. "One of Jack Tennant's daughters (the late 'Lieu' Tennant was an assistant U of L athletic director and the radio play-by-play man) was sitting in front of me and Greg. Suddenly she stands up and yells, 'I love you mommy and daddy. I think the plane's going to crash.'"

Burkman didn't laugh at her. "It was that rough," he said. "We were tossing and turning."

A few people tossed more than their bodies (cookies comes to mind).

"Here we'd just lost to Utah on a last-second shot, didn't play well and we're upset anyway," Burkman said. "Now this."

The plane lurched through the danger safely and landed. But there were five more airborne hours to go.

Touching Down on a Different Planet

The flight from San Francisco to Honolulu was uneventful, but when the squad exited the plane to warm breezes, palm trees and ponds populated with Japanese koi—and that was just in the airport—a lot of the guys thought they had stepped onto Neptune.

The varying degrees of worldliness in the players were stark. For someone like Derek Smith, who had just turned 18 seven weeks earlier and come to Louisville from a village in Georgia, the mind couldn't quite grasp it all.

The Louisville team arrived on December 23. It wouldn't begin play in the eight-team Rainbow Classic until December 28. That left five days to discover how many ways one could spell paradise.

It would be good. And it would be bad. There were monkey pod and banyan trees, all of a rainbow's colors, blue-green water, crashing waves and 85 degrees. And Waikiki Beach, a commercial mix of salt water and humanity—some of it lovely humanity—that could pass for Miami Beach or hundreds of other sun-soaked coastal getaways. Except that Waikiki had been dropped into this alien setting.

"I think we've broken the time warp," Greg Deuser said.

"I came here to watch girls and play ball," Smith said. "Not in that order," reminded coach Denny Crum.

Indeed, some had no reservations about bending a loose rule or two.

"I remember me and Poncho, about 3 o'clock one morning, walking down the main boulevard following these girls," Daryl Cleveland said. "Coach Houston came by in a limousine, rolled down the window and asked what we were doing. We got back to the hotel."

The squad toured the island. It went to a Polynesian Revue where Rodney McCray, Wright, Eaves and Pulliam assisted girls from some of the South Sea island chains with a native dance. The stoic McCray, gyrating like a native Samoan, stole the show.

"Wasn't nothin'," McCray said with a shrug. "Now there's a guy with a lot of confidence in himself," Crum added.

Then there was Smith, a teenager rapidly losing his confidence, his ability to function and his mind.

He was scared of water. He had never even seen salt water.

"Santa Claus will be on a surfboard before I am," he said.

Nevertheless, Cleveland and Brown coerced Smith to sample the three- to four-foot deep water off Waikiki. Cleveland and Brown could swim a little. A nervous Smith expected to drown. Yet he was coaxed into dipping his face in the salty surf. He forgot to close his mouth. He came up gagging and gasping. His bulging eyes said he was terrified. Finally he recovered. Within seconds he was back on the beach.

"The funny thing was, years later Derek would go fishing at midnight or 2 a.m. (on lakes near Louisville)," Brown said. "I'd say, 'Derek, you're afraid of water.' He'd try to get me to go and I'd say, 'You're crazy. I'm not getting on that boat.' He loved to fish. Just fish. Not swim."

That wasn't the worst of it. Smith and Brown had never been away from home at Christmas. Now, suddenly and depressingly, it was Christmas Eve.

"Derek went on strike," assistant coach Bill Olsen recalled. "He went on a fast, wouldn't come to team meals—we had to take him his meals. Worst case of homesickness I'd ever seen." He also boycotted the Polynesian Revue.

"How come these Louisville people bring me all the way over here?" he cried, angrily biting off each word. "I'm going to transfer. My momma expects me home. You can have that steak. I want some cornbread, black-eyed peas, chicken and meatloaf. On Christmas morning I want to see those two cakes my momma puts out on the coffee table with a piece [cut] out of each that Santa took."

Surprising, a Christmas Eve practice was lively and called the best in a long time by Smith. Not surprisingly, a Christmas morning practice was terrible. Smith missed about half his layups and manager Randy Bufford was declared the best player on the floor.

The team still had two days till meeting Pete Carril's maddeningly deliberate Princeton team in the Rainbow opener. The omens were not good.

Calling the Tune in Ig-Pay Atin-Lay

As if there wasn't enough goofiness to go around, it became known before the start of the Rainbow that some of the Cardinals spoke part of the time to each other on the floor in pig Latin.

This, naturally, originated with the Georgia Connection, specifically Wiley Brown. He and his Louisville roommate, Carlton Cherry, had learned it years earlier. Brown taught it to Smith and Cleveland. Another Georgian, manager Randy Bufford, learned enough to withstand pig Latin-speaking raids on his equipment cache. The rest of the guys tried to be tolerant.

Even the McCrays, who wouldn't be caught dead saying "Erek-day, ip-tay ooh-tay aa-may eft-lay" (Derek, tip to my left), picked up enough jargon to understand what was about to happen on the court.

"But when they talk to someone off the court, I don't know what the hell they're saying," said Rodney McCray, his scowl indicating he didn't want to, either.

But the guys did run a decent-sized verbal portion of their basketball operation out of what one dictionary calls "a systematic mutilation of English."

"Erek-day! Erek-day. Ets-lay a-play ough-ray!" Brown calls out.

"Irty-day?" asks Smith.

"Es-yay," answers Brown.

The exchange—"Derek, Derek, let's play rough." "Dirty?" "Yes"—might happen if the Georgians had received one too many stray elbows from the enemy. They would call out a name—"If-gray" for Darrell Griffith—telling him if they got the tip the ball was heading his direction. They announced back-door lobs—"Oot-scray ob-lay" (Scooter, lob)—and offenses—"uffle-shay" (shuffle) and "ard-gay ut-cay" (guard cut)—in the same manner.

"We'd teach Scooter certain words," Brown said. "With Darrell, he didn't really care whether opponents knew what was coming or not because he was going to do it anyway. And with opponents, well, they were like, 'Uh, what? Hey ...?'

"When Derek and Wiley came here I could understand their pig Latin better than their English," coach Denny Crum said. "When I was a kid my sisters and I spoke it. Derek and Wiley's (non-pig Latin) slang was what they grew up with, but they took speech classes, persevered and did well. But that year they spoke pig Latin on the floor, on the bus, on the plane, all the time, all season."

The Eaker-Snay Scheme

The Georgians attempt to pig Latin their way to a sneaker bonanza mostly failed, it seemed.

Always hopeful of adding to their shoe collection from the equipment room, Wiley Brown would say to Derek Smith, "Eak-snay ome-say oe-shay out-ay, erek-Day" (Sneak some shoes out, Derek).

"But Buff (manager Randy Bufford) caught on," Brown said.

"I didn't get into it other than knowing enough so I could communicate," Bufford said. "The sneakers? I don't know. I'd hear them say, 'Here comes Andy-ray,' but I don't remember missing shoes."

And an Ast-Blay from the Ast-Pay

Joe Yates was Louisville's sports information director in 1979-80. His nine-year-old daughter, Jolynn, became one of the kid mascots taken under the wings of most of the players, particularly by Derek Smith and Rodney McCray.

In June of 2003 Yates and wife Kelly rented a house at Virginia Beach, Virginia, for a field hockey tournament involving his stepdaughters.

Jolynn, now 32, husband Jeff and three kids came over from North Carolina for a few vacation days.

The families were sitting outside. Somebody had left the door to the house open. Yates didn't want to embarrass whomever that was.

Instinctively, he called out, "Olynn-jay, ut-shay or-day."Instinctively, Jolynn got up and shut the door.

"She never even blinked," Yates said. "She gets up, shuts the door and nobody even knows what's transpired. I don't know why I did that. It was kind of like a dad with his daughter, something we did years and years ago. It's the only foreign language I know how to speak.

"Later I said to her, 'Isn't it funny how we can still do that from time to time?' She said, 'Aw, Dad, we'll never forget some of those things.'"

Game 8: Princeton, December 28

Finally. Stow the snorkeling tubes, let's play ball.

Let's play bad ball. Let's play boring ball. Let's play stall ball. Let's beat Princeton 64-53 and have no right to feel good about any part of it, except maybe for Daryl Cleveland.

Louisville, the Rainbow Classic favorite over Illinois, Wisconsin, Hawaii and four others, opened against a team that seemingly invented the back-door play. Princeton had its usual complement of fairly slow, not very athletic but clever, smart and mistake-free players—who happened to be 2-6.

Forward Neil Christel, whose high game for the season was six points, scored 10 on back cuts alone against the slumbering U of L defense in the first half. As the Cardinals struggled to stay with the Tigers and were lucky to forge a 32-32 halftime tie, an exasperated Crum called on Cleveland late in the first 20 minutes.

The man who would hardly play again with a game on the line remembers.

"No one could stop this guy," Cleveland said. "Coach Crum said, 'Cleve, you think you can stop him?' I said, 'Yeah, I can stop him. I might foul him a little bit, but I can stop him.'

"I went in, hit him a couple of times, stuck my elbow out there, and in the second half he never went back-door again. Also, Coach took me out of the game and I never got in again."

Louisville slogged to its 11-point victory with a stall the last 12 minutes that Princeton refused to challenge. Princeton sent two guards out of its zone close enough to the Cardinals so it wouldn't be called for a non-guarding technical foul, made no attempt to foul or steal, and that's pretty much how the thing slogged to a conclusion.

The 3,911 fans, mostly islanders, who sparsely populated 7,800-seat Blaisdell Center had come to be entertained by Darrell Griffith and his high-flying friends. Instead, they booed the team. They booed the cheer-leaders. One fan even followed Denny Crum to his postgame radio show and chewed the coach out over the non-dunking exhibition.

Crum jammed his nose into the fellow's nose and said, "I want to tell you something before I lose my cool. If you don't leave right now I might do something you'll regret."

A few seconds later Crum calmed down and tried to explain to the man how he didn't like the stall, either. But by then U of L (7-1) had gone from team excitement to team villain, and would remain there.

Game 9: Illinois, December 29

On top of homesickness, hunger strikes and a preference for sunbathing girls over dribbles, Louisville now was Public Enemy No. 1 in the islands.

Then came Illinois in the Rainbow Classic semis, 8-2 after dissecting Mike Krzyzewski's Army team 75-48. The Illini had speed to go with plen-ty of height. U of L had already handled a supposedly better Big Ten club, but its mental approach against Ohio State hardly compared to the state of mind of the guys on Louisville's listing catamaran.

The Cardinals trailed only 19-17 seven minutes before intermission. Then the Illini closed the half with an 18-2 run. A U of L squad shooting 55 percent prior to the game made 25 percent of its shots during the first half, seven of 28, and trailed 37-19 at the break. Illinois coasted to a 77-64 victo-ry.

"The way we've played since Ohio State, 150 teams could beat us," coach Crum said. "We have to have a burning desire to destroy somebody. We're not big enough or strong enough to play at seven-eighths or three-quarters speed."

"It's been a long road trip and a nice vacation," said Burkman, 0 for 3 with no assists in his 10 minutes against the Fighting Illini. "More vacation than basketball. We lost our spark and haven't kept our perspective. It's easy to forget what you're here for."

Mostly U of L needed to remember what the next three months were for. Maybe they could find a hypnotist to snap them out of their trance.

"I hope this doesn't keep going," said Brown, 0 for 5 with five rebounds in 29 minutes. "If it does, we'll lose a lot of games."

Louisville, at No. 12, was the only ranked team in the tourney. The next week's ratings dropped U of L to 15th and moved Illinois in at No. 20.

A Freshman's Ultimatum, Sort Of

The Louisville team trooped quietly back into its hotel after the Illinois debacle and Darrell Griffith immediately called a players-only meeting.

Everyone was upset, but Griffith was especially angry. He was the one who had put himself on the edge of a cliff four years earlier, who desperately wanted to experience a real March, and now his fourth set of Cardinals seemed on the verge of toppling into another abyss. More nerve-wracking than the losses for this 7-2 squad was the feeling that it had lost its fire and didn't really know why.

While Griffith led most of the session, Tony Branch, the other senior, had more than two cents' worth to say, too.

The next day, Smith said they talked about "hustle, desire, enthusiasm, giving the ball to each other, congratulating each other when we did something good."

"This was it for Griff—his last dance," Brown said. "He needed some help and we had to deliver. Instead we were getting outhustled and had gotten lackadaisical. We knew we were young and we're going to have games like that, but we weren't going to stand it for long. The good thing was we all respected each other. You could say whatever you wanted and air it out. That's what makes a winner."

They all wanted to get the problems fixed. Nearly everybody offered a piece of his mind, reminding one another of goals, of getting a new focus.

Then suddenly, from the back of the room, a low rumble was heard.

"All I know is we've lost two games now, and I never lost two games a season my whole damn (high school) career," freshman center Rodney McCray said.

Burkman recounted the moment as if it happened an hour ago.

"Here's Rodney, quiet Rodney, never says a word," Burkman said. "Still trying to get his legs, still with a bit of baby fat despite how hard he'd been working. For that voice, from that guy, to say that, we looked at each other and we're like, 'Okay. Okay, let's not lose anymore.'"

It was like a stone tablet pronouncement. McCray had lost one game his senior year at Mt. Vernon High, none his junior year.

"It was a serious team meeting," McCray said. "Everybody was all intense. After I spoke, they said, 'Hey, we're trying to be serious here.' I said, 'I am serious.' Everybody started laughing. And we said, 'All right then, let's go.'"

Thief! Thief! Uh, Hold On

The Georgia homies—Cleveland, Brown and Smith – decided to sample the sights and sounds along Honolulu's main boulevard, Kalakaua Avenue, late one night. The long stretch opposite Waikiki Beach is stocked with innumerable open-air stands selling a variety of material, mostly jewelry.

The trio paused periodically to look over the goods. At one stand they were checking out gold chains when Cleveland noticed the vendor slip a necklace into her own pocket. Her English was hard to understand (and you can imagine her challenge with three rural southern guys who might throw some pig-Latin at her) and shortly the players moved on.

But not far. A moment later they heard her hailing two policemen and yelling at the guys to "stop, stop, stop."

They stopped. The vendor approached them, followed by the police.

"Here we are, we've got 'Louisville' written across our backs. [We're] all about 6-8, got everybody looking at us, and she's telling the police we stole a necklace," Cleveland recalled.

Cleveland: "We don't have any necklace."
Vendor: Where'd you put it?"
Cleveland: "You didn't put it in your pocket?"
Vendor (checking her pocket): "Oohhh. I'm sorry, I'm sorry."

The guys got a good scare.

"You know I was [scared]," Brown said. "We're in Hawaii to have fun and end up getting locked up? End up walking around with handcuffs on?"

Not the most sterling image to take back to Kentucky.

Game 10: Nebraska, December 30

Louisville began to reverse directions with an imminently forgettable 65-58 victory over Nebraska in the third-place Rainbow Classic game.

With 13:04 left, Griffith tied Charlie Tyra's school career points record of 1,728 with his 17th point of the game. Sports information director Joe Yates wanted him to break the record at home, coach Denny Crum wanted to win the game and Griffith just wanted it off his mind. He would have to wait until the Cardinals next game—a home contest against Tulsa on January 3—to break the record, as Griffith failed to score the rest of the way. He was honored at the tourney, though, by being named the tourney's most valuable player despite being the second-leading scorer and playing in the consolation game. Fans booed.

"That's the hardest we've played since Ohio State," Crum said. "We didn't play all that well, but we did get after it."

Smith, shooting 67 percent over his first eight games, hit just four of 13 shots during his last two. He still had work to do to escape his funk. Brown, shooting 61 percent during his first six competitions, went two for 17 in his next three before regaining a bit of his touch by hitting four of eight against Nebraska.

Now 2-2 on the 12-day road trip and 8-2 overall, the Cardinals could begin to visualize their own beds. A three-game home stand was next. But they wouldn't get home until the afternoon of New Year's Day and wouldn't likely be over jet lag by the time Tulsa showed up two days later.

Waves with Jaws

The day after Christmas, assistant coach Bill Olsen and eighth-grade son Doug, manager Randy Bufford and players Greg Deuser and Marty Pulliam took an informal tour around Oahu.

The midpoint of the circle was the North Shore, Waimea Bay, where waves easily grow to over 20 feet as they rise over coral reefs. In the late '70s it was considered the best and most dangerous surf anywhere, home to the world surfing championships.

The guys stopped. The waves were about 15 feet high. They pounded through the bay at an angle, and if they caught an unwary swimmer they would sledgehammer him into the sand, grab him with their undertow and drag him back out, performing the cycle again and again as they rolled toward an outcropping of jagged volcanic rocks 300 yards down the beach.

The Cardinals had a slight sense of the danger, but they couldn't resist, even though Olsen warned his son that "it was hard enough to raise three kids without one being a paraplegic or a quadriplegic the rest of his life."

All got caught to some degree in the washing machine. Deuser was probably the strongest swimmer and escaped major trauma, but Pulliam and Bufford had life-flashing-before-eyes moments.

"When you go to Daytona Beach you can walk out into the water as far as the eye can see," recalled Pulliam. "At Waimea it drops straight off. I was playing around, got too far out and the current started carrying me toward the rocks.

"I didn't think I could get back in. Another guy was out there and said I should rest until I saw a big wave coming, then swim as hard as I could and hook my arm into it. I tried that twice and finally rolled up on the beach. I looked up and I was 200 yards down the beach. If I had gotten into the rocks I'd have been in bad trouble. That was my last [time] swimming."

"I was right off shore and all of a sudden it grabbed me," Bufford remembered. "I was going backwards and got to the point where I was calling out for help. Then I started making progress. But I literally fought for my life. The waves throw you down, then step on you. I was never so thankful to get out of an ocean."

So much for body surfing. The next day a surfer got too close to the rocks. His surfboard hit the rocks and split in half. The man also hit the rocks. He died.

Not a Sobering Experience

Louisville didn't fly out of Hawaii until December 31, the day after the tournament ended. It didn't leave until late afternoon, thus losing an overnight (plus five more hours lost to time zones) by the time it arrived back home 12 hours later at 4:30 p.m. on January 1.

So whatever holiday celebration was in order was done over the Pacific.

The airline's personnel were more than anxious to help (or not help, depending on your viewpoint). It was, after all, New Year's Eve, and midnight would come near the time the flight would hit the mainland's West Coast.

Stewardesses uncorked champagne and wine. They offered it free. It was party time for a passenger list that included a basketball team that was in no mood to party. Unless, of course, it was in a drown-your-sorrows kind of mood.

Burkman, Deuser, Branch and Griffith were next to each other in one row.

"Three or four different stewardesses sat on our laps and all had champagne bottles," Burkman remembered. "They kept filling our glasses up. We drank. Griff was the smartest of us. He didn't have more than a glass or so, and he was fine. Greg and I were hurting a little, but nothing like Tony, who had more than any of us."

Unlike teams that came before or after them, partaking in alcohol or drugs was totally out of character for this '79-80 team. Branch was about as unlikely a candidate as you'd find—a senior guard, at the time contemplating a career in law. He said he didn't like beer, didn't like drinking, and had never been drunk. In other words, he was a victim in waiting. He got sick. Really sick. Unstable. Incoherent. He ended up flat on his face.

"He tried to get out of his seat and go to the bathroom, but his legs wouldn't work," Burkman said. "He crawled to the bathroom down the aisle, 20 or 30 feet, and made it before he threw up. It was hilarious."

To some. Branch would like to differ, but his memory of the ride remains (surprise) somewhat fuzzy.

"I was mixing champagne and wine," he said. "I regurgitated, but I thought it was in the bag at my seat. If I crawled to the bathroom, I don't remember. If Roger says I did it, I did it. My initial thought, when I finally had one, was you've got to be crazy to want to drink. All I had ever had before was a slo-gin fizz or a banana daiquiri. I think I wanted to know what it felt like to be drunk.

"Anyway, I fell asleep, much later the plane landed and everybody exited. I was still asleep. Roger and Greg or somebody came back to get me or I'd have gone on to China or somewhere. Those guys saved me a lot of embarrassment. With one guy on either side, they walked me into the terminal and sat me down real quick."

As Branch sat in a stupor awaiting his luggage, Coach Crum walked by. He stopped and looked at one of his two senior leaders. Branch tried to smile. The corners of Crum's mouth began to turn upward, too. He started to say something, then shook his head and walked away.

It had been a long 12 days for everyone.

CHAPTER SIX

Stirring the Embers and Fanning the Flames:

January 3, 1980 to January 31, 1980

Game 11: Tulsa, January 3, 1980

In one sense this was the foregone conclusion game. Darrell Griffith had tied Charlie Tyra's Louisville career points record in the last game in Hawaii. Unless he fouled out in the first five or 10 seconds this night, he was going to break it.

In another sense there was no foregone conclusion at all, as far as knowing what kind of Cardinal group would appear. Not only had they misplaced their attention span, but they should have been jet-lagged as well. Maybe they'd have to be wheeled into Freedom Hall while still slumbering in their dormitory beds.

It took all of 36 seconds for Griffith to swish a 14-foot jumper from the free throw line elbow, giving him 1,730 points to Tyra's 1,728 from 1953 to 1957. The game was halted, Tyra presented Griffith the ball and Griffith presented it to parents Maxine and Monroe. Later he told the *Courier-Journal's* Mike Sullivan, "I think the record means more to my parents. The record I want is to be on the first Louisville team to win the NCAA championship."

In the second half, U of L discarded its sea legs and eased on to a 78-58 victory. Griffith finished with 21 points. Derek Smith ended his four-of-13 brick-shooting with five of seven and 13 points. Wiley Brown seemed fully emerged from his two-of-17 slump with a second straight four of eight and 10 points. Poncho Wright, the top gun off the bench who had gone one for eight in his previous three-plus games, hit five of 10 shots for 11 points in the second half. And Roger Burkman, the defensive irritant in reserve, was back to his untamed self with, as Lou Younkin of the *Times* reported, seven assists, two steals and one sports writer in 19 minutes. One of his pass deflections smacked *Sports Illustrated*'s Curry Kirkpatrick in the face on press row.

Louisville was 9-2. Maybe rediscovery of its rhythm and momentum was around the corner.

Taking a Bite Out of Griff's Numbers

Darrell Griffith was ringing up the cash register all over the Louisville record book. Wiley Brown wants everyone to know this wasn't a solo act. If Scooter McCray was considered the most high-tech assist man, several other Louisvillians were not far behind. Brown was in that group.

"It seemed like every time [Griffith would] do something, like score his 2,000th point (which came later in the season), it was me getting him the ball," Brown said. "A high-low pass or a lob, it'd be me, my assist. I always remind him of that."

A month later at Providence, Rhode Island, six players including Griffith were lined up shooting obligatory free throws at the end of a practice.

A quiet voice near the back intoned, "When Darrell Griffith leaves, it will break up the greatest scoring tandem in university history. Griffith and Marty Pulliam have combined for over 2,000 points. But there will still be half the Dynamic Duo left."

At that moment Griffith had 2,034 career points to 6-9 sophomore center Pulliam's 14.

Game 12: Kansas State, January 5

It seemed appropriate to drop the phrase "all the way back" on Wiley Brown and Louisville after they dealt an 85-73 blow to a strong Kansas State team that was 10-1 coming in and featured star Rolando Blackman. Brown left his Honolulu blues behind with a career-best 21 points that included seven of seven from the free throw line by a low-60 percent shooter.

"When I don't even miss a free throw, I know my luck's gone from bad to good," Brown said.

Darrell Griffith added another exclamation point to the all-around game he enhanced as a senior with 27 points (nine of 11 field goals the second half), five rebounds, six assists and five steals.

And a bad thing-good thing happened. Jerry Eaves went down with a sprained ankle three minutes after tipoff and didn't return. Roger Burkman mostly subbed for him. But when K-State trimmed a 74-57 Louisville lead to 76-69 with 2:24 to go, Tony Branch was called upon. The unrecognized senior delivered two free throws, a pass to Griffith for a three-point play and two more free throws, and it was 83-69.

"It was good to be in there under pressure again," Branch said.

Branch's work against the Wildcats wasn't an omen kind of thing, was it? Leading to a déjà vu moment? Naw. Couldn't be.

My Kingdom for a Healthy Ankle

Jerry Eaves' ankle sprain was severe. He missed the next two games, came back for a forgettable one-point, two-assist performance in 24 minutes at Tulane and started from then on, but didn't get to 100 percent until near the end of the regular season.

Denny Crum decided to replace Eaves with his veteran, Tony Branch, at the point so he could keep the sixth-man energy injection of Roger Burkman intact. It all worked out fine for the team, but it was a three-week ordeal for Eaves and trainer Jerry May.

"We had just gotten a machine called an EGS—an electric galvanic stimulator," recalled May. "It stimulates the ankle to heal with electrical impulses and vibrates the tissue inside the joint. We carried that thing everywhere and worked on the ankle night and day."

"My ankle wasn't 100 percent for a long time," said Eaves. "And I remember Denny telling me going into the conference tournament (February 28), 'If you don't stop limping, I'm not going to play you.' That's when I said, 'Uh-oh.'"

Game 13: St. Louis, January 8

Basking in its full athletic glory, Louisville disemboweled St. Louis 94-65, improving to 11-2 with its fourth straight victory in its first Metro Conference game.

It was a Globetrotterish exhibition filled with half-court lobs, behind-the-back passes on breaks and eye-watering slams. The Cardinals had runs of 19-6 and 20-6, and it was over when U of L expanded a 44-33 halftime lead to 64-39.

Tony Branch started in place of injured point guard Jerry Eaves, ran the team for 20 minutes and scored nine points. But he quickly bowed afterwards to the head-shaking exploits of Roger Burkman. In a 50-second span of the second half Burkman scored 11 points and fouled out the two best Billikens players. He scored 19 points in 20 minutes, hit 13 of 14 free throws and had five steals and five assists.

"Roger covered so much ground, they must have thought there were two of him tonight," Branch said.

Jeff Schneider was a Billikens freshman sixth man who had played for DeSales High School in Louisville and knew many of the Cardinals well.

U of L had runs of 19-6 and 20-6 and Schneider remembered one simple guard-to-guard pass he threw toward David Burns followed by a fuzzy, warp-speed image.

"There was this blur in the middle," said Schneider, now author of sports books *The Fix* and *The Games*. "Rodney (McCray)! I turned around, the crowd's going nuts, and there's Rodney, elbows above the rim, throwing it down. I said, _____! I went back, got the ball and David said, 'Don't do that again.'"

Highlight Moment? Sorry, Try Again

Steve Clark, Louisville's walk-on freshman who bent a rim the first day of practice and received the Denny Crum reprimand, "If you can't dunk the ball, lay it in," had few opportunities for crowd-engaging moves. He dressed only for home games until after the Hawaii trip and wound up playing a total of 11 minutes in six of the 36 games.

But three of those minutes came against St. Louis, and with them a possession that was his best chance to hit the highlight reel. Billikens rookie and displaced Louisvillian Jeff Schneider apparently had a piece of that action, too.

"Rodney (McCray) steals the ball near the end of the game and I take off downcourt," Clark recalled. "Rodney throws it to me. In the back of my mind I'm going to go up for a dunk here at Freedom Hall, and the crowd's going to go crazy.

"I went up and Jeff kind of fouled me and knocked me down, but they didn't call anything. I fell on my hip. It hurt. The next day I couldn't sit on that side."

Several days later the team was watching tape of the St. Louis game when the Clark flash to the basket came up.

"If you can't dunk it, Steve, you need to lay it up," Clark heard Crum say.

A good laugh was had by (nearly) all.

Gimme a Body-Bending 'C—A—R—D—S'

As the Louisville Cardinals expended high energy on the court, so too did the voltage level increase in the Freedom Hall stands. This was thanks in great part to a 1973 business school graduate named Rob Hickerson, who sensed a lot of promise in the '79-80 team and set about to give it some help.

U of L had had a hard-core following of 6,000 to 8,000 fans for decades. But it had never had full-season sellout support in the 16,613-seat Hall, and it never had the sort of raucous, intimidating crowd for opponents that Louisville had to deal with at several stops on the road.

Hickerson, a season ticket holder since 1974 in Section 141, was excited about that season's prospects.

"We had a pretty well thought of team in preseason polls," he recalled. "I was a huge fan of Darrell Griffith's. He had promised a championship and, by golly, it was time."

Hickerson settled into his seat for the sold-out South Alabama opener in an advanced state of anticipation. With 3:55 left, the visitors had rallied to go ahead 71-69. Time out.

"The crowd was just dead—you could hear a pin drop," Hickerson said. "You would think that would be the time to really get it going—you know, 'We're behind, we've got a preseason ranking, these guys don't, let's make something happen.' I stood up in my seat and kind of encouraged the crowd to follow me. A few of them did."

Hickerson continued to try to get his neighbors up and at 'em for another game or two the conventional way. One night he and his (then) wife were having dinner at a restaurant and talking about his antics.

"I don't know how the heck it came up, but Wild Bill Hagy, the cab driver who stood on the Baltimore baseball dugout and spelled out O-R-I-O-L-E-S (in body language) came to mind," Hickerson said. "I said, 'You know, I can do that with C-A-R-D-S.' I gave it a try. At first the crowd didn't know what I doing exactly. But then they picked up on it."

For the fifth home game against Ohio State on December 19, 1979, he rented a tuxedo and a red shirt, and C-A-R-D-S went big-time. At first he did it at his seat, climbing up on the arms of the chair, turning around and spelling.

"They were permanent seats that had sturdy armrests," he said.

Then he moved a couple of rows up to the concrete walkway that encircled Freedom Hall before the current renovation.

"It had a metal railing, and I could spread my legs, rap them around the tubular railing and hold myself there," he said.

Not all fans joined in Hickerson's hijinks, especially at first. But by mid-January, the crowds—particularly those in six sections surrounding Hickerson—had come alive. Thanks in part to a team full of life itself, but also to Hickerson.

During the St. Louis game, Hickerson split the seat of his pants during his routine, thereby giving *Courier-Journal* sports columnist Billy Reed the opportunity to write, "Hickerson proceeded to 'moon' his followers, proving that (1) nothing can stop him, and (2) some cheerleaders don't always wear underwear."

"There was a group of eight or so people who sat behind me throughout the years," Hickerson said. "The next game they brought a pair of red U of L gym shorts with a U of L pennant sewn into the seat, and in an extra-large size so I could wear them over my pants. Which I did."

And when *Times* news columnist Bob Hill mentioned that Hickerson drank some champagne before games to loosen his tonsils, fans made it a ritual to bring him some bubbly.

Denny Crum had no time to turn and watch someone gyrating at the other end of the Hall, of course. But he knew there was a romance going on between his guys and those guys.

"Kids respond to positive things," Crum told Reed. "This team has nice young men, not jerks and dingbats, who want to do the right thing and get the job done. When the crowd gets excited in a positive way, [the players] get excited and want to please the people and please themselves."

Hickerson continues his act to this day, though not quite as much, he said. The official Cardinal cheerleaders have added a C-A-R-D-S to their program. The Cardinal Bird mascot does it, too.

For the last home game of '79-80, Hickerson was recognized at halftime for his contributions on a sold-out night that pushed Louisville's average home attendance over the 15,000 mark for the first time. It's never dipped below that since.

Games 14 and 15: Memphis State, Tulane

Next came two coming-of-age tests—January 12 at Memphis State, Louisville's most hostile rival, and January 19 at Tulane, where U of L would compete in a 4,400-seat shoebox.

Each provided the most definitive answers about the potential of the Cardinals since Ohio State.

Dodging projectiles from the stands and venom from the opponents (four Memphis technicals), Louisville smacked the 8-3 Tigers 69-48. Turning away from verbal instigators seated within touching distance of the bench, U of L whacked the Green Wave 76-59.

At Memphis, Louisville led 66-35, astounding considering the struggles these rivals usually engaged in. The Cardinals disrupted the Memphis offense and helped force 21-percent shooting in the first half.

"We're getting older by the day," forward Derek Smith (22 points, 10 rebounds) told the *Courier-Journal's* Mike Sullivan. "We appreciate what's been going on back home, with our fans and the good publicity, and we wanted to show everybody what we could do in a tough road game."

At Tulane, where the Greenies were 5-0 as opposed to 0-9 on the road, and in an eardrum-bending environment, Louisville dropped a 20-6 anvil on the Greenies to expand a 56-53 lead to the final margin.

Darrell Griffith scored 23 points and Wiley Brown had 14 points, six rebounds and five steals.

"They beat us the way all good teams beat you—they adjust, they compensate, they get you out of any kind of game plan, and before you know it you just got your __ beat by 17 points," Tulane coach Roy Danforth said.

Welcomed with Confetti, Heavy Version

As much as Louisville was unshaken by the Memphis State environment, the same could have been said for the game officials. No home-cooking, or even home-leaning, for this one.

The Cardinals had 14 team fouls to Memphis' 13 and shot 23 free throws to Memphis' 20, six resulting from four technical fouls.

Hank McDowell and Dennis Isbell were "T'd" up for mouthing off to officials. Memphis coach Dana Kirk picked up technicals three and four for entering the playing area after being warned twice by referee Dave Phillips.

"We didn't get any of the usual home-team breaks," Tigers center Hank McDowell said. "It would have been a lot closer if the refs hadn't jumped on us in the first half. The crowd was a lot wilder than usual, but if I had been up there and had brickbats, I'd have thrown them down on the floor."

The crowd of 10,899 had plenty of other stuff to unleash, and did so after an incident late in the first half involving U of L's Roger Burkman and Memphis' Jeff Battle.

Battle was rising for a layup when Burkman hit him and sent him crashing to the floor. Kirk went out to check on Battle, exchanged words with referee Phillips and was rung up twice. Battle wasn't injured and said Burkman was "just hustling."

Memphis fans, already fuming, aimed their wadded-up paper cups, popcorn boxes, paper "snowballs" and a few coins Burkman's way, but a Memphis timeout limited the damage.

One irate customer yelled, "What you got, a bunch of kamikazes?" at Louisville's Denny Crum. Burkman, with his defensive rampage through opponents well underway, could appreciate the sentiment.

Louisville made it to their locker room unharmed, dodged a couple more missives on their way out of Mid-South Coliseum and escaped in their getaway vans.

"Remember two years ago here?" senior Darrell Griffith said. "They threw baby shoes and flashlight batteries."

"And quarters," senior Tony Branch added. "Don't forget the quarters. Those hurt."

Said Burkman: "At the end of the game, a guy came up to me and said, 'You got no class, 34.' I'm wondering, who's got less class, him or me? As far as I'm concerned, they can read the score (69-48) and weep."

Poncho's (Mis)Adventures

Sophomore Poncho Wright walked into Mid-South Coliseum a couple of hours before game time and came upon a cage holding the animal version of Memphis State's mascot, a 400-pound Bengal tiger.

Wright thought that was neat. "Raarrr," he growled, raking his hand in the shape of a claw across the glass. "He can jump 16 feet," an unsmiling security guard said. "Oh," Wright answered. "I'm going inside now."

Inside, during the game, a less-furry but no less mean version of the tiger hit Wright in the eye with a wadded soft drink cup from the stands. He went on to commit three turnovers and four fouls but grab three rebounds and score six points.

"That's why I made those three turnovers," Wright said. "I started looking at what was coming at me. That's no excuse, of course. Everybody else had things thrown at them."

Nevertheless, it was a sobering experience for a 19-year-old, one he was reluctant to repeat anytime soon.

"I'll come down here again when they put a cage around the whole thing," he said. "Just get me back to the 'Ville."

Cubbyholes and Mad People

First there were the irritated islanders, deprived of a Louisville dunkathon. Then came the angry and dangerous hurlers at Memphis.

Now U of L had to deal with the taunting students of Tulane, screaming unprintables from directly behind the U of L bench while classmates sat within tripping distance of any enemy fast-breakers in 4,400-seat Tulane Gym.

This time some of the Cardinals responded in kind, or nearly so, as they attempted to exit the floor through narrow walkways as instigators continued to yammer away within arm's length.

Scooter McCray, injured, finished for the season and on the bench in street clothes, was the most animated Louisvillian, although coach Denny Crum, Darrell Griffith and assistant Bill Olsen got in their licks, too. Decades later, McCray still remembered the scene.

"They were all over Denny, talking about his mother, sister, everybody—bad," McCray said. "I said, 'That's enough.' I stood up and said some words, like, 'If you want to talk to me, we can talk (he didn't really mean "talk"), but I'm tired of hearing that about Coach.'"

Griffith gave the students some incentive. He drilled a 28-foot bank shot at the buzzer to close a 20-6 run and the 76-59 victory.

"I guess the long bank shot at the end got to them," Griffith said. "If they didn't like it, so much the better. I guess it wasn't good for their egos."

The Cardinals felt like a quarterback trying to call signals at an opponent's two-yard line in an enemy stadium.

"Those students were on us every second," Wiley Brown said. "We tried to ignore it, but we couldn't hear anything. We started using hand signals to tell each other the plays and the defenses we were going to use."

Games 16-19:
Marquette, St. Louis, Florida State, Tulane

Louisville finished up an unbeaten January with four more victories, rising to 17-2 and 6-0 in the Metro Conference. It now owned 10 straight triumphs and was up to seventh in the Associated Press poll from 15th at the beginning of the month.

On January 22, Marquette and U of L staged their typical body-bumping roller derby, the Cardinals using a 16-2 spurt to grab a 76-63 decision. Derek Smith was listed with 12 rebounds. "I think I had about 17," he said. "I think I have about 18 bruises, too."

It was coach Denny Crum's 200th victory, achieved faster than John Wooden, Adolph Rupp and Bob Knight. At 200-54, his .787 winning percentage was No. 2 among active coaches.

"I'm told I got to 200 faster than any of them," Crum said. "If that's so, and I can last 65 more years, I guess we've got a chance to do something."

On January 25 at St. Louis, the Cardinals delivered an even more withering steal and dunk-a-thon than in their 29-point blowout at Freedom Hall. They won 99-74. They had 15 steals out of 19 St. Louis turnovers.

Poncho Wright had four dunks, one in which he transferred the ball from one side of the basket to the other, re-grabbed it with both hands for a reverse jam and another 20 seconds later where he materialized from out of nowhere in front of the rim, caught a lob and whipped it down behind his head. There was a whoosh as the net barely riffled. One could imagine a jet breaking the sound barrier.

"The dunks were ridiculous," Wright recalled recently. "I have a friend in St. Louis who saw the game on TV and still talks about it to this day."

Remembered Jeff Schneider, the St. Louis freshman from Louisville: "Poncho had those long arms. They were all like that. You go in and, one, you're intimidated. Then it's, 'You mean they're going to press us all night long, too?'"

"They have to be one of the top teams in the country," St. Louis coach Ron Ekker said. "If they aren't, my God, I'd have to see the others."

On January 27 Louisville met up with the first of its two main league challengers, Florida State. The Seminoles were 10-4, losing three times in a total of nine final seconds. They had cut a 10-point U of L lead to four when Wiley Brown and Darrell Griffith scored in a four-point trip that stretched it to 68-60 and an eventual 79-73 victory.

On January 31, playing as if they were in a mud pit, the Cardinals lurched past Tulane 64-60 after trailing for 21 minutes.

"We've been so lackadaisical in practice that I've had a hard time getting their attention," Denny Crum said. "Maybe it's national ranking, girlfriends, I don't know. I just hope we've learned something from this."

It was not a pleasant sendoff to the rugged month of February.

Nom de Plumes, Nom de Guerres, Aliases

It would be hard to find an athletic team anytime, anywhere, that didn't have a few nicknames for its players. But it would be harder to find an many athletic team that had a nickname for everyone, some with multiple sobriquets, some that were created in October and changed in January, some that came from birth and were spelled funny, some that were partially discarded out of embarrassment.

Long names, half-names, single-letter names, mystifyingly goofy names.

That was Louisville, circa '79-80.

They even had names for stuff, such as a "Free the Hostages" dunk, a hard one-handed jam for the people being held hostage in Iran, and a "Freako Bob" for the best one-on-one move of a game.

Newspaper beat writers were not immune. Coaches decided Mike Sullivan and this author were "Hustle" and "Muscle," although neither could ever figure out who was what or how degrading they were intended to be.

The players called one "Sully" and the other "Hune," "Hune-y" (by Darrell Griffith) or, if you were Wiley Brown and possibly miffed at a written transgression, you'd take a hard plop onto the author's lap and follow it with a snappish, "Ta-hoon, I'm gonna hurt you bad."

Jack Tennant, the radio play-by-play man and assistant athletic director, was "Lieu."

Denny Crum, the head coach, was "The Brain" to players and "Cool Hand Luke" after ex-coach John Dromo offered that comparison.

Here are the players and their stage names (make sense of some of them at your own risk):

Griffith: Griff, Dr. Dunkenstein, Stein, His Griffness.

Brown: Wilo.

Derek Smith: D, Smittybob (Cleveland didn't know why the "bob") or Sweets or Sweet Beady (Scooter McCray didn't know where those came from, either).

Rodney McCray: Baby Huey (a derisive reference to his early-season conditioning and work ethic), then Hard (for how hard he worked, intimidated bigger people and reinvented himself by mid-December).

Jerry Eaves: Weeble, for the way he walked and dribbled, as in Weeble Wobble, because a childhood accident made one leg shorter than the other.

Roger Burkman: Roger Dodger (athough opponents did most of the dodging).

David Wright: From the womb—Poncho or Ponch. "When I was in my mother's belly she thought she had a paunchy belly," Wright said. Somehow "paunchy" misspelled its way to Ponchy and became Poncho (a cloak with a slit for one's head), then Ponch, but never Pancho (the Cisco Kid's buddy).

"My wife (Wonna) only knows David," Wright said. "At reunions it amazes her (that no one ever uses his given name). She's like a deer in the headlights, saying, 'You guys must have really been something.'"

Later, his helpful U of L mates added Regis Wrong (because, said Scooter, he was forgetful and would be in the wrong spot for some offensive plays) or Yeahyeah (his answer whenever coaches or teammates would get on him about a mistake).

Carlton McCray: Scooter Pie. An endearing suggestion his mother's sister made when Shirley McCray was pregnant. "I told her when I got older we'd have to drop that 'Pie' thing," Scooter said. He became Scooter, and Scoot, and Scoo, and eventually the self-described Iceman, borrowing from another long-armed, lanky, play-any-position guy named George Gervin.

Tony Branch: T or TB.

Greg Deuser: Deuce (Deus if you like).

Daryl Cleveland: Cleve—"With friends in Louisville I still never hear Daryl," he said. Or Seawolf—he had a CB in his car and his handle was "Wolfman" or, as Scooter said, "He was like a mascot in Alaska (for the Seawolf Classic in 1978)."

Steve Clark: Stevie or Clarkie.

Marty Pulliam: Henry Marshall Pulliam IV once was "Hank," then "Big-Un" (he was 6-9). But with blond hair turning white, and listening to Scooter call himself Iceman, he chose at midseason to become the "Snowman." "I wasn't getting enough publicity so I gave myself some," he said.

At a morning shootaround in February, Pulliam sauntered up to Dr. Dunkenstein and asked, "Any hostages freed yet? I'm going to free some today." "Do it, Snowman," ordered Stein.

Rough House, Indeed

Louisville's trainer wasn't Jerry May. He was "Rough House" or "Rough," names as common to the guys as Poncho was to Wright and Scooter was to McCray.

For very good reasons. In charge of the care, feeding and safety of the Cardinals, not to mention regular taping, repairing and bionic thumb-installing duties, Rough House was rough on his own house and any other houses, hotel clerks, chefs or rental-car attendants who got a bit cockeyed with him.

"If you told Rough a meal would be prepared at 5:45, and it came out at 5:46 or 5:47, he would jump all over those hotel people," Roger Burkman said.

"Jump" was a mild way of putting it. May got his nickname from Rick Wilson, a guard-forward in the mid-'70s.

"Wilson didn't like to practice, and (former trainer) Jim Bible always let him leave the floor to put ice on his leg," said May, who assisted Bible from 1975 to '77. "He (Wilson) would stay down there (in the training room). Several would do stuff like that."

Bible left in 1977 and May took over.

"I locked the damn training room door and wouldn't let them in," he said. "I'd throw a bag of ice up on the (practice) floor and say, 'Put ice on your leg and watch what's going on. You keep ice on it here because you ain't going down in the training room and go to sleep.' That's all they wanted to do.

"Well, they had a song out then called 'Brick House,' with a line like, 'She's a brick house.' They'd substitute 'Rough House.' And they'd sing it that way."

May brought new meaning to the phrase "take no guff."

"If I'd knock on their door for room check and get no answer, I'd (all but) kick it down," he said. "We had a lot of characters (in earlier years) and it was a rough group. But don't ever not open the door when I knock on it."

May was just as hard line about meals. They needed to be nutritious and absolutely on time.

"Say you have a pregame meal at three o'clock," he said. "It's based on how many hours before you play, so the food is digested and you are in a state of readiness to put your body to use. If you get there at three and don't get the damn food till 3:40, you've lost. That means the first part of the ball game you're looking for energy that ain't there. So if they didn't have it ready, by gawd they paid for it.

"Before every meal I went by and tasted everything. I figured it'd give us a chance to have something decent, or at least I'd be the first to die."

The Backup Electric Company

There have been terrific sixth men, sometimes sixth-through-eighth men, for hundreds of powerful basketball teams across the years.

Those people need to make room on their devastating bench for Roger Burkman and Poncho Wright, who may have given the 1979-80 Louisville Cardinals as unique a lift as any two-man sub machine ever has.

Burkman, a 6-5 junior guard, was called Instant Defense for his steals, deflections, charges taken and anger and frustration instigated with a touch of offense thrown in.

Wright, a 6-5 sophomore forward, was called Instant Offense for his rainbow-arching pre-three-pointer perimeter shots, blink-of-the-eye jumping quickness for rebounds and dunks with a smidgeon of defense thrown in.

Both were from Indianapolis. Wright's Marshall team eliminated Burkman's Franklin Central club from the 1977 state high school tournament. Appropriately, they would be forever linked as the supersub patrol. And without them, U of L probably would have come up empty in 1980.

"They were definitely critical," assistant head coach Bill Olsen recalled. "The 'chemistry' a team needs might not just be getting along, but how all parts blend to bring something together that, as a whole, is better than all individual parts. Griff (Darrell Griffith) was an exception, but all the rest were so much better for the way they blended."

No better examples exist of the havoc they could wreak than the St. Louis games of January 8 and January 25.

In 42 combined minutes, Burkman hit 16 of 18 free throws, and delivered seven assists, seven steals and 28 points. In 47 combined minutes, Wright hit 12 of 17 shots, grabbed 13 rebounds and scored 27 points.

"There seems to be a pattern of the other teams getting physically exhausted five minutes into the second half," Derek Smith said. "Then they tell you reporters about how much depth we have. It's mostly Roger and Poncho. I think they believe those two are four or five guys."

A look at each of the "instants" follows.

Instant Defense...

Roger Burkman was a scoring champion in high school, averaging 27.2 points in a county that included all the big teams from Indianapolis.

Still, college recruiters weren't bumping into each other to get to his door. Louisville, Purdue, Wyoming and a couple of mid-majors were sort of interested, but there were plenty of doubting Naismiths who questioned whether he had enough stuff for Division I.

So Burkman signed on at U of L with things to prove, and almost instantly discovered that the path to playing time was not through points. The Cardinals were stocked with scorers.

Gradually he redirected his ego toward floor burns, ball slaps and becoming a defensive wasp with a long and dangerous stinger. He came to relish his role. He even relished coming off the bench. He became a superb anticipator, giving coach Denny Crum a weapon not many others had.

"At Florida State, I remember a guy taking the ball out of bounds, their big man stops at the top of the (backcourt) key while the other guard has run down to the other end," Burkman said. "I'm back there, glancing over my shoulder, looking for opportunities. The guy has to pass it in to the big man. I automatically know he's going to throw it back, so I take off before he catches the ball. I got a hand on it and deflected it. I couldn't save it, but it was that close to a steal and layup.

"Little things like that helped me as a defensive player that other guys might not have had. I thought about those things all the time, like anticipating a reverse dribble, stepping over and taking the charge."

Players saw Burkman coming in and muttered, "Oh, no."

"He was a hell of a player, doing all the things nobody else wanted to do," said Jeff Schneider, a St. Louis guard from Louisville. "He covered a lot of ground with those long legs and arms. You see somebody like Roger come in, you're dead tired, you make a pass and say, 'Wait, that wasn't supposed to happen.'"

Coaches marveled at his instincts.

"Roger was like a great defensive back who before a pass was thrown had already made a decision on where the ball was going and was one or two steps closer to get the deflection or steal," Olsen said. "He had the ability to focus. A lot of players have long arms, but they're a step late. Roger had long arms but was a step early. It's immeasurable the value of that. Even on plays where he didn't get the steal, the pass is altered so much that they throw it away or put the receiver in a spot where he can't do anything."

Focus, indeed. Burkman would become so transfixed that he would become, as a Memphis fan hinted, kamikaze-like, appropriate perhaps because his great aunt was a full-blooded Hawaiian familiar with the business end of Japanese aircraft.

Crum tried to get him to stop passing after he became airborne, and to back off an opponent who still had his dribble left. Manager Randy Bufford was always on the lookout to calm him down. But when Burkman went maniacal, not much helped.

"I get so caught up in things I leave the world," Burkman said then. "Randy sees a light or star in my eye. Then it's watch out, because I'm going to go berserk."

...Instant Offense

David "Poncho" Wright had to sit out his freshman year at Louisville because he was a non-predictor.

"I never cut a class, I just wouldn't study," he said.

He had to work harder in preseason because he was out of shape and 10 pounds too heavy from his year off.

He was the only viable front-line backup, subbing—at six foot five—for center Rodney McCray or forwards Derek Smith or Wiley Brown because academics, injury and the completion of eligibility wiped out the 1978-79 front and coach Denny Crum didn't trust any other big person with quality minutes.

Finally, he was the designated piñata, at least verbally, for his coaches and teammates because on more than one occasion he would be found in the wrong spot on the press or out of alignment in the set offense.

One would think these items were a sure script for transfer. Instead, he got his grades going, got in shape, let his immense athletic gifts handle any heavy labor inside and gradually began to discover the right positions at the right time.

On top of it all, he not only took the abuse better than most players ever would but actually felt it was beneficial.

Thus Poncho Wright became a vital piece of the 12-man puzzle. He never started in his three seasons, and the limited playing time bothered him but, even from the distance of 24 years, he still understood.

"When I came out I was one of the better players in the state of Indiana," he said. "I felt I should have been playing a lot more. But we had some great players. Derek (Smith) was an outstanding player who so happened to play the same exact position I did. If I was honest with myself, there's no way I could have said I should have been playing ahead of him."

His honesty, composure and ability to handle the slings and arrows was no different that season. After a narrow escape at Providence in February, Crum ripped his squad more than he had even in Utah and Hawaii. The target was Wright, who was glad-handing teammates afterwards.

"I think he misunderstood what I was doing," Wright said at the time. "I was congratulating everybody on the win and he said, 'Poncho, what do you think you're laughing at?' Well, he was right. I might as well have not been there that game (one point, one rebound, three fouls).

"The thing is, he's not a Bobby Knight-type coach, yelling at you all the time. If he did, it'd probably get on your nerves. But he barely gets on you, so when he does get on you, you know you've done something. He doesn't treat you like a little-bitty boy."

Wright launched baseline missiles and executed Dunkenstein-rivaling slams.

"He had great range," Crum recalled, "and it didn't matter if he hadn't been in, because he didn't know you needed to get warmed up. He had the green light to shoot it out there, he did, and he made them."

And he made himself a strong, quirky part of the 1980 run performed by strong, quirky guys.

CHAPTER SEVEN

Scattering Demons and Fanning More Flames:

February 3, 1980 to February 18, 1980

The Evil Spirits of Februarys Past

The Louisville Cardinals had aced nearly all the tests put before them: Tough road game at Tennessee while losing a key player, home game with rugged Ohio State, perilous trip to rival Memphis State, hazardous contest in Tulane's tiny gym, game with one of the Metro's top clubs in Florida State.

But those were physical exams or trials of poise and concentration.

Now came their biggest challenge yet – casting aside the ghouls of recent Februarys, the fiends that infected their games on national television and the fatiguing rigors of long road trips.

Coach Denny Crum had raised the fans' (and maybe journalists') bar of expectations considerably with Final Four treks in 1972 and 1975, the second and third for the school. In each of the next four seasons, such anticipation was pronounced as U of L apparently was riding an elite thoroughbred as it turned for home. Anticipation turned to exasperation as it spit out the bit every time.

1976: Louisville was 18-4 before February losses to Marquette and Wichita State, an upset loss at home to Memphis State in the first Metro tourney that cancelled an NCAA ticket and a first-round loss to Providence in the NIT. Final record: 20-8.

1977: 18-2 and on a 15-game win streak. Crum is remarried in Las Vegas before UNLV snaps the streak 99-96. Forward Larry Williams breaks a foot the next game, necessitating three position changes, including forcing Crum to start his formidable sixth man, freshman Darrell Griffith. The Cardinals lose four more, including a first-round NCAA game to UCLA with a hobbled, bandaged Williams playing remarkably well, considering. Record: 21-7.

1978: 16-3 before three straight road losses in mid-February, followed by seven victories, followed by a 90-89 double-overtime NCAA regional semifinal loss to DePaul in which center Dave Corzine scores 46 points and Louisville misses four critical free throws in the extra periods. Record: 23-7.

1979: 21-3 and on a 13-game streak when Marquette stops the momentum on February 10 in the second of five straight road games. Cardinals lose four more, including a near embarrassment to Arkansas in the NCAA regional semis. Record: 24-8.

Crum was his usual rigid stone wall when the words "collapse, foldup, letdown and disappearance" were tossed his way on February 1.

"I don't think we've had a collapse," he said. "One team may be better than the other. One team may play better than the other on that day. Sometimes we just weren't playing well. A slump is a slump. It can happen early, in the middle or at the end of a season. Do hitters only go into slumps in the middle, or do some of them have slumps in the World Series?"

But the signs and numbers were ominous.

U of L was about to meet St. John's on national TV in its 6,000-seat campus gym, then play Iona on a coast-to-coast hookup 15 days later from Madison Square Garden.

These were prehistoric times for sports on the tube and sports. ESPN was in its start-up season and other cable channels for sports were nonexistent. U of L was on a lot of local and regional stations, but rarely on a semi-national feed and rarer still on a full national circuit that had NBC's Dick Enberg, Al McGuire and Billy Packer as the only country-wide announcing team out there.

Good thing. The Cardinals were 1-6 in national games, including 0 for their last 3.

Also: Because of the major shows booked annually into Freedom Hall in February, Louisville found itself on extended out-of-town journeys (three road games in eight days in 1977, four in nine days in '78, five in 11 days in '79).

It would be no different this time—four games in eight days (February 9-16) with two at rivals Virginia Tech and Cincinnati.

U of L was 17-2 with 10 straight successes, but large obstacles lay ahead, and some ghosts were flitting about somewhere.

"It'll be a tough deal no matter how it goes," Crum said. "But I wouldn't mind having a good February."

Game 20: St. John's, February 3

St. John's had every conceivable thing going for it. It had won 17 straight games, was 19-1, was ranked ninth nationally to Louisville's seventh, had NBC in for a national telecast and was playing at its tiny bungalow (6,000-seat Alumni Hall) instead of its big house (Madison Square Garden).

U of L had scheduled the contest as a going-home treat for Rodney and Scooter McCray, who hail from Mt. Vernon, N.Y., a few miles away. Coach Denny Crum had always made it a practice of scheduling difficult non-conference foes, but the Redmen at this time of year might be a bit much.

The sign behind one of the baskets that greeted the visitors set the tone: "Hello, America, Welcome to Alumni Hall, the Real Looie-ville."

The Johnnies' bantamweight coach, Lou Carnesecca, certainly deserved to have this Ville nicknamed for him, and his team was out to show a big sea-to-shining-sea audience why.

However, the Louisville that stalked Tennessee, Ohio State and Memphis State was the one that showed up.

Four minutes of hard-bitten full-court defense ignited a 12-2 first-half run that gave the Cardinals a 32-22 lead, some of it without a surprisingly uptight Darrell Griffith. "He wanted so badly to play well," Crum said. "I sat him down to get him to relax and quit pressing."

U of L secured a 32-25 halftime edge and stretched it to 55-38 in the throes of the obscenity-laced taunts of a packed house with some dominant work by Wiley Brown (18 points) and Derek Smith (13 points, 13 rebounds) in the paint.

Had Louisville been able to do any good from the free throw line, the advantage would have been much greater, and St. John's would have been cooked. U of L missed the front ends of seven one-and-ones or two-shot chances and hit 12 of 27 for the game. Brown missed his first six, then clapped when the seventh rolled in. "I just had to give myself a hand," he said.

That allowed the Redmen to keep the door from closing completely. They saddled up in the last 10 minutes, staging rallies of 10-0 and 5-0 and closing the deficit to three points on three occasions, the last at 74-71.

But U of L stunningly found an eye or two from the free throw line when it counted most. Jerry Eaves hit three, Brown miraculously went two for two, and the Cardinals won 76-71, their 11th straight in an 18-2 season.

Of Louisville's goal-line stand, Carnesecca said, "They didn't get scared, but they did feel the wind down their backs. We had played them with nails in our shoes the first half, then we began climbing the mountain like mountain goats."

Crum had something else on his mind—February critics.

"We beat a good team at their place on national TV," he said. "We could have folded six or eight times, but we showed character instead."

Foldup? Not this time.

An Alley-Oop with a Capital A

Denny Crum sat Darrell Griffith down to calm him in the first half against St. John's. Louisville's star guard would play only 27 minutes.

Would he be remembered for that? No.

Would he be remembered for springing from underneath the right side of the basket on an outward angle to the left side, catching a line-drive lob pass near the front of the rim, cradling it with his fingertips, and, with spinning rotor blades keeping him high enough and controlled enough, flushing it backward and straight down through the net from behind his head? Yes.

Cameras captured every split second of the *Guinness Book* achievement, an eye-popping feat even to Griff watchers whose eyes had been popped for years. NBC would use it as its featured promo for the next seven weeks.

For a man who needed to relax, it wasn't a bad move. Neither were the three other dunks he delivered, or the 10-of-13 shooting, 23 points and four rebounds in the victory.

"I've only tried that in practice before today," he said. "It's all a matter of where you catch the ball. But since you're throwing it backwards, you can't be completely sure of where it's going."

An Alley with a Capital OOPS

There was one group of people not prepared to get excited over Darrell Griffith's wham-bam-thank-you jam.

His teammates.

The teammates who had come to take Griffith's supernatural deeds with a collective shrug because they'd seen that and more in practice.

Jerry Eaves' teammates.

Eaves lofted the pass toward Griffith where he had to reconfigure his body and execute a burned-in-the-memory highlight. Other Cardinals remembered the throw first, the catch second.

"The lob was thrown too short and he dunks it backwards," Scooter McCray recalled. "I say that because of the spectacularness of the play, but also because we were such adept passers. From then on (to Eaves) we were like, 'I've never thrown a pass so short a guy had to dunk it backwards. Who the hell caused this? That's why we can't put you back there (to throw any more).' That's the type of joke we'd shoot at each other."

Eaves could grin (now) at the thought.

"I was at the top of the key, going to throw it right, and instead threw it over here," he said with a gesture to the left. "I don't remember what I did to cause that. Horrible pass. Terrible pass. We'd be watching it on tape and they'd go, 'Look at that pass.'"

And then it becomes NBC's primary promotion.

"Absolutely," Eaves said, and grinned. "From the bad comes good."

Talk the Talk in Practice, Walk the Walk in Games

Although hard to imagine in these days of fists pounding into chests, fingers pointing skyward, screams into hand-held cameras and mouths yammering into enemy faces, Louisville almost never trash-talked opponents in 1979-80.

That's because the Cardinals would rather have their steals and dunks speak for them, and also because they had used up all their put-downs, challenges and unprintable phrasings during workouts.

"It wasn't a trash-talking team on the floor, it was a trash-talking team to each other," Scooter McCray said.

Only under extreme provocation, such as Dexter Reid vs. Darrell Griffith and Jerry Eaves in Virginia Tech games or Louisiana State taunts in a more vital circumstance later, would U of L respond.

But each day, from the moment any two of them would meet up walking to Crawford Gym until they split up after training table that night, the verbal dustups were relentless.

"'I'm telling you, I'm going to kick your butt all day in practice, you know you'd better step up to the plate, because if we go down to the locker room and sit in the whirlpool together, you're going to hear, I just kicked your butt all day today, didn't I?'" said McCray, picking out an imaginary teammate. "And it'd keep going on until the next practice."

Rodney McCray remembers the walk to the gym.

"(Jerry) Eaves would come up and say, 'Wiley (Brown) really worked you out yesterday. What you going to do today?'" Rodney said. "I'd be like, 'Okay, watch me.' It was always about who was going to get dunked on today. Guys looked forward to 3 o'clock coming around, sprinted over to the gym and wanted to start the battle with each other."

Eaves knew about those dunks.

"I always tried to dunk on Scooter, Wiley, Derek (Smith) and Rod and they'd block every one," Eaves said. "'Don't try to dunk on me,' they'd say. 'I'm going to get you, I'm going to get you,' I'd say. Never did. Derek and I fought each other tooth and nail."

"If people could have attended practice every day, they would have seen some amazing feats," Poncho Wright remembered.

But on game days, the smiles went away and the ego-deflations stopped. The guys got their jollies a different way, by undressing the other team.

"It was all business then," Scooter said. "Because we played hard and played well together, a lot of teams feared us. That was half the battle. Some talked trash to us. We didn't say anything. We knew the press was eventually going to crack 'em. After the game, they'd shake their head like, 'Damn, where did that come from?'"

Jeff Schneider, a Louisvillian who played for St. Louis in two thrashings by U of L, was asked if showboating and smack were part of the dunkathons they staged against the Billikens.

"Those (1980) guys never did that," Schneider said. "To me, they were like quiet assassins."

But there was no place for glass egos during U of L practices.

"You had to have a strong sense of personal confidence to be a part of the Cardinals, because the way we played and approached things was so different," Scooter McCray said. "We could shoot jokes at each other and they'd almost rip the most sensitive person apart. But that team knew it was nothing personal. It was just the way we were."

Games 21 and 22: Memphis State, Cincinnati

Even though Louisville had about 15 seconds to celebrate the St. John's success and two old unfriendlys were next, the snowball continued to gain size and momentum.

On February 4, about 28 hours after the Johnnies' demise, Memphis State pulled into Freedom Hall and worked up a 37-35 halftime lead. Coming off a national TV high, the Cardinals were vulnerable, right?

Wrong. U of L put on its best stealing-blocking-dunking clothes and erupted in its most prolonged lightning strike of the season. It went on a monstrous 40-9 run to win 88-60. Memphis coach (and former U of L assistant) Dana Kirk called four timeouts in seven minutes trying to stop the avalanche. "He could have used four more," Louisville guard Greg Deuser said.

Darrell Griffith was one off his career high with 31 points, plus seven rebounds and three assists, vindicating Kirk's earlier admonition that "he should dip his wings twice in salute as he passes over the rest of us."

On February 6, Cincinnati motored in, a rival over which Louisville had a 20-18 series lead. This time Griffith, eight points shy of the magic 2,000 career point mark, had to pry No. 2,000 out of himself with a crowbar. He hit four of 12 shots and scored 13 points, passing the standard with 5:31 left on a two-hand dunk after a shovel pass from Wiley Brown.

Brown noted he also made the pass when Griffith broke the school scoring record on January 3, then added, "I don't want any trophy."

U of L won 88-73 as Derek Smith got a career-best 26 points plus 10 rebounds. The Cardinals would soon have more chances to prove that, for them, the whole would be greater than the sum of its parts.

Up, Up...Then Darkness

Two plays from the pages of the 40-9 Louisville firestorm that consumed Memphis State were testament to what remarkable stuff these Cardinals could dream up. Neither resulted in points, just indelible images for the mind.

The first: With 5:47 remaining and the game decided, 6-4 Memphis guard Jeff Battle was pounding in from the left side on an apparent breakaway. Obviously thinking dunk, he was soaring, two-plus feet off the floor, hands cocked and ready to jam, when something materialized to his right. An apparition? Nope, 6-7 Rodney McCray. His undetected appearance was a surprise to Battle, and a surprise to everyone else.

Rising straight up with the form of a diver, McCray's hands clamped on the ball a split-second before Battle was to begin his throw-down. The sky disappeared from view. McCray snatched the ball completely out of Battle's hands. Battle continued out of bounds. McCray returned to the floor and squatted over his prize.

It was more than a block. More than a steal. It was a ball-jacking.

"I was mad coming down the floor because I had just been hit in the mouth by some other guy," McCray said. "I wanted that one. But I don't know where the guy went. It seemed like when I came down, nobody was there."

"If I had seen him, I wouldn't have put it up," Battle said. "He got it clean, because he didn't touch me with any part of his body. Geez. He's a super dude."

The second: At another moment, McCray rebounded a missed shot and fired a long outlet pass to Darrell Griffith. The pass carried Griffith close to the right sideline and was a hair long.

Griffith fought to control the ball with one hand. A defender was waiting in front of him. He got his fingers around it, but if he tried to dribble he would probably be calling for palming. If he didn't sail out of bounds first.

So, in one continuous motion, he gained control and whipped a 35-foot, one-hand, behind-the-back bounce pass with his right hand to a cutting Derek Smith. The ball met Smith deep under the basket. He had a split-second before he, too, left the court. He launched the best layup he could under the circumstances, but it missed.

"I knew he'd be there, because it was two-on-one," Griffith said routinely.

"I was moving too fast and shot it too hard," Smith said. "But that shows you what talent the guy's got that no one else has got. And we haven't seen it all yet."

The Woe Trip:
On the Road Again, Accompanied by Rasputin and Other Evil Mystics

There was something sinister about every stop on the 10-day, four-game forced march Louisville was obliged to attempt from February 8 to February 17 while a trade show occupied its home court at Freedom Hall.

First up was Providence, (February 9) a mediocre outfit but one running a deliberate offense that gave U of L seizures in the past. Next was carving out a path from Rhode Island to Blacksburg, Virginia, one of those you-almost-can't-get-there-from-here destinations. Awaiting was Virginia Tech (February 11), the second hottest team in the Metro Conference and the Cardinals' prime challenger.

Third was Morgantown, West Virginia, and West Virginia (February 14), headed by one of Denny Crum's bitterest coaching rivals, Gale Catlett, when Catlett was at Cincinnati. Last came Cincinnati (February 16), a nemesis that could identify with Memphis State when it came to ugly extracurricular moments.

So there was plenty of work ahead without any outside interference. Would it be strictly business? As it turned out, Homer had nothing on this odyssey and Gulliver could probably identify with the travels.

Providence, Saturday, February 9: Two planes, four stops and five hours after departure, U of L arrived in the Rhode Island city. The next day, appearing to still be extracting themselves from their little coach seats, the Cardinals stumbled past an 11-10 Providence team 79-73.

Denny Crum spent extra minutes in the locker room giving his platoon an indignant piece of his mind, then said, "We played horrible. No enthusiasm." Georgians Wiley Brown (career-high 24 points) and Derek Smith (20) saved an embarrassment. "We weren't quite clicking," Darrell Griffith (15 points) said. "We'll get the click back."

Virginia Tech, Monday, February 11: Nothing spelled end of winning streak (Louisville had now captured 14 in a row for a 21-2 record) like its six-hour trip by plane, cab, van and rental car from Point P (Providence) to Point B (Blacksburg).

Virginia Tech was 17-3 and on an eight-game string, was 6-1 to U of L's 8-0 in the Metro Conference, had a pair of approximate six-nine, 230-pound frontmen in Dale Solomon and Wayne Robinson, the grim prove-it mentality of a team unranked by the polls and a large advantage playing in cozy Cassell Coliseum.

The Hokies quickly set about making it all come true. They sliced easily through the Louisville press, Dexter Reid helped unsettle Griffith into making only six of his first 18 shots and the Cardinals wound up with two steals (season average: 10), three assists (season average: 18) and one dunk in regulation.

The outcome was surely written in stone. Sorry, Techies. U of L, 56-54 in overtime. How? Louisville's small fry front line outrebounded Tech's counterparts by a staggering 32-14. Derek Smith (6-6) and Rodney McCray (6-7) had 11 each and Wiley Brown (6-8) 10. And McCray had six blocks in the first 29 minutes, two each on the Hokies' forward wall.

"Robinson dunked on me early," McCray said. "Had to get him back." Said Robinson: "I really think they miss Scooter McCray. But then they've got Rodney. Their stuff must run in the family."

McCray missed a 22-footer at the end of regulation with the teams tied 48-48. For all his troubles, Griffith felt it was an affront that coach Denny

Crum had not called his number. The situation reappeared near the end of overtime, game tied at 54, timeout.

"Which play do you want me to run?" Griffith remembered saying to Crum. "I'm taking this shot." The lead gun had one silver bullet left in his chamber, a 22-foot fadeaway from the dead left baseline corner with Reid challenging him with hands up. Swish. One second was left.

"As we're walking off, I put my arm around Coach Crum and said, 'If you'd let me take the last shot in regulation, we'd have been out of here five minutes ago,'" Griffith said.

West Virginia, Thursday, February 14: If one were flying on the back of a crow, it was about 170 miles due north from Blacksburg to Morgantown. If one were traveling with Louisville's road gang February 12, it was rental cars to Roanoke, plane to Washington, D.C., another plane to Pittsburgh, bus an hour and 15 minutes to Morgantown's St. Francis High School gym, work out, bus to hotel.

Total hotel-to-hotel time: nine hours. Grand totals for first three legs of trip: six planes; eight intermediate city stops; four fleets of rent-a-cars; two buses; two victories; one 15-game win streak.

They were now spelling road warriors with a capital R and W. "We've had some interesting road trips, but this is the toughest," said the senior Griffith. "If we had even one direct flight . . ."

The Cardinals gave over a hundred awestruck kids, mostly pre-teens, a "Best Dunks of 1979-80" show at St. Francis on the 12th. Two nights later they gave 10,136 mostly hostile adults a dose of the "Best Griffith of 1976-80."

He was mission control with a career-best 35 points, hitting 16 of 23 mid-range jumpers, dunks, reverse-pivot scoops and deep rainbows. He also had eight rebounds, seven assists and three steals in a 90-78 victory over the Mountaineers. It was No. 16 in a row, breaking a tie with the 1971-72 and '76-77 squads for longest school win streak.

"The 16th straight was something we all wanted, especially me," Griffith said, ignoring his own numbers. "I was on the team ('76-77) that won 15. And we aren't planning for this thing to die at 16."

That's if they could find their way to No. 17 and beyond.

Tight Defense, Loose Tongue

Dexter Reid was more than just a defensive specialist for Virginia Tech. He was a throat specialist, too.

He pretty much kept up a running larynx battle with Darrell Griffith throughout the Louisville game. It escalated with 6:15 left in regulation.

When a timeout was called, Reid shouted and shook his fist in Griffith's face for several seconds. Griffith didn't respond, later saying, "I accept it as part of the game. You know that guys might try to get you upset. It's something you have to deal with, that's all."

But when told later that Reid called himself "the best defensive guard in the country," Griffith said, "He couldn't guard my little brother, if I had one."

A couple of decades later Griffith hadn't forgotten. But after 10 years in the pros, 30 or so years on the playgrounds and billions of trashy words, it was hardly a major memory, either.

"He was just running his mouth," Griffith recalled. "I was the type of person who didn't say too much, because I was going to embarrass you with my play. You can talk all you want to, but you're going to shut up quickly without me opening my mouth."

Griffith didn't have the type of game (seven of 19 shots, 14 points) that would put Reid's voicebox under lock and key, as he would see seven days later.

Hoops or Hospital Rules?

Kathy Tronzo, administrative assistant in the sports information department and the director's right-hand woman, picked the wrong season to deliver child No. 2.

She gave birth to Derek the day (February 8) before Louisville left to play Providence and was still recovering in Baptist East Hospital when the Cardinals got to Virginia Tech. Her husband, Mike, visited and decided to stay and watch the game with his wife on the little black-and-white TV in the room the night of February 11.

The game started. The game continued. And continued. Curfew for visitation passed.

"That was when fathers couldn't stay as long as they wanted," Kathy remembered. "Nurses came in and told him visiting hours were over and he had to leave. He said, 'I'm not leaving.' The game went into overtime. They came back in and said he had to leave. He refused to leave. They came back in and were pretty firm, saying they were going to kick him out. Mike was firm, too. He said, 'When the game's over, I'll leave.'"

Mike stayed until the game ended, about 10:30. The nurses may have been unhappy, but they were kind enough not to call for hospital security.

Searching for Cincinnati

Louisville's Corps of Discovery was about to breathe a collective sigh of relief.

Its travel itinerary had just one more page: One bus to Pittsburgh (about 60 miles), an hour or so flight to Dayton, a puddle-jumper (maybe 20 minutes) to Cincinnati, a welcome from several hundred hometown fans expected to populate 12 buses coming up from Louisville, a ride home on the university's bus.

And, wow. Three victories, maybe four.

The ride to Pittsburgh went routinely. Except snow had begun to fall, temperatures had begun to drop and patchy fog had begun to roll in.

The U.S. Air bird loaded up at 3:15 p.m. February 15, 25 minutes behind schedule. Not bad. It taxied to the runway, and stopped. It was sixth in line to be de-iced. Just as its turn came, the pilot announced there was zero visibility in Dayton and that airport was closing.

Options: Alternate air routes; ordering a private plane to come and take the team to Cincinnati; stay overnight in Pittsburgh; bus.

The snowstorm was shutting down airports all over the Midwest, so getting airborne in time to make the next night's game was unlikely. If they waited till morning, the weather might be worse.

Solution: Bus.

Sure. Four hours after the decision, a bus finally extracted itself from expressway traffic and arrived at the terminal at 8 p.m.

It left Pittsburgh on Interstate 79 at 8:20 p.m. It overheated at 8:40. It stopped, cooled down, resumed and overheated at 9. It stopped, cooled down, seemed better, and resumed. In minutes it suffered a flat tire. By now it had reached I-70 and a snowy wilderness. It limped into a gas station a few miles from Prosperity, Pennsylvania, at 9:15. No one thought the name of the village was funny or ironic.

Jerry Eaves was especially upset. He was hooked on the night TV soap *Dallas*, and the series was at the critical point where bad guy J.R. Ewing had been shot, leaving fans to ask the question, "Who shot J.R.?"

A lot of the Cardinals were addicted to the show, so much so they'd started a $1 pool on the gunman's (or gunwoman's) identity. A lot was at stake, and they were going to miss an episode.

"Mad? No question," Eaves remembered. "Everybody wanted to know who shot J.R. We were going to stop that damn bus."

Then the bus stopped itself. The team piled into the station, which had a TV set—and a 140-pound German Shepherd named Charlie.

"Eaves was scared to death of that dog," assistant Jerry Jones recalled. Others were scared somewhat close to death. "Well fed, isn't he?" assistant Wade Houston said. But Darrell Griffith knew about big dogs. He had a Great Dane named Clyde at home. He walked up to the small horse and made friends immediately.

"I thought he was going to eat us up," Eaves said. "But I said, 'Damn the dog, I'm watching Dallas.' Then Darrell made friends with him. He laid right there with us and we all watched."

Oh, yeah. Trainer Jerry May won the pool. "It was a dollar pot," May recalled. "They thought I cheated, like I talked to CBS (which carried the show) when we were in New York or something." May insisted he just had a good crystal ball.

At 10:30 p.m., an hour and a half later, another bus brought a replacement tire. After some discussion, it was decided to send the first bus packing and bring the second off the bench, thus changing driver, team and luggage.

It was still snowing, sometimes sideways. It was now very cold. The "good" bus managed to get about 160 miles in three hours under its belt, but after exchanging I-70 for I-71 and making it 30 miles out of Columbus, it lost gears two, three and four.

An exit for Mount Sterling, Ohio, still 80-some miles from Cincinnati, beckoned ahead. The bus, whining in first gear, jounced toward the ramp, then precariously coughed and sneezed its way down the snow-covered asphalt. May passed among the people, offering cough syrup and treating Denny Crum's bronchitis.

"Put a bandage on it," assistant Bill Olsen called out to the driver. "Badger Bus Lines," he added, a reference to a devious plot obviously concocted by Cincinnati coach Ed Badger.

Luckily, the LK Motel sat at the foot of the exit. Not real fancy, but an oasis. The bus made it off the ramp and slid into the lot. It was 2:30 a.m. Saturday, February 16. The driver thought about calling a mechanic. The coaches thought about calling the school's bus, already in Cincinnati.

They decided to call it a night, or at least a bit of a night. It was now 3:30 a.m. The Cardinals were to take the floor against Badger's Bearcats in 16 hours. They still hadn't found Cincinnati.

"Greg (roommate Deuser) and I get in our room, dead-dog exhausted," Roger Burkman recalled. "I don't know if we even took our clothes off. Just closed the door and lay down on the bed. We weren't there 10 minutes when all of a sudden a big, howling wind comes and actually knocks the door open, like someone breaking in. Snow, wind comes running in there. Perfect."

Blacksburg wasn't the remote outpost on this trip. Cincinnati was. Where were Lewis & Clark when you needed them?

Finding a City, Losing a Thumb

Trainer Jerry May had had enough. He called Robert "Bosey" Thrasher, equipment coordinator for all Louisville sports. Thrasher was staying in the Cincinnati hotel room May never got to. He told Thrasher to have the university bus, scheduled to take the team back to Louisville after the game, come to Mount Sterling.

Thrasher did and, after a few hours' sleep, May and the troops boarded a familiar vehicle. With a Kentucky state police car as an escort, the team finally made it to the city on the river in the afternoon.

All but Wiley Brown's prosthetic thumb.

At 6 p.m., an hour and a half before tipoff, May and manager Randy Bufford realized it was missing. Brown, who never liked the thing much anyway, thought he had packed it. If not, oh, well.

"But this was Jerry's main thing," Thrasher recalled. "He sent me back to the (LK) motel in the state police car (that was to lead the bus home), lights flashing, as fast as we could go."

Thrasher and policemen Steve Manning and David King got to the LK Motel safely, rushed to the front desk and learned the room had been cleaned.

"We tore it all to pieces again," Thrasher said. "No thumb. We looked everywhere. Then, just as we were getting ready to leave, I decided to give it a final once-over. I got down on my hands and knees and looked under the bed again. There, inside the front headboard, right beside the bedpost, was the thumb. Standing up."

The digit-hunters made it back before the game started, and Brown was fitted and pronounced good to go.

Game 26: Cincinnati, February 16

A bronchitis-riddled Denny Crum hacked into his rolled-up program. Darrell Griffith, who said he slept "an hour, maybe two," had 14 points and six turnovers. The team's second-best percentage shooter, Rodney McCray, went three for 13. Jerry Eaves, the first five's top free throw shooter, went two for six.

Still...here one needs to shake one's head a bit in disbelief...Louisville found another way, 61-57.

"We take a bus from West Virginia to Pittsburgh, then they say we're going to take a bus from Pittsburgh to Cincinnati, and I'm like, 'What?'" McCray remembered. "We woke up that morning, and the Cardinal bus is waiting for us. We bus into Cincinnati. We're tired. We could have easily lost that game and nobody would have said a word. We didn't, and I knew then and there that there was something special about this team."

The Cardinals had a 57-55 lead with three minutes to go, got its usual free throws, rebounds, defense and delay game and pushed its win streak to 17 and its records to 24-2 for the season and 10-0 in the Metro.

This after Crum was forced to play a chuck-and-duck game in the first half with Cincinnati fans sitting behind him. They threw wadded-up paper at him, then coins.

"The first six or seven times Coach didn't pay any attention to it," remembered equipment man Bosey Thrasher. "But when they started chucking nickels and quarters at him, it made a different impression. He turned around a couple of times. Finally we got security to come over and stand behind him, and they stopped throwing."

There couldn't have been a more fitting end to the 10-day gauntlet run than that, or a scoreboard that showed a more fitting testimonial to a squad's resiliency.

"I could feel it a little bit at the end," Griffith said. "The trip took it out of us. But we don't lay back because we're No. 3 or No. 2 (U of L was expected to move from No. 3 to No. 2 in the AP poll after Syracuse lost to Georgetown). We carry on like we're No. 30. We all know that No. 2 ain't no good at the end of the year."

Game 27: Virginia Tech, February 18

Louisville had one full day to take a deep breath and draw a hot bath before resuming a couple of skirmishes—one with Virginia Tech the team and the other with Dexter Reid the guard—in its final regular-season home game.

The Cardinals were shooting for a 14-0 Freedom Hall record. It was Senior Night—plaques were given to Darrell Griffith and Tony Branch before the game. It was "Wear Red Night"—a sellout crowd of 16,613 was decked out in more red-colored stuff than people should be allowed to wear.

For 32 minutes it looked like "Worn Out Night" for the homeboys. But at 54-54, Griffith fired up the engine with 11 of his 23 points and U of L pounded out a 77-72 triumph, No. 18 in a row.

"We were tired physically, tired mentally, not playing very well, needing to regroup and playing a very good basketball team," Denny Crum said. "But these guys have a burning desire not to lose."

The guards had many desires to burn something or someone.

Reid guarded Griffith and Jerry Eaves guarded Reid. It was strange to see the bursts from an unprintable dictionary as the backcourts journeyed up and down the court. It wasn't U of L's normal way. But Griffith unleashed a stream of words in Reid's face when he whipped around him for a three-point play. At one timeout Reid fired the ball into Eaves' stomach and Eaves threw it into Reid's back.

What did Reid say to Griffith?

"He was making wisecracks you couldn't print," Griffith said.

What did Griffith say to Reid?

"I'm not going to comment," Griffith said. "I'm not going to get anything started and be projected as that kind of person."

Griffith's "he couldn't guard my little brother" offering after the first game a week earlier hardly made Reid a happy camper coming into the sequel.

"I didn't think he was that hot-dog kind of player," Reid told *Courier-Journal* columnist Billy Reed. "At times, I wanted to take a pot-shot at him. I had him below his average (the first game) and I'm only six foot one. If he's the Doctor of Dunk, I'm the Doctor of Defense."

Countered Griffith: "At the end I was asking him where his defense was."

Years later, Eaves said he didn't limit his dislike to one Hokie.

"For me, there was a lot of hate, but it was for the entire team," he said. "Virginia Tech was just one of those situations where they'd rub you the wrong way."

At least it was done with—unless they met for round three in the Metro Tournament less than two weeks away.

CHAPTER EIGHT

A Fat-Cat Infection, Quickly Treated:

February 20, 1980 to March 1, 1980

Eating Up the Big Apple

With a newly minted No. 2 national rank, an 18-game win streak, a 25-2 record and a sweep of four pothole-filled road games, Louisville felt as if it had become an impenetrable fortress.

Everything—gods, breaks, coaching, talent, poise, focus, execution—was on its side. Now U of L was off to New Yawk and the Gahden for an old-timey doubleheader in tandem with No. 1-rated DePaul (23-0). The foes were New York City squads Iona and Wagner in a throwback to the days when Madison Square Garden was college basketball's Valhalla.

In the Garden's storied history, dating to when the National Invitation Tournament was bigger than the NCAA, never had the nation's Nos. 1 and 2 teams been on the same card.

Things could hardly get much sweeter.

Asked recently what he remembered about the Iona trip, reserve center Marty Pulliam quickly brought up a preseason discussion by a team that was not very tall and not very bulky.

"Coach (Denny) Crum called us together and asked, 'How many teams on our schedule are we going to physically manhandle?'" Pulliam said. "Some players said, 'Maybe Iona.' Nobody else was mentioned."

Armed with this "knowledge," U of L jetted into the Big Red Delicious ready to take a big bite. This was a truer homecoming for Scooter and Rodney McCray than the St. John's game February 3, because New Rochelle (Iona's base) and Mt. Vernon (the McCrays' hometown) were about two miles apart, and the Garden was another 10-12 miles down the road.

The team was happy to let Scoot and Rod give it some New York schooling. The coaches were happy to give the guys a dinner at Mama Leone's and a tour of the Empire State Building.

And Denny Crum and Darrell Griffith got a taste of another side of New York in a speeding, weaving cab ride to the restaurant.

"I thought I saw traffic when I lived in L.A., but that was an experience to last you a lifetime," Crum said. "We must have just missed killing six or seven people."

Said Griffith: "Once a lady was about to push her baby carriage over the curb. Then here we come in the cab and – whoosh! – she barely pulls the kid back."

"We got out of our regular road routine in Hawaii," assistant Jerry Jones remembered. "Same thing here. When we played St. John's, we didn't."

Which was fine for wide-eyed Georgia whippersnappers Derek Smith and Wiley Brown. First the sophomores discovered paradise and other stuff in Hawaii, now they were getting a big dose of the big town.

"We were unbeatable," Brown remembered feeling. "We were killing everybody. We were getting the big heads, getting cocky and just knew we were going to beat Iona.

"We were going to have a ball in New York and not worry about the game. Derek and I, the whole atmosphere, we were blown away by it. Imagine, two kids from south Georgia, rural Georgia..."

And, hey, this was little Iona. Unranked Iona. What could go wrong? Well, little Iona was 23-4. It was coached by the late Jim Valvano, who would win a national title three years later with North Carolina State.

It was piloted by a couple of deadly long-range shooters and a press-piercing guard and driven by a tank in the pivot, 6-10, 260-pound Jeff Ruland.

It was playing a big-time team in a big-time place with some big things to prove.

Game 28: Iona, February 21

Louisville had dispensed with Ohio State's pillar-sized Herb Williams and Jim Smith. The Cardinals had twice fought off Virginia Tech's Dale Solomon and Wayne Robinson.

But this Iona guy was an entirely different kind of roadblock. Jeff Ruland was about an axe handle and a half wide across the shoulders and carried the same thickness down through his hips. The tissue in between was not made up of fat grams, but sinew. The Cardinals looked shriveled in comparison.

He was Rocky Mountain Ruland. After No. 1 DePaul slapped Wagner 105-89 in the first game of the doubleheader, Ruland powered—and we mean that literally—the Gaels to a crushing 77-60 victory over No. 2. He snatched 21 rebounds, six fewer than the whole Cardinals team, and scored 30 points.

Goodbye, 18-game victory streak. Hello, red alert.

"I'm amazed it didn't happen long before this," Denny Crum said afterwards.

The U of L press that had bumfuzzled so many others was greedily dismembered by Iona guard Glenn Vickers and backcourt friends, who not only beat it but attacked the rim with a man- or men-advantage. Darrell Griffith lit up Madison Square Garden for 32 points, but the rest of the Cardinals scored 28 points and shot 28 percent.

Long jump-shooters gave the Gaels a 53-42 lead, then turned it over to Ruland and his sledgehammer. Of his 13 field goals, 10 were layups, two were four-footers and one a gorgeous eight-foot hook.

In his three-year college career, Ruland tore apart two rims and two backboards and exploded a scoreboard with an outlet pass. He became a successful bull in the NBA's china shop for many years and is now back at Iona as its head coach.

We're you pretty much an Empire State high-rise landing on Louisville?

"In my three years, very rarely would a team play us man to man," Ruland recalled, referring to Crum's base half-court defense, a switching man to man. "There's not really anyone who's going to guard me one on one, being very frank. I do want to thank Coach Crum for playing the man to man."

Remembered Crum: "Our team was out socializing and didn't think there was any way they could beat us. I could have played 12 different defenses, and it wouldn't have made any difference."

Afterwards, U of L paid homage to the big fellow.

"He's huge, the biggest guy I've ever seen," Wiley Brown said. "He backs over you, he runs over you. He does anything he wants."

"Best big power center in the nation," added Griffith.

Ruland remained an awesome specter in some Cardinals' minds 23 years later.

"Coach always talked about fronting him, but you couldn't get around him to front him," recalled Brown.

Said Daryl Cleveland: "He treated Wiley like a little kid."

"I could have gone anywhere out of high school," Ruland said, "but this is New York City, and part of the dream Coach V (Jim Valvano) sold me on was to play a nationally ranked team in a nine o'clock game in front of a sold-out (18,592) Madison Square Garden. Someone said the (point) spread in the paper was 17 (favoring Louisville). You don't need any more motivation than that. And *we* won by 17."

For U of L, there were a couple of burning questions. Did Iona expose a major weakness due to be exploited by a Joe Barry Carroll or Sam Bowie down the road? Or was it a noisy wake-up call?

Close the Door, Time to Talk Again

The resounding loss to Iona was definitely a shock to Louisville's motor, which had been humming without a hiccup for over seven weeks.

The Cardinals were now 25-3, sure to cough up their No. 2 slot in the poll and headed to a treacherous regular-season windup against tough Florida State in the Seminoles' one-car-garage-sized gym.

But the players didn't feel like they had thrown a rod, one that would put the vehicle on lifts in a repair shop for a couple of weeks.

So U of L did what it always did when it lost, shoo the coaches away, gather in a hotel room and have a gripe session. The team met that night at their headquarters, the Statler Hilton, across the street from Madison Square Garden, with seniors Darrell Griffith and Tony Branch and sophomore Derek Smith loosely in charge.

"Everybody talked, and nobody was afraid to say things," Wiley Brown remembered.

This defeat was different, though. Utah was part altitude, lack of focus and a last-second shot. Illinois in Hawaii was part bikinis and a few guys singing that mournful song, "I Won't Be Home For Christmas."

Iona was the result of (a) a team getting the invincible feeling of a long winning streak, (b) another mournful song, "Sidetracked in New York," and (c) an opponent with the game but not the name.

It was as if Ralph Kramden walked into the Garden, mistook Alice for someone in a Cardinal uniform and snapped, "Pow! Right in the kisser."

"The game really smacked us hard," Daryl Cleveland remembered.

"It took a lot of pressure off," assistant coach Bill Olsen said. "In some respects, Iona was underrated and playing at home. And it was more than just Ruland. It was a well-coached team that was highly motivated."

Recounting the "maybe we can physically manhandle Iona" meeting, Marty Pulliam said, "Well, we handled them good, right? Jeff Ruland crushed our whole front line. But we wouldn't have gotten a (championship) ring if it wasn't for Iona. We were fixing to get beat, but after that we said we won't lose another game."

No one was in better position to see and feel the shock and distress of U of L's demise than injured forward Scooter McCray, back in his hometown before family and friends.

"They gave me a standing ovation even though I didn't play," he remembered. "We get to this mecca of basketball…and these guys just blew us out. Leveled us. We were embarrassed. It was a deflating, humble feeling. We weren't as great as we thought we were. It was a major reality check for us. It brought us down off that high horse. We got rededicated and back on track."

Could an Ink-Stained Wretch Abort a Season? Certainly

The Louisville Cardinals were happy to jump on a plane the morning of February 22 and exit Not-Very-Much-Fun City for the balmier (and hopefully regenerating) climes of Tallahassee, Florida.

This Sunday bout with an athletic Florida State team in microscopic Tully Gym, where its 3,000 permanent seats had sold out earlier than any game in history and 500 folding chair additions went in minutes, was supposed to determine all kinds of things in the Metro-7 Conference. But U of L had clinched the title (and first-round tourney bye) eight days earlier.

Not much more was on the line except bragging rights for both and recovery for Louisville. Unless, of course, disaster struck in the strangest of forms.

On Saturday, February 23, the Cardinals went to Tully for a workout. While U of L was running a routine practice on the main court, the author attempted to play some one on one on an adjacent side basket with sports information director Joe Yates.

At one point the basketball got loose and rolled onto the main floor. Without thinking or looking, I chased down the ball. It and I were maybe 15 feet onto the hardwood. The team was into its three-man full-court fast-break drill. I didn't notice.

As I secured the ball and began to stand up, a voice behind me said, "Don't move." It was Darrell Griffith. It was Griffith at full throttle. I froze in a semi-crouch, somewhat petrified. Griffith scissored over me, sort of as he had done nearly three years earlier to a stand-up guy in the World University Games, and sped on to complete the play.

For over a couple of decades, I've had flashbacks of a 39-year-old chap with a two-inch vertical standing up cluelessly, catching one of Griffith's legs with his shoulder, spinning him to the court and blowing out a knee, blowing out his last title hope, blowing out an NBA career.

Remember that, Griff?

Griffith laughed. He laughed some more. "No, I don't," he said. He shrugged, indicating how ludicrous it would be to think some no-skills sports writer could get high enough to ruin a four-foot leaper's life.

Scooter McCray didn't remember it, either, but he knew what would have happened if I had stood up.

"Griff would have just adjusted and said, 'I've got to go a little higher,'" McCray said.

After a few other tries, thinking maybe he had imagined it, the author found someone who remembered. Rodney McCray.

"Like it was yesterday," he said.

Really?

"When you bend down like that on a break, I've seen guys jump over other guys," Rod said. "It's one of those things where you could have let the ball keep rolling and caused more injury than what you did. A ball can roll any old kind of way."

'Preciate that, Rod. Still, if the unthinkable had come to pass, the wretch would have been stained with more than ink after Griffith's mates had rolled him any old kind of way.

Game 29: Florida State, February 24

Louisville was able to get in two days of solid work, especially on the flagging 2-2-1 press, and it was rewarded.

With Darrell Griffith having perhaps the finest all-around game to date of his terrific career, Louisville shook off Iona's uppercut and bounced Florida State 83-75. It wound up a 26-3 regular season and became the five-year-old Metro Conference's first undefeated squad at 12-0 before a lusty record "crowd" of 3,700 in the Tully Gym sweatbox. The Cardinals played 10 games in February, seven away from home, and went 9-1.

"See what practice can do for you," Roger Burkman said. "We had the best practice before a game in three or four weeks."

In a strange town, in a strange gym?

"A floor's a floor," Burkman insisted.

Griffith scored 29 points (not his high) and hit 11 of 22 shots (under his shooting percentage of 56). But he had nine assists, eight rebounds, seven steals and a blocked shot. He was so overwhelming that the two Seminole guards forced to try to defend him were surly and combative in the locker room afterwards.

"He scored, what, 30 points?" noted Tony Jackson, a six-foot senior from Lexington, Kentucky, who had gone against Griffith for seven years. "That's how you all judge everything anyway, don't you? There's a size difference there."

Rodney Arnold (6-4, the same as Griffith) took some swats at the big Cardinal for eight minutes. "I fouled the _____ out of him, and he'd get it anyway," Arnold said.

The three Georgia Cardinals had people there, especially Wiley Brown, whose 11 relatives and friends from Sylvester, about 80 miles from Tallahassee, bought $135 worth of tickets and were able to sit together in the folding chairs thanks to Florida State coach Joe Williams.

Brown dunked twice, the second after Derek Smith got a lead pass and still shoveled it off to his buddy.

"My mom said every dunk was for her," Brown said. "Derek gave it to me and said, 'Tear it down, big fella.'"

The team collectively exhaled. It was nice to reverse course. U of L now had five days before it would play in the Metro tourney semifinals in Freedom Hall. Five days of doctoring to get ready for the postseason, and there was more tinkering and fine-tuning to be done.

Okay, Wiley, Start Us Up

Darrell Griffith didn't take the first shot of most Louisville games. Neither did Derek Smith.

Wiley Brown did. He wanted it. His mates wanted it for him. Not a big complicated play, just something that would free the 6-8 forward for a jumper in the free throw circle.

If it went down, and the majority of them did, the effect was that of a guy slapping aftershave on his face in the morning. Bracing. The team was now awake and rolling.

"Wiley wanted the first shot because he happened to hit a lot of them," Tony Branch said. "We'd all be thrilled if we'd run a little pick, get it to Wiley and he'd hit that left-hander about 18 feet out. Because then we'd hear him go back upcourt yelling, 'Oh, they in trouble now. I'm hot, I'm hot.' It put us in a fun mood to play."

Wiley, would you say that?

"I would," he said. "They were (in trouble). It was just my psyche and it was an iron rule. We'd all talk about it. You've got to give it to me because I'm going to hit it. I'm not going to say I was perfect, but I hit that shot almost every single time."

And after that?

"We'd give the ball to Griff."

Pranks, Capers and Tomfoolery

Aw, They're Just Being Grown-Ups

Seven of the 13 players were still teenagers for most or all of 1979-80—all the starters except Darrell Griffith, plus Poncho Wright, Scooter McCray and Steve Clark.

Aside from rare moments of levity such as Wiley Brown's first shot, they were all business and effort on the court, mature well beyond their years. The instant they got off the court, they became people mature not well beyond their years.

There were months of practical jokes and deceptive skullduggery that may have set new standards for longevity, goofiness and stupidity.

It would have been easy to stand in front of the kids, hands on hips, and shout, "Grow up!"

Except that the kids were usually the victims. The perps were assistant coach Wade Houston. And assistant coach Bill Olsen. And, once in a while, assistant coach Jerry Jones and, mostly, reserve center Marty Pulliam, who turned 21 on January 9, 1980.

"There weren't a lot of big pranks," Houston recalled. "Subtle stuff, just to keep guys loose more than anything else."

Were there more than in other years?

"I think so," Houston said, "because it was such a good group to be around."

Some examples:

Wright stood at a Salt Lake City carousel, awaiting his luggage. From Utah the team would go to Hawaii. Wright was wearing his snorkeling outfit, a black mask and tube protruding a foot above his head.

In Salt Lake, Derek Smith was holding a book called *Sex and Marriage*. Inside it was a buzzer. Anybody who opened it was shocked. Except the buzzer didn't work. Nobody was shocked.

In the Pittsburgh airport, Pulliam put on dark glasses, picked up an umbrella and put his hand on Tony Branch's arm. Branch led the "blind man" through the security checkpoint, where he fumbled the bumbershoot onto the conveyor belt and groped for the guard's hand trying to find it. "I guess that's either sick or good humor, depending on your point of view," Pulliam said.

In seemingly one airport after another, Houston had Brown and Smith paged "to the nearest white courtesy phone." "They were new guys who basically hadn't flown," Roger Burkman said. "They didn't know. They'd pick up the phone and say, 'Yeah?'" No one was on the other end, of course. "Not every airport," Houston said. "Eventually they caught on. But I'd pick the right time to do it."

Pulliam was a big World Wrestling Federation fan who would vehemently argue with anyone that the sport was legit. The next season in Los Angeles, Burkman remembered Pulliam deciding to show Smith how wrestlers body-slam an opponent. He may have had a few sips of something stout before he weaved over to Smith, picked him up and slammed him onto the bed in the hotel room. "The bed just exploded," Burkman said. "The legs were sticking out to the sides and the frame was just a mess."

"To me," assistant Jerry Jones said, "one of the best unifying factors of that team was Pulliam. He was so funny with those guys. They all picked on him and he took it. Then he instigated things back at them. They loved him. Here's a guy who hardly ever played and maybe he's the most popular guy on the team."

Herewith, then, are a few excerpts from the devious life of Henry Marshall Pulliam IV, the once straw-blond 6-9 center from small-town Kentucky, better known as Snowman.

A Special Kiss for This Piece of Chocolate

In Blacksburg, Virginia, Roger Burkman and Pulliam checked into adjoining rooms in the hotel. A double door with a bolt lock separated a side entrance to the two.

Pulliam went to visit Burkman. When Burkman wasn't looking, Pulliam slipped the bolt lock off the side door. They went to dinner.

"I leave early, go to my room, open up my half of the doors, push his open and rifle through all his stuff," Pulliam said. "I find a big half-pound Hershey's kiss some girl had given him. I opened that up, bit the end off, took bites all the way around it, wrapped it back up, put it back in his bag, locked his side door, went out into the hall, went back into my room and laid down to watch TV.

"About 8:30 at night I hear Burkman hollering, 'Marty, did you break into my candy?' I said, 'I don't know anything about it.' He found out later, but he never knew how I did it."

Pulliam got a 5:30 wakeup call courtesy of Burkman the next morning.

Tickets Here, Any Hour of the Day

In the elevator of a hotel at one tournament site, Pulliam posted a sign saying there were two or more tickets available for that night's game. Jerry Jones' room number was written on the sheet.

"He must have gotten 50 calls and thought Wade (Houston) did it," Pulliam said. "He called Wade and told him they were going to watch film at such and such a time, and gave him the room number across the hall from where the coaches were."

Houston said it was assistant Bill Olsen, not Jones, who called him.

"He was the culprit on that one—he was worse (in general) than I was," Houston said. "I kept knocking on 'Jerry's' door. A guy came to the door, in his pajamas, obviously had been asleep, and he was frosted. They were watching through the peephole. I just stood back and watched as this guy went off—on and on and on. He was steaming."

Care for Some Dog Droppings with Your Regurgitation?

Houston always carried a briefcase with him on trips. Along with unimportant stuff like scouting reports and recruiting logs, he packed rubberized renderings of dog doo-doo and vomit.

"You always knew something was up when Coach Houston pulled that briefcase up and set it on his lap," Burkman said. "On one flight, Marty was on one side of the aisle and Wade on the other. He pulls out the fake puke, throws it on the floor and says, 'Marty, Marty, act like you're sick.' He calls for the stewardess, she comes down and Marty is acting like he's dying. She says, 'Oh my gosh, are you all right, son?' We start laughing. Wade picks it up. She rolls her eyes."

Houston pretended to be asleep.

"She tried to show a lot of poise," he said. "I think at first glance she thought it was real. Then after she looked hard at it she knew something was going on. I had one eye opened looking at her. Marty was rubbing his stomach. She walked back up the aisle shaking her head."

Worthless Insider Trading

Pulliam was wandering around a hotel lobby in Hawaii when a man came up and asked if he wanted to go to dinner.

"Sure," Pulliam recalled saying. "Free food. Two words I understood."

The man, "Bob something," treated four Cardinals to supper. The next day Denny Crum cornered Pulliam and told him the man was a gambler, which neither Pulliam nor his mates realized.

"Coach said, 'Don't be doing that,' Pulliam said. "'He's looking to get a little bit of information that'll make a lot of money for him and get you in trouble.' I'm thinking, 'Well, if he's looking to get information from me, there's no one here who knows less about it than I do.'"

Waterworld

Pulliam and others bought squirt guns in Tallahassee. They commenced to squeezing off rounds at each other, and heading out of town after the Florida State game brought some innocents into the mix.

Pulliam and Derek Smith were in one rental car going to the airport when it pulled up at a light next to a pickup. A boy was riding in the truck bed sitting next to the cab. Smith was next to the car's window.

"Shoot that boy, Derek," Pulliam ordered.

"Wait till the light changes," Smith said.

"It was one of those lights with an arrow and we didn't realize it," Pulliam said. "We got to watching the light for the other direction, saw it change to yellow, Derek rolled down the window and got the kid good. He went to squalling and hollering, and his momma got out of the truck wanting to know what was going on.

"And our light didn't change because of the arrow! So there we sat, thinking, 'Oh, no, momma's going to come over and . . .' Just then the light changed, and we got on out of there."

Nobody confiscated the guns, and the water battles made it back to Louisville unresolved. In fact, they escalated. In fact, the shooters outgrew the squirt guns. Two weeks later it would all come to a head in more ways than one.

More Disturbing History Lessons?

After ripping up its voodoo dolls from Februarys past, Louisville now faced a couple more historical obstacles.

No host school had won any of the first four Metro Conference tournaments, and U of L had this one, starting February 28. However, no school had ever gone through the league unbeaten, as the Cardinals had. Louisville would have to play two games to win it, all the others three, but the expanded NCAA Tournament—up to 48 from 40 in 1979—figured to include three Metro squads regardless.

Denny Crum's club also had a shooting mystery wrapped in an enigma. It was tracking a school-record field goal percentage at .524 vs. the standards set in '78-79 of .504. But it was also in the throes of mediocrity at the free throw line, .676, a stat that could get you beat in March.

It was such an odd contrast. The Louisville team it was compared to in so many ways (1974-75), set (and still holds) the school freethrow percentage record of .752.

"That team was mostly seniors and had a lot more poise at the line," Crum said.

Tony Branch was 13 for 13, but was averaging three minutes a game. Marty Pulliam was four for four, but was averaging 90 seconds a game. Senior Darrell Griffith had to hit seven of eight free throws at Florida State to climb to 71 percent. Roger Burkman was at 72 but had once been at 87.

Some inconsistencies were grotesque. The team hit 90 percent at St. Louis and 53 two days later against Florida State. It hit 44 percent at St. John's and 80 against Memphis State 30 hours later. Wiley Brown missed his first six at St. John's, then hit 16 of 21 a week later on the brutal four-game road trip.

"We'll prove we can shoot them," Derek Smith said.

That would be at the top of Crum's wish list.

Meanwhile, the Cardinals collected nearly all the Metro hardware. Griffith was named player of the year, Crum coach of the year, Smith made the all-league first team, Brown the second and Burkman and Rodney McCray honorable mention. McCray was part of the all-freshman team as was Louisville DeSales High grad Jeff Schneider of St. Louis.

Metro Conference Tournament:
Memphis State, Florida State

Memphis State, February 29: Looking like a flamingo standing on one foot, properly named Memphis State freshman Bubba Luckett hit a 21-foot semi-jumper at the buzzer to beat St. Louis 62-60 in the first round the previous day and advance to meet Louisville for the third time.

It was not a charm. The Tigers played about perfect for a half, hitting 74 percent from the field and 86 percent from the free throw line – and trailed 37-34 at the break. That was because Derek Smith, Darrell Griffith and Poncho Wright went 16 for 20.

U of L went on to an 84-65 victory, outrebounding Memphis 22-9 on the offensive boards. "The ball goes up on the board," Tigers center Hank McDowell said. "You block them out. You look up for the ball and they're already up, from behind, and they haven't even touched you. Incredible, man."

For the league title the Cardinals would get Florida State, which escaped Cincinnati 79-69 in double overtime.

Florida State, March 1: As sort of a final "thank you," Louisville treated its Freedom Hall supporters to one more thunderburst, a 20-3 run that wiped out Florida State's 42-35 lead with under 17 minutes to play and headed the Cardinals to an 81-72 decision and the Metro crown.

Griffith stuck an exclamation point onto his farewell collegiate performance in the Hall with 30 points, four rebounds, five assists, three steals and one turnover in 37 minutes and probably wished he could play the Seminoles another dozen times. In three games he averaged 28.7 points, 6.7 rebounds, six assists, 4.3 steals and one blocked shot, hitting 36 of 63 field goal attempts and 14 of 22 from the line.

Now 28-3 and apparently fully revitalized after the Iona difficulty, U of L expected to be sent to its usual NCAA Tournament region, the Midwest, as its No. 1 seed, when the committee announced its brackets the next day.

Parental Hotheads—the Anti-Stereotype

Redshirt sophomore guard Greg Deuser was probably more obvious in his distaste for the amount of playing time he was getting than anyone on Louisville's team, even demoted senior Tony Branch or junior Daryl Cleveland.

He made no secret of it to coach Denny Crum, the assistants and to his parents. But when he went to gripe to Glenn and Thelma Deuser, he was not met with a "Yes, son, I can't believe what they're doing to you." He was met with a straight-arm.

"My parents were always a lot more sensible than I was," Deuser said. "If I complained, they'd say, 'Hold on a minute. You've got Darrell Griffith, Jerry Eaves, Roger Burkman, Tony Branch—do you really think you should be playing ahead of them?' It was essentially the reverse of what you might expect to hear."

It got Deuser to wondering if the connection established by the parents—with their sons and with each other—was maybe one more ingredient in the bond that enveloped the '79-80 Cardinals.

They all sat in a section in the second deck behind the U of L bench. Deuser's folks were at most every home game, as were Monroe and Maxine Griffith, Frank and Ella Eaves and the parents of Marty Pulliam and Steve Clark.

Roger Burkman's mom, Juanita, was always in from Indianapolis accompanied by her husband, Elvin, when his health permitted. Thomas and Shirley McCray got off work at their respective New York paint and telephone companies for one in-season game and the NCAA Final Four. The families of Tony Branch and Poncho Wright came when they could and the mothers of the Georgians once in a while.

"It would have been interesting to listen in on conversations in that area," Deuser said. "Was there a lot of dissension about playing time? Someone saying, 'Why put him in?' From what my parents have said, it was all very positive.

"We (the players) always had a strong feeling of what was right and wrong, although it was never clearly defined for anybody. We may have had more shared values than our backgrounds implied. I always thought that was a parental impact."

Eaves found the situation different, too.

"The parents were very close—unusual because, being in coaching as I have, I know it doesn't happen all that much," he said. "They pulled for each other's young men."

A smile creased Pulliam's face.

"There was no better person than Monroe Griffith," he said. "Me being the least person on the team, he treated me and Steve Clark no different than his son or anybody else.

"And I remember Mrs. Burkman . . . One time Poncho came in with his collar turned up because he'd seen it like that in *GQ*. Mrs. Burkman said, 'Here, Poncho, you've got your collar messed up,' and turned it back down."

"Roger's mother, she was the best," said Daryl Cleveland, one of the Georgians. "Indiana Momma, that's what we called her. She had a CB (Citizens Band radio) and that was her handle. Roger had one—he was Blue Flash. So did I, and I was Wolfman. We had a lot of fun with that."

A typically soft chuckle came out of Wade Houston's throat as the ex-assistant thought back.

"Great families—to me, anyway," he said. "I don't know how they were to Denny."

Will These Tactics Work? No Sweat

Louisville coaches weren't the only ones who needed a gameplan for the enemy. Trainer Jerry May had a couple of strategies in mind, too, for home games. Neither involved taping ankles or gluing on Wiley Brown's artificial thumb.

With the players milling about the locker room prior to games but before the coaches arrived, May walked to the blackboard. He drew a basketball court. He drew a row of chairs on its side.

Then he grabbed a pointer, summoned his best Vince Lombardi voice and began, as then-student trainer Steve Donohue, in his best May voice, recalled:

"All right, fellas, I'm going to sit right here. Marty (Pulliam), you sit next to me 'cause I know you ain't gonna play, so you ain't gonna sweat on my suit. (Daryl) Cleveland, you sit over here next to Marty. (Greg) Deuser, you sit over there next to (coach) Jerry Jones.

"With two minutes to go, Cleveland and Deuser, you switch with each other. When the student section sees Cleveland walking toward Denny (Crum), they'll think he's going in the game. They'll go crazy."

Cleveland was that season's fan favorite. May performed his ritual every game. He also judiciously chose someone to sit next to him who was either not going to get in or wouldn't get in until near the end.

"I didn't want to get all sweaty," May recalled. "And you probably never noticed us (the bench) go crazy when we finally did get Cleveland in a game. The students would also go nuts. And when we faked putting him in, they'd go nuts then, too."

▲ The 1979-80 Louisville Cardinals: Seated, from left—manager Randy Bufford, Greg Deuser, Jerry Eaves, Roger Burkman, head coach Denny Crum, Darrell Griffith, Tony Branch, Poncho Wright, assistant manager Lambert Jemley; Standing, from left—assistant coach Jerry Jones, graduate assistant Mark McDonald, Rodney McCray, Daryl Cleveland, Marty Pulliam, Scooter McCray, Wiley Brown, Derek Smith, assistant coach Wade Houston, assistant head coach Bill Olsen, student trainer Steve Donohue. *University of Louisville Archives and Records Center, Louisville, KY*

▼ Guard Greg Deuser was one of the second-team maniacs who made things tougher on the first unit than several of Louisville's actual opponents. *University of Louisville Archives and Records Center, Louisville, KY*

Homespun center ▶ Marty Pulliam was No. 12 on the Cardinals in minutes played, No. 1 in pranks played. *University of Louisville Archives and Records Center, Louisville, KY*

◀ When Darrell Griffith elevated for a jump shot with his 48-inch vertical leap, a defender could do little more than wave goodbye.
Photo by Bill Straus

Tony Branch was demoted ▶ from starter to guard No. 4 for his final season, but that didn't prevent him from saving Louisville's hide against Kansas State in the NCAA Tournament. *University of Louisville Sports Information*

U of L grad and frenzied fan Rob Hickerson created the C-A-R-D-S body-language chant from the stands in '79-80 before the official cheerleaders added it (and sometimes him) to their routines. *University of Louisville Sports Information*

Reserve forward Daryl Cleveland claims to have invented the high-five at the beginning of the '79-80 season, and his teammates back him up. *University of Louisville Sports Information* ▶

▲ St. Louis U. could testify to the running, leaping, and dunk-
ing abilities of Louisville skyriders Poncho Wright (left) and
Darrell Griffith (right). Griffith scored 52 points and
Wright added 27 in two blowout victories over St. Louis.
Rich Clarkson/NCAA Photos

▲ When a knee injury ended Scooter McCray's season
early in the third game, the loss was potentially devastating. Not so fast, said Scooter's brother, Rodney, who
was quick to fill in. *University of Louisville Sports Information*

▲ Freshman Rodney McCray, battling one on three against UCLA in the title game, dramatically changed his work ethic and attitude when brother Scooter went down. *Photo by Bill Straus*

◀ Poncho Wright, whose physical gifts were in the Darrell Griffith neighborhood, was "Instant Offense" as the first forward off the bench.
University of Louisville Sports Information

▲ Roger Burkman (with ball) was called "Instant Defense" because of his incessant harassment. Most opponents had other names for him, none printable here. *Rich Clarkson/NCAA Photos*

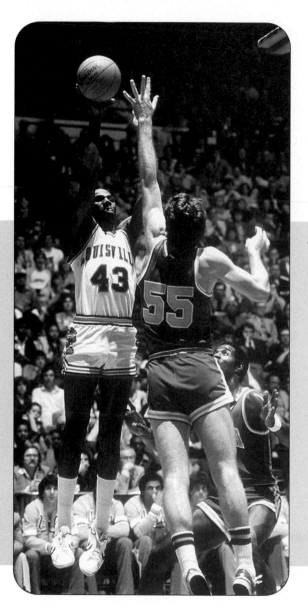

◀ Derek Smith was U of L's leading percentage shooter and rebounder. Only Darrell Griffith's overwhelming presence kept the sophomore's star from shining brightly on the '79-80 NCAA stage. *Rich Clarkson/NCAA Photos*

Point guard Jerry
Eaves spent three
months searching
for more minutes
and recognition,
then found all he
could ever hope
for in March.
*University of
Louisville Sports
Information*

▲ After being allowed to drive an Indianapolis 500 pace car, Wiley Brown was in ecstasy, just as he was after helping drive U of L past worthy foes such as Louisiana State. The team visited the speedway the day before the championship game. *Photo by Bill Straus*

▼ The Cardinals draped themselves over an old Indy 500 racer at Indianapolis Speedway Museum. That's assistant coach Bill Olsen's son, David, in the middle. *Photo by Bill Straus*

◀ When Denny Crum picked up a piece of chalk, such as here before the championship game against UCLA, he wasn't kidding around. *Photo by Bill Straus*

▼ Denny Crum didn't get rapt attention from all his teams during pregame talks, but he did with the devout believers of 1979-80. *Photo by Bill Straus*

▲ Wiley Brown's aunt came up with this fake newspaper for her nephew and Brown's Georgia buddy, Derek Smith. While the grammar in the headline could have been better, the thought could not have. *Photo by Bill Straus*

▲ Seniors Tony Branch (left) and Darrell Griffith (right) accept the national championship trophy from NCAA Tournament Committee chairman Wayne Duke after Louisville's 59-54 victory over UCLA. *Photo by Bill Straus*

▲ Darrell Griffith was denied Player of the Year honors, which were distributed before the end of the season. But he picked up the John Wooden Award in voting that occurred after the NCAA Tournament.
University of Louisville Sports Information

CHAPTER NINE

Mates Flame Up to Sustain Their Smoldering Leader:

March 2, 1980 to March 16, 1980

To the Midwest (Right) As a No. 2 (Huh?)

On Sunday, March 2, the NCAA Tournament committee announced that Louisville's 28-3, fourth-ranked Cardinals would get a first-round bye (expected) to the Midwest Regional (expected) as the No. 2 seed (not expected).

Louisiana State was handed No. 1 in the Midwest, even though the powerful Tigers (rated fifth in the Associated Press poll and 24-5) had won the Southeastern Conference's tourney and its automatic bid. That league's champ had always taken the Mideast route in the NCAA.

But the committee had a dilemma. LSU beat second-ranked Kentucky (28-5) in the SEC final. Kentucky was due to host the Mideast semifinals and final in Rupp Arena. And Louisville's 17-point haymaker from Iona was more painful than people knew.

"It was a concern of the committee that, even if all the tickets are sold, it would hurt the tournament if nobody showed up to see LSU play in Lexington," NCAA spokesman Dave Cawood said. "Plus, Louisville's loss to Iona was so much more decisive than any of LSU's losses, and the committee members were swayed by that."

In one sense, it reinforced Cardinal coach Denny Crum's long-held belief that wire-service polls are meaningless. Now someone agreed with him—the NCAA. But as usual, he shrugged.

"Why did they put (top-ranked and Chicago-based) DePaul in the West?" he asked. "Maybe balance was more important. I can see 20-some teams in there that could win it all. It'll be who plays best and gets the fewest bad breaks."

The Cardinals would head to Lincoln, Nebraska, for a Saturday, March 8 date with either the team it beat by 12 points January 5 (Kansas State) or the team that knocked it out of the 1979 NCAAs by 11 (Arkansas, minus Sidney Moncrief).

Fewest bad breaks, indeed. Maybe one or two good ones would be needed, too.

A Crazy New Dance

The NCAA Tournament's clichéd nickname, "Big Dance," didn't come along until later, but this might have been the year that led to it.

For the first time, the committee (1) had 48 teams to disperse, up from 40 in 1979, (2) had the right to put them anywhere they wanted, and (3) could take more than two teams from a conference.

It sent No. 1-ranked DePaul to the West Regional for the second straight year along with ninth-rated Ohio State, causing Ralph Miller, coach of Pacific-10 champ Oregon State (also there), to mutter, "I don't think this is a very fair proposition."

It steered Southeastern Conference tourney winner Louisiana State to the Midwest. It left runnerup Kentucky near its home in the Mideast. It left out worthies such as Virginia and Nevada-Las Vegas. But it welcomed UCLA which, despite its deified basketball stature, was only 17-9 and had finished fourth in the Pac-10.

Still, despite all the usual debates and protests, the regionals looked about as balanced as they ever had and the whole field seemed to have a lot of unpredictability to it.

How much parity was there?

Example one: Because the event hadn't yet reached the must-be-there status it would a few years later, the NCAA had trouble getting schools to offer their arenas as regional sites. Those that did hoped to qualify for the tourney and expected to be given a slot that would land them on their own floor. For financial and attendance reasons, the NCAA complied.

In 1980 the NCAA had four such first- and second-round sites (Purdue, Western Kentucky, Arizona State and Weber State) and one such regional proper (Kentucky). All five played on their home courts (UK reaching Rupp Arena via Western Kentucky's Diddle Arena).

"There was concern by the committee about leaving UK in a position to potentially play on its home floor," NCAA spokesman Dave Cawood told *Courier-Journal* columnist Billy Reed. "Obviously, the concern was not so great they decided to move them. There's no guarantee, you know, that UK will get to Lexington. Last year, when the East was held in Raleigh and Greensboro (N.C.), everybody said North Carolina and Duke had it locked up. Instead, they both got beat in their first games."

Prophetic man, Cawood. Kentucky reached its home base but couldn't leave it. Three other homies failed to escape their floors. Only Purdue made it out of the friendly confines.

Example two: The committee chose its four No. 1 regional seeds, then its four No. 2s, then four No. 3s, then four No. 4s, in that order, like today. All would receive first-round byes. Of those 16 teams, one would reach the Final Four.

Example three: In the 26 years since the seeding procedure has been in place, only once have all four No. 1s failed to reach the Final Four. The year was 1980.

Then there's the school that many thought didn't belong. Risking provincialism, a Californian and former UCLA grad and coach named Denny Crum admonished those who disparaged the Bruins. "Better watch out," he said. "They may be young and their record may not be real good, but they have a lot of talent."

Sure, Coach. Why don't you go on and say too-young, overachieving Louisville and eighth-seed UCLA could win nine tourney games and play for the national championship? Insane.

Well, there turned out to be a lot of lunacy in 1980. As the dementia unfolded, the Charleston, jitterbug and mashed potato stepped back to make room for the zaniest dance yet.

The Ascendance of Rodney

As Louisville mounted up for its NCAA drive, Rodney McCray was now 18 years old going on about 25.

He had been a reluctant participant, had been thrust into a major role by his brother's injury, had matured into manhood overnight, and now had averaged 32.4 minutes while starting 28 of 31 games. Pretty much a career rolled into three months.

But he was still in the semi-hidden category, stuck beneath Darrell Griffith's exploits, Denny Crum's accolades, Derek Smith's fiery demeanor and the unique contributory roles of others.

He was still in his rookie season. He was steady, but none of his numbers leaped off the page—fifth on the team in scoring at 7.6, second in rebounding at 7.3, also second in turnovers with 76, a good shooter at 54 percent, an average free thrower at 65.

He led the team in blocked shots with 53, a remarkable stat for a 6-7 guy who operated in a baseline forest, but with people like Griffith jumping four feet off the ground, McCray's elevator hardly stood out.

By March an aura had begun to emanate from McCray, a commanding presence that would be strong medicine for the next three U of L seasons. His brother and the other '79-80 youngsters joined him, and it seemed that then they began drafting a bill of rights into the Cardinal basketball constitution, amendments on what's important (winning), what isn't (what the individual does) and how hard to play the game.

Scooter McCray addressed the family approach years later.

"Part of the attitude of being a complete player is knowing you have to sacrifice your ego," he said. "A lot of guys just think they want to score, score, score. If that's what makes them happy, that's fine. The attitude of Rodney and me is, if I'm on the court playing, I'm happy."

Don't assume the McCrays and others came without egos, though. They just happen to be in plural form: What "we" accomplished, what "we" brought to the university, how the school grew because of "us."

"Me and Rodney were in Freedom Hall walking around during our reunion in 1990 for an open house," Daryl Cleveland said. They were checking out the $13.3 million 1984 renovation that added 24 private boxes and over 2,000 more seats.

"This lady came up to us and said, 'Who are you? Who you with?'" Cleveland said. "Rodney said, 'I'm probably the one who built your suite.' And he was right. Three Final Fours. That's a lot."

Rodney scored in double figures only his senior year, averaging 11 points. He had a 10-year NBA career with four teams, was a regular in the first nine, averaged from 10.3 to 16.6 points in eight of them and between six and eight rebounds in seven. He became a world champion in 1993-94 with the Chicago Bulls.

John Crawley was the assistant sports information director in '79-80. He spoke for a lot of folks when he said, "By the time he got out of there, I thought he might have been the best all-around player who ever played at U of L."

Honed in on a Zone

Kansas State threw a 3-2 zone at Arkansas and won easily 71-53 on Thursday, March 6, in the NCAA's first round at Lincoln, Nebraska.

A much more controlled, intelligent club would get a second shot at Louisville. Like going to school on an opposing golfer's putt before having to follow a similar line, the Wildcats now had a much better feel for how to approach U of L in the sequel.

"They were wild the first game," Cardinal Wiley Brown said. "They're under control tonight."

They figured to be a pain.

Kansas State suffocated the Arkansas offense and handed coach Eddie Sutton a 71-53 loss, his worst in six seasons with the Razorbacks, to move on to round two with U of L, which rose to second in the final AP poll of the season.

This would not be the same bunch of Wildcats who were outsprinted 85-73 by U of L on January 5 at Freedom Hall. That team played mostly a man-to-man defense. This one spread three guys across the defensive perimeter with 6-7 Jari Wills steering the operation from the top of the free throw circle.

It flustered Arkansas, which triggered only 20 shots in the first half, made nine and scored 21 points, and a much-improved K-State club executed smoothly and disappeared from sight.

But would the Wildcats go zone or go back to the man to man? They liked to run some, too, just not as much or as explosively as Louisville.

"I'd tell you what we'd use, except I don't know yet," K-State coach Jack Hartman said, and he seemed to be sincere.

A Crummy Decision in the Water Wars

Marty Pulliam was delighted to see that his relatively innocent purchase of a squirt gun in Tallahassee, Florida, two weeks earlier was thriving.

On Friday, March 7, as Louisville bused to practice in Lincoln, Derek Smith, Darrell Griffith, Wade Houston and Wiley Brown took turns wetting down busmates. Tony Branch was as big a victim as anyone, finally dodging enough water shots to attack Brown with a headlock.

Back at the Lincoln Hilton Inn that night, the combat graduated to hotel room ice buckets. Six or seven players were involved, Pulliam, of course, in the lead.

"Tony was rooming with Griffith," recalled Pulliam. "We went down, knocked on the door, Tony opened it, we threw water on him. We went down again, he wouldn't open it, we got ready to leave, then he opened it and threw water on us. We had a couple of rounds of that."

Branch picks up the narrative:

"I had a habit of harassing the Georgia contingent, and after somebody got me I said, 'Okay.' I put the chain on the door. There's a knock on the door. I thought it might be Derek. Coaches were nowhere to be seen.

"I knew it was one of the guys coming to get me. I had a bucket filled up. I opened the door as far as it would go with the chain on it and just threw the water."

Denny Crum was hardly ever one to check up on his troops or even go talk to them in their rooms. But knowing the NCAA Tournament would ratchet the performance level up a notch, he was worried about how his young team would respond.

Crum decided to call upon his seniors. He knocked on the Branch/Griffith door. He was greeted by rainman. Branch's toss through the four-inch opening got his coach a bit wet, but it could have been worse.

"The next thing I heard was, 'Tony, what are you doing, son?'" Branch said. "All I could think of at first was, 'Am I going to get any minutes (which couldn't have dropped much lower—he averaged 1.5 in the previous four games)?' And second was, 'How far down in the doghouse am I going to be now?'"

Crum not only shrugged it off but maybe saw it as a tension relaxant.

"If he had known (who was at the door) he'd have thrown it straighter," Crum said at the time. "No player likes to miss a shot."

It took an awful lot to get Crum angry. It didn't take much at all to get him plotting revenge.

Game 32: Kansas State, March 8, NCAA Midwest Regional Second Round

By the time Tony Branch got the ball, seven seconds were left in overtime.

Louisville and Kansas State were tied at 69. Darrell Griffith was gone, banished with his fifth foul over two minutes earlier.

Branch, the senior vet, the man who had started 22 games in 1978-79 only to play a piddling 92 minutes in 20 games in '79-80, the man who washed down his head coach hours earlier, was in to run U of L's delay game. He wound the clock down from 2:20 to 1:57 and called time. He wound it down from 1:57 to 0:14 and called time again.

Coach Denny Crum devised a set that would give Branch three options—a pass to Poncho Wright or Derek Smith if one was open as they came off a double screen, or a shot by himself.

But K-State defenders jumped Branch at the whistle to start play, forcing in-bounder Rodney McCray to desperately look elsewhere for a receiver.

It took seven seconds for the ball to go to Wiley Brown to Smith to Branch. It left the six-foot Branch facing 6-6 Rolando Blackman, the Big Eight Conference's three-time defensive player of the year, and 5-11 Glenn Marshall, who was having a lights-out game.

Six seconds...five...Branch dribbled to the free throw line and Blackman and Marshall stepped up to trap. Branch knew he was out of options, except one.

Like a move from a ballet class, Branch one-stepped forward, off-balance, splitting Marshall and Blackman, who wanted to harass but not foul. Left leg forward, right leg cocked behind, he launched a soft quasi-jump shot from 15 feet out.

Four...the ball hit the front of the rim, caromed delicately to the back brace...three...bounced delicately once, twice on the iron...two...and fell through. The Wildcats, down 71-69, called time at 0:01. A length-of-the-court pass from Jari Wills sailed out of bounds.

The Cardinals had escaped an opponent they in many ways had no business beating in a game that dripped with so much irony, breaks and luck that film directors would have rejected it as too implausible.

Branch and Blackman revisited the game in 2003.

"When I got trapped, my experience said to me, 'I've got to get a shot up,'" Branch said. "They weren't quite in front of me, so there was a little gap. I didn't know if I could get the shot off or if Blackman could block me with his size. I leaned in because it was the only way I could get it off, but when I let it go I thought it was going in. Soft. Right on target."

"It was all miracle..." said Blackman, now an assistant with the Dallas Mavericks. "We knew he was a doggone good player, that's for sure. But no one can say what's going to happen when you split a double-team like that, throw it up in the air and the ball bounces up, bounces up, then bounces and bounces, and then bounces through. I wish it would have bounced in faster and given us more turnaround time. But I can't say that shot was anything more than what it was—a good player getting a lucky break."

Griffith didn't have a scrapbook game—eight of 20, 18 points, four turnovers, zero steals (but eight assists and six rebounds). Smith helped with 20 points, but as tough as K-State was, the Wildcats still needed a Blackman 10-footer to tie it 67-67 at the end of regulation.

Maybe an angel and not a devil was sitting on Louisville shoulders this time.

"We played bad, like we were all freshmen," assistant coach Bill Olsen said. "But since I've been here, I can't remember getting any lucky breaks in the NCAA. Today was the first time."

Thanks to the right arm of the most improbable of heroes.

A Love-In for the Branch Who Became a Mighty Trunk

Outside a euphoric Louisville locker room, Darrell Griffith wrapped his arms around Tony Branch, pointed him out to all onlookers and exclaimed, "This is my roommate!"

Inside the locker room, Poncho Wright was exclaiming, "He saved our jocks. We had to rely on TB's one-on-one A-BIL-A-TEE."

And Scooter McCray was gushing, "He was our Curly Neal (the Globetrotters' sleight-of-hand dribbler). The wizard of U of L, the master of the hardwood. You see Tony Branch in practice. He's bouncing two balls, three balls. He spins 'em, whirls 'em, takes 'em around his neck. Ah, Tony Branch."

If this had been the Oscars, there would not have been a dry eye in the house. The band of Cardinals could not have been more incandescent, more impassioned, more beside themselves for one of their own.

The senior guard had planned on being one of the team's guiding lights. Instead he was consigned to non-playing teacher/cheerleader duties.

Now, in a moment of monumental vindication, in his 95th minute of action out of a possible 1,290, with his 10th field goal out of 26 tries in three-plus months, Branch was neither Griffith's valet nor Griffith's roomie. Griffith was Branch's roomie. Griff loved every second of the reversed spotlight. And Branch felt so good.

"Sitting on the bench is something I've had to constantly work on," he told *Courier* columnist Billy Reed. "This season was awfully difficult. But my teammates respect me as a basketball player and as a person. They tried to keep me up. In practice I'd make a good move, show them some of the old razzle-dazzle, and someone would say, 'Get down, Tony!' That helped me a lot."

Expressions of delight appeared on the often stoic face of coach Denny Crum.

"There's nobody who likes or respects Tony more than I do," he told Reed. "It (the demotion) was hard for me. I got a lot of criticism for it."

There was no truth to the rumor that Crum had ordered Branch to win the game as punishment for the water toss the night before. But there was reason to think in terms of omens.

"The things I always remembered about Denny's (tournament) philosophy were (1) you've got to be good, and (2) you've got to get lucky and get some breaks," Rodney McCray said years later. "That shot stands out as the most glaring example of that. The bounce goes our way, and we go on. We could have been right back home."

Splish, Splash, Let's Take Another Bath

On Tuesday, March 11, Roger Burkman was warming up for practice when he heard Denny Crum call him to the lobby at Crawford Gym.

"He says, 'Come here, holler at Tony, tell him you want to see him,'" Burkman recalled. "I say, 'What you talking about, Coach?' He reaches around and has this bucket of water. So, of course, I say, 'Hey, TB, come here, man, this man wants to see you.'"

Crum was poised on the step behind the door that opened into a cage leading onto the gym floor. Branch entered the cage and opened the door.

"I duck out of the way and Coach drills him," Burkman said.

Crum also made sure a TV news crew was there to record a man not getting mad but getting even.

"I didn't like it for a second," Branch remembered, "but then it was okay. In hindsight, I think he was trying to relax me. But Denny's highly competitive. He wanted to get me back."

"Turnabout's fair play," Crum recalled thinking. "After it happened (in the hotel) I decided to pay him back." He grinned. "They (his teammates) were shocked," he said. "It was okay for them to do it, but . . ."

That brought an end to waterworld, at least as far as squirt guns and ice buckets were concerned. Of course, things like showers were still available.

Suddenly a Rash of Doubters

Funny what one shaky, tentative performance with a lucky outcome can do to a team's rep.

In half a week, a Louisville squad harassing enemies on the ground and bombing them from the clouds had gone from 29-3 and second-rated to overrated in the minds of many NCAA Tournament geeks.

You might have even included Denny Crum among the club. In a hard-line message driven home two days after the 71-69 survival of Kansas State, the coach gathered his guys around him before a Monday practice and said, "We played like a bunch of dogs. We were passive, tentative. We choked."

No player likes to hear the "c" word, but Crum made it a bit more palatable with further explanation.

"We'd do something good one time down the floor, then we'd stand around," he said. "That's why Kansas State shot so well. Nobody challenged them. We didn't get one breakaway basket, one turnover on the press. We let them set up in their offense and run it.

"You've gotten into habits you don't even realize, and we can't beat any team like that. You've got to force things, make them happen, push the tempo, and that has to be done on the defensive end. There's not a team left in the tournament you can't beat if you do the things you have to do. But if you play like you did Saturday, we don't have a prayer Friday.

"Now let's get after each other in practice and get in a groove."

Friday would be March 14 and a date in Houston's Summit with Southwest Conference champ Texas A&M (26-7). The Aggies were an unranked and unrecognized No. 6 seed despite devouring third-seed North Carolina in a second overtime by 17 points, 78-61, in the second round. Louisiana State and Missouri would meet in the second game of the Midwest Regional semis.

LSU had increased its stature as the hot horse. Louisville was watching its bandwagon jumpers climbing off, not on.

Game 33: Texas A&M, March 14, NCAA Midwest Regional Semifinal

Darrell Griffith made up for lost time lickety-split.

Throwing his downbeat Kansas State game into a landfill, he dunked, hit from 20, 18 and 18 feet and added two free throws before Texas A&M couldn't draw a deep breath at The Summit in Houston.

When Jerry Eaves scored on a driving layup, Louisville had a 12-2 lead 2:48 into the conflict. At that rate, Louisville would win 160-27 behind Griffith's 133 points.

In their dreams.

A&M coach Shelby Metcalf called time at 17:09. Saying later that the "game started at 7:07, we started at 7:10," he switched from a zone defense to man to man. Normally the Cardinals' eyes glow at the sight. But they had not seen one in three weeks.

Staggering resumed. Griffith's candle was snuffed out by David Britton, Rudy Woods or Vernon Smith, who brushed, tipped or actually blocked a half-dozen of his shots. Griffith went three for 16 the last 37 minutes of regulation, then two of four in overtime.

The Aggies caught up just after halftime, 35-35. They led by four with 11:49 to play at 47-43. Neither team could manage even a point in the next 3:35. Finally Wiley Brown hit a five-foot baseliner and a six-foot hook, and the Cardinals soon headed to another overtime tied 53-53.

Denny Crum switched Griffith to a new spot low on the weak side. Griff responded with six points, and U of L scored the last 10 of OT to win 66-55.

Louisville shot only .397, its worst percentage since December, but survived again.

"We won not playing great against a good team, so give us a pat on the back," Griffith said.

Multifaceted Louisville State eliminated Missouri 68-63 in the other semi.

"That's a lot of talent," Derek Smith said, thinking of LSU, "but there ain't no rinky-dinks left."

Ejecting Another Psychic Phenomena

With 11 seconds to go and survival assured against Texas A&M, Kansas State hero Tony Branch was fouled and stepped to the free throw line for Louisville.

Nothing big about this moment, except . . . Branch was 16 for 16 for the season. Nothing too big about that, except . . .

Five years earlier, Terry Howard had gone through U of L's season 28 for 28. In the 1975 NCAA national semifinals against UCLA, he stood at the line with a one-and-one that could wrap up a glorious victory over the final battle group of John Wooden's armada.

Howard calmly went through his normal preshot ritual. The first free throw was on line. It looked true. Somehow it rolled off. UCLA won in overtime 75-74. With astounding unfairness, a fifth-year senior who had been a starter and reliever for the Cardinals, who had been solid, dependable and had won them games over his career, would be remembered for needing 29 free throws to hit 28.

Now Branch was rowing the same boat. Coach Denny Crum, ever vigilant about such things, brought the Howard subject up to Branch before the A&M game, when Branch was 13 for 13.

"I knew I was going to ask him to miss one," Crum said. "I didn't want him to be under that kind of pressure the last two to three games. I knew if there was a situation at the end, he'd be in there to get fouled and shoot free throws just like Terry was. I told him I wanted him to miss one, and he said, 'Whatever you think's best, Coach.' That was Tony's typical attitude. Never questioned it, just did it.

"I understood the history," Branch said. "He felt that there might have been too much pressure on Howard—not that that caused him to miss that one. So he's thinking of me and the team."

But Branch remembers himself telling Crum, "I really think I shoot them better without having missed."

So Branch was at the line at 0:11.

"I received the ball, and he (Crum) stepped into my peripheral view," Branch said. "He called my name. I was surprised because I had learned to block everything out but him. I thought this was kind of weird, and he said, 'Do you think you want to miss this one?' And I said, 'No.' And I hit it.

"I line up for the second one, and he stepped into my line of vision again. I decided to miss it just to take the pressure off him. I thought he was worried about it. So I told the guys on the free throw line, 'I'm going to miss this.' They started laughing. I said again, loud enough for everyone to hear, 'I'm going to miss this one.' And I did."

A week after the Branch episode, Howard was at a pep rally and was asked (of course) about the miss.

"I'm in sales and, at least once a day, somebody reminds me," he said. "At least once a day."

Regional Finals—Who Are These Guys?

As Louisiana State and Louisville arrived at Houston's Summit arena for practice and press conferences on Saturday, March 15, before their Midwest Regional championship the next day, the NCAA Tournament had stripped off almost all of its makeup to reveal a remarkably unglamorous face.

LSU was the lone remaining No. 1 seed, U of L the lone remaining No. 2.

Gone was Mideast No. 1 Kentucky, nicked on its own court 55-54 by Duke when Kyle Macy missed a jumper and no whistle blew on a disputed was-he-fouled-or-wasn't-he? play with five seconds left. Gone was Mideast No. 2 and Big Ten big-dog Indiana, dominated from the get-go by fellow Big Tenner and archrival Purdue 76-69.

Gone was East No. 1 Syracuse, at the hands of Iowa, and East No. 2 Maryland, undone by Georgetown.

Long gone were West No. 1 DePaul, punched out by UCLA, and West No. 2 Oregon State, knifed by Lamar, both in the second round. For good measure, Clemson took out West No. 3 Brigham Young in round two. For extra good measure, UCLA stunned powerful No. 4 seed Ohio State in the semifinals, then stopped Clemson in the final.

This was, of course, a UCLA squad bent over like Quasimodo trying to carry the Bruins' invincible John Wooden legacy on its back. The four previous seasons would have been glorious almost anywhere else—102-17, one national semifinal and a regional final. But no crowns. Terrible. The chant "Off with their heads" was heard.

Enter Larry Brown from the pros in the school's third leadership attempt A.C. (After Coach). This one was, well, geez, pretty bad. The Bruins lost nine games. They finished fourth in the Pacific 10. "Off with his head" was practically a compliment compared to other stuff Brown was hearing from the stands.

Yet, in a bewildering display of karma, luck, guts or something, UCLA was headed for Indianapolis and the Final Four.

Brown stifled a chuckle years later as he recalled the upheaval in Tempe, Arizona, on March 9 in the West subregional. UCLA had just shocked DePaul 77-71. Ohio State was taking the floor against Arizona State, a fellow Pac-10 squad and "a wonderful team," Brown said, that was ranked 18th nationally, was playing at home and had beaten UCLA twice, 92-80 and 78-76.

"I had to go to a press conference and my assistants, Larry Farmer and Kevin O'Connor, went out to scout," Brown said. "I got out there and Arizona State was getting beat like 25 at the half (heading toward an 89-75 defeat). I told my coaches, 'Look, guys, let's stop scouting this game. We're not going to beat Ohio State. Let's go home and celebrate beating the No. 1 team in the nation.'

"I thought Ohio State was unbelievable. But I didn't tell my kids that."

Five days later Ohio State was more believable. UCLA, 72-68.

Louisville coach Denny Crum was asked about all these surprises.

"They're upsets only if you're enough of an idiot to believe the rankings," he said. "Things are so even that if you swapped two or three teams from each region to another one, I believe you'd come up with a different eight."

Could be. But the truth was that on this regional final weekend only one of the NCAA's top eight seeds would make the last roundup.

Louisiana State? Or Louisville?

Griff and Rudy—Chums Before Rivals

Darrell Griffith, Louisville's guiding light. Durand "Rudy" Macklin, Louisiana State's captain and hopeful stabilizing force.

How strange that they would collide at another intersection, especially one of this import. It was like they were joined at the jump shot.

They grew up a mile or so from each other. Griffith started playing basketball at age 11 when his dad nailed a hoop to the back of the family garage. Macklin picked up the game about two years later.

Soon they came together on the same court. Soon they became friends. Soon, though not many blocks apart, they headed in different directions. Griffith played for DuValle Junior High and Male High, Macklin for Shawnee Junior and Senior High. Griffith's teams never lost to Macklin's.

But in the summertime they combined forces, first for a squad called Chocolate City in the high-velocity "Dirt Bowl" battles at Shawnee Park when they were in high school, then at U of L's Crawford Gym for the summer pickup bruisers when they were in college.

"Every time he comes home, I'm the first one he calls," Griffith said. "And when I go out, it's either me and Rudy or me, Rudy and Bobby."

Bobby was Bobby Turner, Griffith's Male and U of L teammate until academics knocked him off the 1979-80 team. Together with another friend, Bobby Stewart, they would tool around town and across the bridge into Southern Indiana, hunting up games on weekends.

"Like musicians looking for a gig," Macklin recalled years later. "Once we were in the Jeffersonville (Indiana) High School gym. This one team had a 6-8 white guy on the team. He looked slow. We got on the floor and he was making no-look passes and hitting long jumpers. They beat us like 24-12 and never left the court (because they never lost). A long time later we're watching a game on TV and it's like, 'Hey, see that white guy. He's the one who kicked our butts in Jeff.' It was Larry Bird."

Now they were hunting a gig again, but only one would get to play it. Yet even in the high-tension, high-pressure atmosphere of a berth in the NCAA's Final Four, first things first.

On Saturday night, March 15, about 20 hours before their teams would tip it off for the Midwest Regional title, Griffith and Macklin went out to dinner.

"We didn't talk about the game," Griffith remembered. "We just had a good time."

"We were just chilling out and catching up," Macklin recalled. "Two good friends getting together. From junior high to high school to college to the NBA, it seemed like chemistry. We wouldn't let anybody get between us."

Macklin said his college choice came down to LSU or Louisville and he decided "to crease my own path." Later his high school coach, Ron Abernathy, and Shawnee High product Gus Rudolph joined him.

"It ought to be fun for the folks at home to see how we do against the local boys," Rudolph said on Friday.

There were a lot of folks in a lot of places who could hardly wait.

Still Looking to Reconnect

Louisville was now 30-3. Magnificent, really, considering where it began.

But its followers were so used to seeing its energy converted into electric, dominating performances that its first two NCAA games were practically downers.

The Cardinals had overcome tentativeness with good shooting, bad shooting with aggression and escaped twice in overtime with their star not shining as brightly as usual. They had probably run out of feline lives. If they remained disjointed against somebody with as many skills as Louisiana State, they could turn out the lights.

Denny Crum said so the day before the regional final.

"We played poorly against Kansas State but shot better than 55 percent," he said. "Against (Texas) A&M I felt we played extremely well the whole way, yet shot 39 percent. We still haven't put the kind of game together that was typical of our play in reaching this tournament.

"I'm convinced we won't have a chance against LSU unless we do both things—play well in all phases and shoot well, too."

LSU's Dale Brown was not about to be out-badmouthed. He, too, was disturbed by his team's shenanigans. The Tigers had won at Kentucky, beaten Kentucky for the Southeastern Conference tournament crown, were 26-5, ranked third in the final poll, had lost to eventual national champ Michigan State in the NCAAs the year before and had most of their guys back.

But against Missouri the night before they were content to pop long outside jumpers, shot 39 percent the first half and trail by a point before collecting enough of their former selves to win by five.

"We had shown such control in our previous 13 or 14 games that I was really shocked," Brown said. "We were putrid. We really stunk. We better be much more conservative in our shot selection against Louisville. If we try to change personalities, we'll be back in Baton Rouge for good."

Brown had gotten mysteriously tricky this season, reining in his thoroughbreds at odd times for delay/control games. But he also knew he had immense athleticism in 6-8 DeWayne Scales, 6-9 center Greg Cook, 6-6 Rudy Macklin, point guards Ethan Martin and Willie Sims and a deep-shooting stroke in Jordy Hultberg.

"Louisville might be the toughest (of anybody LSU played)," Brown said. "They match up with our quickness, they run the way we do, and they've shown they can sit on the ball when they want to.

"But we're not a flash in the pan. It's been a very hard eight-year climb to build what we have. I think we'll be national champions if we can play our game for two halves every time out."

Time to discover if one of these folks could actually do that.

Game 34: Louisiana State, March 16
NCAA Midwest Regional Final

Pregame

Louisville's players received a special welcome when they arrived for pregame warmups in Houston's Summit. Practically ringing the court, Louisiana State fans, dominant in the crowd of 15,400, began chanting "Tiger Bait," "UK Rejects" and "Wildcat Rejects."

"Tiger Bait" was familiar, even expected. The Kentucky stuff was a bit more personal. Roger Burkman thought the chanters were mostly LSU football players.

"I kept smiling at them," he recalled. "Wiley (Brown) and Derek (Smith), though, I could see on their faces it was getting to them a little bit. I remember telling them to 'stay focused, stay focused.' But they were saying, 'Man, Rog, they're calling us Wildcat Rejects.' I just said that what we had to say would be on the floor."

The smack wasn't just coming from people in street clothes. Everybody knew the LSU Tigers had a card-carrying membership in the trash-talk society. They apparently reserved some of their best lines for U of L.

Brown and Smith, the sophomores from Georgia, were getting a snootful, a good portion of it from DeWayne Scales, it seemed.

"Reject this and reject that, then, 'We're going to kick your ass, we're going to do this and that,'" Brown remembered. "Derek and I are looking at each other like, 'You talking to us?' But we weren't going to back down from anybody. We didn't care. We're still going to play the game. We're still going to be here."

Some of the irritation had been set in motion the last two summers in the campus gym, when LSU forward Rudy Macklin, Darrell Griffith's buddy from Louisville, got into some back-and-forth with Smith and Brown, leading to Smith saying later that "there's something that kept us from being friends."

Eaves said he heard some mouth the day before the game, too.

"Rudy was telling me Ethan Martin was going to eat me alive," Eaves said, referring to the impending battle of point guards. "He said Martin had already killed Kyle Macy (Kentucky's counterpart), so he's already killed half the state, and now he's going to kill you.

"At the introductions, Martin and I shake hands, and he says, 'I can't wait to take the ball from you.' I was so mad. I could not believe all the stuff."

The teams moved to the center jump circle and Brown had had his fill. As the players positioned themselves for the tip, he leaned toward Scales.

"'Let's stop all this talking,'" the Cardinals' 6-8 forward said he told the man he would be trying to check. "'You want to fight, let's go ahead and fight, get it over with, take the edge off, then play the game.'"

After the deluge, though, Brown was left with sort of an appreciation of the LSU verbal assault.

"I'd never seen anybody talk trash like these guys," he said. "But they backed it up. They played good."

You mean backed it up until that day.

Wiley Brown smiled. "Exactly," he said. "Absolutely."

First Half

Darrell Griffith and Rudy Macklin wasted no time getting together again. This time it wasn't for supper.

On the tip, two seconds in, Griffith was whistled for bumping Macklin. Rodney McCray's unexpected 18-footer then ignited a six-field-goal flurry, three by Wiley Brown, that gunned Louisville to a 12-2 lead, the same as two nights earlier against Texas A&M.

But in the middle of that burst, with only 3:27 gone, Griffith picked up personal No. 2, a needless reach-in against Ethan Martin. Griffith out, Roger Burkman in.

Griffith sat for 4:52 as the Cardinals held their own, leading 17-10 when he returned. But 2:08 after that, charging in seeking a rebound, he banged into Louisiana State center Greg Cook for foul No. 3 and was gone again.

This was much more worrisome than the NCAA opener against Kansas State. The Tigers were now growling like the beasts of the regular season. Seconds before Griffith's third, DeWayne Scales drilled a 10-footer, cutting U of L's lead to 21-15. With bombing specialist Jordy Hultberg in the line-up for jumpers from 20, 20, 18 and 18 feet, LSU saddled up for a 16-0 run and took a solid grip on the reins at 29-21.

There was trouble for the guys from River City, and Brown sought out Burkman, the junior guard and season-long turbocharger.

"Griff is our leader, and it hurts when your leader is on the bench," Brown said. "But I turned to Roger Burkman and said, 'Roger, handle the ball and make us play our game.' Roger has been around, and we all looked to him."

Astonishingly, the Cardinals reared back and delivered an uppercut of their own. Brown got a layup, Tony Branch touched off a 24-foot set shot, and Burkman made two free throws. Then, in a gamble with enormous implications, Denny Crum reinserted Griffith and his three fouls. What?

"I dreaded the negative feeling we'd take off the court if we were several points down at the break," Crum said. "I didn't want us doubting ourselves in the locker room."

Recalled Branch: "Denny had the biggest decision to make in the tournament. We were tense and they had chances to lengthen their lead. If Darrell picks up his fourth foul, they go after him, he gets his fifth and then we're done. It would have been terrible, because if we got beat we wanted to get beat at full strength."

With 3:21 to go to intermission, Griffith returned. Twenty-seven seconds later he was fouled, converted two free throws, and exited with the score 29-29. Then, just before the buzzer, Burkman ripped a 20-footer from the top of the key for a 31-29 Louisville lead.

My goodness. U of L 12-2, LSU 16-0, U of L 10-0. What cataclysmic deeds remained to be performed?

"Talk about going to war," Burkman said years later. "I'd never heard so many hits and jabs or saw so much extra effort."

The Cardinals bounced vigorously off the court. They had been a shadow of themselves, but they had looked the big, bad wolf in the eye and found him vulnerable.

Intermission—Louisville Side

"Our locker room was just wild," Louisville manager Randy Bufford remembered. "We had played so bad. Before the game our fans—*our fans*—were telling us it had been a good year. We heard a lot of that around the hotel beforehand, too.

"Now here we are and there's a lot of screaming. Good screaming, like, 'Damn, we can kill 'em, Let's quit doing this, quit doing that.' (Denny) Crum was like, 'Hey, pipe down.' But it was a positive thing."

Once some order was restored, Crum calmly began to talk. He was tired of seeing his squad fail to rise—for the third straight NCAA game—to the roaring level it had sustained so much of the season.

"I told them we were not playing like the Louisville team that got us to this point," Crum recalled. "I said it was a shame to play so well to get here and then blow it because we weren't playing Louisville basketball and doing the things we needed to do to win. I didn't yell or scream, but I did say it was a shame to let the pressure of the moment take focus away from what they should be doing."

The lecture was mere reinforcement. The Cardinals were already in the process of putting steel back into their game.

Intermission—Louisiana State Side

LSU faced problems of a much different sort in its dressing room.

A dispute between roommates DeWayne Scales and Willie Sims that had been simmering the previous few weeks suddenly spilled into the open at the worst possible time.

Rudy Macklin said it started in the moments right before tipoff. Sims said it didn't break out until halftime. Scales could not be located to tell his version. Here's Sims' account from Israel, where he owned and operated a health club in early 2004:

"DeWayne had a real big ego and a bad temper. His girlfriend had been calling me trying to find out what he (Scales) was doing when we were on the road. He must have got jealous to some degree. When we were in our room (late in the regular season), I told him, 'You got to stay cool and relax.' He pulled a knife. Then he put it down, came over to me and we got into it."

As the Tigers entered the locker room on March 16, Sims said he tried to take a leadership role. Too much of one.

"First of all, the whole team was not mature, even myself," he said. "I told him (Scales), 'You've got to pick yourself up, man. Don't let those guys rebound.' He said, 'No!' He told me to shut my mouth, and other stuff, then there was some pushing and we got into it a little bit."

Macklin was a redshirt junior forward from a high school in Louisville. He said as the team's captain it was his job to keep emotions on as much an even keel as possible. He remembered the incident beginning as a tease and moving quickly into very personal territory.

"Ethan Martin got involved as a friend of Sims and Scales wanted to fight them both," Macklin said. "Then he got angry with me, and I told him, 'This is why you're not included in anything.' As captain it was up to me to keep the peace as much as possible, and this time I failed. It was very disastrous. I'm probably to blame."

Coach Dale Brown didn't assess blame but said the blowup was costly.

"It didn't almost end up in a fight," Brown recalled. "I want to say DeWayne threw a shoe over at Willie's locker. Regardless, I could tell it really let the air out of our team."

Sims and Macklin had high praise for Scales' skills, for the skills of most of the Tigers.

"We had a lot of talent," Sims said. "DeWayne was so talented, 6-8 with a good jump shot, handled the ball well enough to get himself freed up, moved well without the ball—had everything going for him. But we had a bunch of individuals who didn't want to hear you (another player) telling them what to do. DeWayne's head was so big he couldn't see teamwork.

"Durand kind of let us down, too. He was talking about (Darrell) Griffith (his boyhood pal) so much, how good he was and how he could do this and that. He should have been talking about his weaknesses. That was his good friend and I could understand that, but I was like, 'C'mon, he's the enemy.'"

The comfort zones in the two locker rooms had taken severely opposite turns just as winning time arrived.

Second Half

Darrell Griffith had one rebound, four points on one-of-four shooting and three fouls as the second 20 minutes began, and his Louisville team had connected on only 33 percent of its shots.

The Cardinals were thankful Wiley Brown was in a mean and nasty mood, because his 12 points kept them out of a deep pit.

Louisiana State managed ties at 33 and 35 in the first two minutes, but U of L now had all its pistons pounding.

Griffith hit from 20, 15, 14 and 20. Brown converted a tip. Derek Smith dunked. Denny Crum backed up his 2-2-1 press into a half- to three-quarter-court trap that he had added to the mix just that week. It didn't yield steals and turnovers as much as disrupt what little remained of LSU's offensive rhythm.

"I believe we panicked," Tigers guard Willie Sims recalled. "I felt during the season I couldn't be touched, but when they threw the press on me I kind of froze. We broke presses like they were nothing during league (SEC). We knew about Louisville's press. We were ready for it.

"But this time we stopped talking to each other. They threw the ball to me and everybody left. Instead of continuing to run our drill, I'm looking for guys cutting, and no one's cutting. Plus we were all talking about Griffith and forgetting about guys like Wiley Brown. Being mature enough, being man enough and taking control, it didn't happen."

A layup by Griffith with 11:43 to play drew LSU center Greg Cook's fifth foul. Thirty seconds later, a Poncho Wright shot block sent the ball Smith's way, whereupon he shoveled a pass to a breaking Griffith for his 40th dunk of the season in 40 tries. Called the "windjammer" by teammates, he tapped it two-handed on one hip, then the other, then back to the first before windmilling it down.

The NBC-TV analyst stood up in his chair. "Al McGuire called it the Bingo-Bango-Bongo dunk," Scooter McCray remembered. "He took it from his right hip to his left hip to his right hip, then, boom."

Louisville led 57-45, and LSU was on the run. Griffith and his henchmen went on to bury the Bengals 86-66 in as splendid a display of all-fingers-in-one-glove basketball as anyone could draw up.

Griffith scored 13 of his 17 points in the second half and finished with seven assists and eight rebounds. Brown, Smith and Rodney McCray scored in double figures. Jerry Eaves had nine points and no turnovers in 31 minutes. Burkman had eight points and seven assists in 26 minutes. Smith and McCray had 10 rebounds each. The team shot 72 percent in the second half, 18 of 25.

The Beatles' song "I Get By with a Little Help from My Friends" played on a stereo in the locker room afterwards. The Cardinals could have written it.

It couldn't have ended more negatively for the No. 1 seed.

DeWayne Scales, LSU's leading scorer, never got himself in sync. He played only 10 sporadic minutes in the second half, and was jerked out twice by coach Dale Brown, going back in only when someone fouled out. He scored two of his 12 points in that period.

"Scales tried everything," Sims recalled. "He wanted the ball, he'd get it, then he couldn't make it. He was like, 'Give me the ball, give me the ball,' but he couldn't come through. Then he got angered by something and Dale took him out."

Macklin, seeking his first victory ever over a Griffith team after losses at the junior high and high school levels, was turned away again. He had nine points and eight rebounds and sat on a locker room bench afterwards, his head dropped into his lap, crying.

"They (mostly Derek Smith) did an excellent job of keeping me in one area," Macklin recalled. "They played one hell of a team defense that pushed us to the middle, and there was always more than one person there to greet me. The trap got us out of our stuff. Coach Crum is a basketball genius."

With 37 seconds left, Dale Brown cleared his bench and removed Ethan Martin. Thoroughly harassed by Eaves, he made one of 11 shots and had five turnovers to go with eight assists. As he walked toward the bench Eaves, with Martin's pregame taunt of "Can't wait to take the ball from you" still ringing in his ears, sauntered past and said, "When you going to take the ball from me?"

And, Eaves said, "He didn't say a word."

Postgame

David "Poncho" Wright, naturally, turned out to be the wisest Louisville Cardinal of them all.

It was going on four months since he uttered the seven-word pronouncement that at the time seemed to be more typical Poncho nonsense than some sort of prophecy: "The Ville is going to the Nap."

Yet as it is spoken, so shall it be done. The (University of Louis)Ville was heading for (India)Nap(olis), joining Iowa, Purdue and UCLA in Market Square Arena for the NCAA Tournament's Final Four.

"I don't know if we can win it or not, but nobody is going to come away ashamed and everybody is going to play their hearts out," proclaimed the sophomore from Indianapolis Marshall High School. "And . . . WE . . . MIGHT . . . DO . . . IT!"

U of L had unceremoniously tossed aside the NCAA's last No. 1 regional seed by 20 points. Mighty Louisiana State. Out of the mighty Southeastern Conference. Rapture was everywhere.

But is there more to consider today now that we know about the Tigers' inner turmoil? Would the second half have produced a different result had LSU performed the way it had much of the season?

Afterward, DeWayne Scales said, "We're as quick as Louisville. We're as big and strong as Louisville (if not bigger and stronger). They just outplayed us. They wanted it more than us."

"It wouldn't have made any difference," U of L guard Jerry Eaves said. "Derek (Smith) was all over Rudy Macklin. Scales was a bully, but Wiley Brown had him locked up."

Willie Sims veered back and forth.

"I believe we would have won," he said 24 years later. "We had a lot of talent. We would have boxed (Darrell) Griffith out." But he also said, "Guys wanted to showcase. Guys couldn't showcase the way they wanted to and got upset. Our fans gave us some bigheadedness. And the head grew."

Which is the real point. Had Scales and Sims not tangled in the locker room, LSU would have still been populated with guys who "had their ways." U of L had guys who "had their ways" in other seasons. Not this one.

Did the incident affect LSU on the court?

"I've never asked any of my guys, but I didn't think we were as crisp," coach Dale Brown said. "I thought it took an edge off the team. It was a goofy game and a disappointing situation. But it didn't have anything to do with the outcome. I would never take anything away from Louisville—they were a well-drilled, good team and talented, and Darrell Griffith was a superstar."

Joe Yates, then the Cardinals SID, drove home the point of separation between the two teams recently.

"I could see it (the incident) happening to LSU because Macklin, Scales, Martin and those guys thought they should be getting the headlines," Yates said. "You say something wrong, and all of a sudden it does become a grudge with a he-really-did-mean-it-type attitude.

"It wasn't the case with our guys. We had one star and everybody knew it. They were so young and goofy that everybody knew they were kidding around with one another."

A joyous flock of Cardinals reveled in their LSU rout and prepared to see if they could fulfill another prophecy, the title Griffith promised four years earlier.

However, he would only be able to tie Poncho Wright, who had a 1-0 lead on Griff in the crystal ball department.

"I'll need about 700 tickets," Wright said. "The scalpers could make a million off my family."

Today, one of the big T-shirt items sold in the U of L section of stores is one that simply says, "The Ville." Even though there seems to be a Ville around every corner—Knox, Nash, Jefferson, Gains, even Hogans and Thomas—everybody knows which Ville this one is.

Thank you, Ponch.

One Final Watery Journey

In 1980, Louisville's *Courier-Journal* and *Times* newspapers not only had competing staffs despite living in the same building and being owned by the same family, but two columnists from the top brass.

Paul Janensch was executive editor of both papers and wrote a piece for Sundays. *Times* managing editor Leonard Pardue knocked out one that appeared on Wednesdays in the afternoon publication.

On Monday of the week the *CJ* and *T*'s three Division I schools marched into the regional semifinals (Louisville in the Midwest, Kentucky and Indiana in the Mideast), Pardue asked sports columnist Dick Fenlon and the three beat writers on the *Times* for a brief biography and their predictions for the Final Four.

This book's scribe, thinking of Louisville's narrow escape from Kansas State and the ominous presence of No. 1 seed Louisiana State, attempting to think logically, picked LSU out of the Midwest (which would soon make him 0-4 for the weekend).

U of L had left for Houston and the regional before the *Times* and Pardue's column hit the streets on Wednesday, March 12. But assistant Wade Houston got hold of an early edition, cleverly tore out the column and made sure the team got an eyeful.

When I arrived at the arena, the guys I had been covering all season, riding in a variety of vehicles, refused to consent to interviews. How could this bozo jump off our wagon now? They weren't mad. They were really mad.

"A knife in the back," Roger Burkman said, and he meant it.

It was hard—impossible?—to explain to these teens and barely 20-year-olds that a journalist had to try to be objective about what they did on the court. He couldn't root for them to win, even though he kind of thought it was okay to root for them to succeed in life.

It was a tough time in Houston. I tiptoed carefully through the weekend, able to cobble together enough nouns and verbs to avoid being fired as the Louisville-LSU regional final approached.

Which U of L won, of course. Impressively.

I entered the locker room. The guys were talking to me again, too jacked after the 86-66 victory to carry the grudge any further. Or were they?

As I surveyed the scene and picked out my first interview subjects, I felt myself leaving the floor. I can't pinpoint the perps today, but guess they might have been named Burkman, Rodney McCray and Wiley Brown with backup from three or four others.

I was pretty sure where I was going. "Someone take my notebook, please," I begged.

They obliged. I took a shower.

Upon emergence, I realized the crotch of my pants was ripped stem to stern. Giving new meaning to the word em-barr-ass-ed, I managed to complete my interviews.

Tony Branch was kind enough to loan me his warmups for the four-block walk back to the hotel. Otherwise, I would probably still be in a Houston hoosegaw, serving out a long sentence for really indecent exposure.

Dunkenstein Unmasked

For two and a half NCAA Tournament games, Darrell Griffith was somebody else.

He fouled out against Kansas State and got in deep trouble against LSU. He shot nine for 24 against Texas A&M. He had 13 assists but nearly as many turnovers, 11. His shooting percentage in 92 minutes was .375.

He was forcing some shots, forcing some passes, too loose on some dribbles, reaching in sometimes instead of playing solid defense.

Was it tension? Did he feel pressure? Was he trying too hard? Was the weight of promises made and unfulfilled bearing down?

"It was probably in his mind that he needed to do more and ended up getting in foul trouble," Louisville coach Denny Crum said years later.

The team as a whole was a shadow of its regular-season self, too. There was plenty of uptightness to go around.

Then, perhaps in response to Louisiana State's intimidation techniques, a riled-up U of L rediscovered its old armor-piercing weaponry and Griffith again became Dr. Dunkenstein—six-of-eight shooting, 13 points, seven rebounds and four assists in his 18 second-half minutes.

Looking back now, does he think he felt special burdens going into the tourney?

"I remember the Britton guy—he ran his mouth a little bit," Griffith said of A&M guard David Britton. "I never did get uptight. I felt confident. The first two games went overtime, and you've got to have a little luck, but I just knew this group of guys was going to pull them out."

He trusted his mates. They trusted him. All had reboarded the barreling locomotive. For a half, anyway. Could the engineer and his firemen keep stoking the boilers for another 80 minutes?

New Definition for Empty Trip

The Piedmont Airlines flight bringing the Louisville basketball team back from the Midwest Regional was due to touch down at Standiford Field at 10:45 p.m. Sunday, March 16.

No, wait. 11:10 p.m. No, wait. 1:30 a.m. No, wait. Probably later. Maybe never.

The Cardinals could only shake their heads and accept the inevitable. It wouldn't be right for them to actually board a plane, have it take off at its appointed hour, fly smoothly over a few states and land safely at the moment it was supposed to. A trip like that wouldn't even belong in this season.

One would think they had exhausted all the ways the travel beast could bite them. Au contraire. U of L and Louisiana State had been originally scheduled to play the 12:08 (Central time) regional final that Sunday, followed by the East Regional at 2:08. Louisville booked a 4 p.m. flight home. On Tuesday, NBC television decided to switch the two finals. The Cardinals couldn't make a 4 p.m. plane, and by then all other commercial flights were booked.

There was, however, a Piedmont charter carrying 130 Louisville fans. So the solution (here's where you might want to become speechless) was this: Take the fans home. Turn around. Fly the plane—empty—back to Houston. Pick up team. Bring team home.

And that's what happened. The fans' flight arrived at Standiford at 11:10 p.m. The players straggled in around 4:10 a.m. Coach Denny Crum, sly devil, had hitched a ride on booster Bob Shaw's private plane, and was already at the airport awaiting his squad, as were about 750 very hardy supporters.

"I'll tell you one thing," Crum said when his presence was detected. "If anybody is going to beat us now, they're going to have to play awfully well."

Unless, say, the university bus taking the team to the Final Four confused one polis with another and wound up in Minne instead of Indy. The U of L folks were keeping their fingers crossed.

Guard These with Your Life, Lady

Each NCAA Tournament regional champion in 1980 was given 1,600 tickets immediately after its victory to be taken back to the school for distribution to administrators and politicos and for sale to fans.

This was before superdomes became must sites for Final Fours. Market Square Arena in Indianapolis, the location for this one, had a capacity of 16,637.

Betty Jackson was the assistant ticket manager at Louisville. She made all the big road trips while ticket manager Don Belcher stayed home to run things in-house.

Jackson was handed boxes containing the 1,600 ducats and gulped. She had to get them from The Summit in Houston to an airport where she would sit for who knows how long, then from Texas to Kentucky, then through a bunch of people at another airport who were already holding up "need two tickets" signs, then home in the middle of the night, then to an office safe three or four hours later.

Good luck, Betty.

"I knew I had in my hands something worth a great deal of money," Jackson said of the cardboard with a face value of $34 but who knows how much more if illegally scalped in Naptown. "We got black garbage bags at the airport and put the tickets in them, hoping to look inconspicuous. There were no police on the plane."

"I thought she was carrying dirty laundry," recalled the athletic director's administrative assistant, Debbie Young.

The team party arrived at Standiford Field after 4 a.m. Jackson slipped through the welcoming crowd with her goods undiscovered except by a daughter, a son-in-law and a few people in the know. They got her home. She needed to be in the ticket office four hours later.

"I was the only woman in the department doing a man's job," she recalled. "I wanted desperately to do it right, worried about doing it right. I could hardly sleep until I got them in the safe the next day."

She got them to the safe. Then she went into high-security mode.

"I didn't know whether I'd be able to get tickets as a staff person," said Kathy Tronzo, the sports information department administrative aide. "I called her the next night at 10 and David (Jackson's son) would not let me talk to her. I'm like, 'It's Kathy, let me talk to her.' And he says, 'Nope, she's not taking calls from anybody.'"

"He was like her bodyguard," Young added.

The ticket personnel would all come close to needing one the next few days.

Climbing into the Upper Bunk

College basketball in the Kentuckiana (Kentucky-Indiana) region had been pretty much a religious rite for close to five decades.

The University of Kentucky had five national titles and two seconds. Indiana owned three crowns. Louisville had a third-place finish and a couple of fourths, but despite the outstanding work of Peck Hickman (1940s-'50s-'60s), maintenance by John Dromo and upgrade under Denny Crum (1970s), U of L was still a downstairs program to be waved away with the back of a hand by the upstairs fans.

UK had always refused to play Louisville, except when forced to in a tournament. To nearly all of the Wildcats' statewide fleet of supporters, the Big Blue was the only team in the bluegrass. Even as Crum's teams grew more dangerous seemingly by the season, and came within an eye-blink of meeting Kentucky for the 1975 championship, U of L's band of hardy followers usually had to settle for, well, crumbs.

So as the stepped upon, disregarded Cardinal faithful gathered in the airport to await the return of their undervalued Louisiana State conquerors, it was not surprising that some couldn't resist trying to rub it in the face of the colossus down Interstate 64.

"L-S-WHO, L-S-WHO," was one chant *Times* reporter Rick Bozich heard. "Big Blue, Where Are You?" was another.

A man asked if anyone could spare a dime. What for? "So we can call (UK guard) Kyle Macy to see if he wants to carry Griff's bags off the plane."

Gloating, of course, wasn't going to change anyone's addiction to UK basketball. Instead it would provide more fuel for the next one-upmanship faceoff. But at least the Louisville folks could sample the uptown revelry for a while.

Maybe for a lot longer, if their heroes could climb two more treacherous hills.

Hey, Look, We're Over Here

Scooter McCray called them "toos" and "fews."

As in "Louisville gets on TV sometimes, too," and "Sure, there are a few good things about U of L."

As in "you guys are an afterthought, and you're not going to get a lot of respect."

This bothered the Cardinal players as it did their fans. Not to the degree that they hated the other guys, though. Not to the extent they wanted them to lose. They weren't even asking for equality in the hearts and minds of Kentuckians. Please, just a little consideration.

If the door to recognition and respectability was slightly ajar, the 20-point battering of Southeastern Conference strongman Louisiana State, a team that took two of three from Kentucky and won its league tourney, enabled Louisville to jam a size-15 shoe into the opening.

"We're hearing the fans, hearing 'Tiger Bait,'" remembered Scooter's brother, Rodney. "We're saying, 'These guys are good. They got crazy (DeWayne) Scales, Rudy Macklin, Ethan Martin, and they play in the SEC. Okay, this'll be a tough game.'

"Then we dismantled them, destroyed them. This is supposed to be the SEC's best, people talked about how the Metro [U of L's league] isn't that good, the Metro champ just beat the SEC champ, and it wasn't even close. If people didn't believe in us before then, they believed in us after."

Three years later the NCAA set a bracket in motion for the two schools to meet for the Mideast Regional title in 1983. By the next season enough pressure had been exerted by people with clout that an in-season series was started. It exists today, an annual vibrant example of how exciting the game is when two teams are expending every ounce of energy.

Scooter thinks some of the meanness and arrogance has left the rivalry.

"It's real good competition, and a lot of diehards have accepted it as good state competition, not a live-or-die thing," he said. "Especially with Pitino here coaching now [Rick Pitino left UK for the pros after a national title and second place in the '90s, then left the pros for U of L]. Some will always call him a traitor, but others appreciate his style of coaching and like watching U of L though they're still UK fans.

"And players don't have a problem. We get along with their players and they with ours. We try to compare how crazy some fans are to theirs and some of the wild things we've heard, like families torn apart and some people refusing to talk to other people. Why? They [fans] don't even play. It gets so ridiculous. It's two different worlds. But us players, we just co-exist and move on."

Roger Burkman is the senior development officer for a big Catholic high school in Louisville, Trinity, and wife Judy is a judge. They move in circles that include fans of both schools, some close to a rabid state. Burkman will not pull many punches in trying to educate those with a narrow view.

"I'll be out with my children, and a person might come up to them and say, 'I knew your daddy, he was a great player, I guess you guys love those Cards and hate those Wildcats,'" he said. "I tell them, 'I'm not raising my children that way. I'm not so shallow that I'll make my child pull for one and hate the other. They can pull for Kentucky, for Louisville, for Western Kentucky, Centre, for all those schools.'"

Now this, of all things, has happened. The day after NCAA Selection Sunday, on March 15, 2004, a Denny Crum—Joe B. Hall radio call-in show was begun on Louisville station WXXA-AM (790).

For 10 seasons the Louisville and Kentucky coaches loudly defended their programs while remaining at either end of the 80-mile demilitarized zone between Louisville and Lexington. Then came the monumental 1983 meeting, two Rupp Arena UK victories in '83-84 and a U of L triumph in '84-85 to make the modern rivalry 2-2 in Hall's final season.

Twenty years later they joined forces for a 10 a.m.-to-noon, five-day-a-week year-round yak session on the state of whatever sport is in season. One reason they got back together is that neither of the fishermen and hunters held the animosity for each other their fans did.

"Maybe Joe B. and I can bring the state's fans closer together," Crum said.

How far we've come.

CHAPTER TEN

The Ville Really Is in the Nap, and It's Wide Awake:

March 17, 1980 to March 24, 1980

Three 'Don't Belongs' and Those Nutty Kids from River City

Louisville, Iowa, Purdue and UCLA.

It had been a long time since the NCAA had seen a Final Four like this.

Louisville—ranked 2-4 by Associated Press and United Press International, respectively. Purdue—rated 20th by AP and zilch by UPI. Iowa? Nowhere. UCLA? Huh-uh.

Two consensus first-team All-Americans—U of L's Darrell Griffith and Purdue center Joe Barry Carroll. Of all the other guys on the four squads, only Iowa's Ronnie Lester was mentioned on the first, second or third teams of five awarding organizations. Lester's selection must have been based on his worthiness and the preceding season. A knee injury had kept him out of 15 of the Hawkeyes' 27 regular-season games.

The teams combined had lost 29 games (UCLA 21-9, Purdue 22-9, Iowa 23-8, Louisville 31-3). Only the 1954 Final Four had more defeats (33: Bradley 18-12, Southern California 19-12, Penn State 17-5, LaSalle 24-4).

The 97 victories were the fewest since 92 in 1965.

Winning percentage for the 1980 group was .770. Only three of the previous 41 Final Fours had a worse number.

Al McGuire's last Marquette team of 1976-77 held the record for most losses, seven, by a champion. Only Louisville could prevent that mark from going down.

And no No. 1 tournament seed got there (U of L was 2, Iowa 5, Purdue 6 and UCLA 8). Since seedings began in 1979, at least one No. 1 has reached the big four every year through 2004. Except in 1980.

On the other hand . . .

When the tournament expanded from 40 to 48 teams this year and the committee was given the power to put them wherever it wanted, four were handed "don't belong" tags by critics. Clemson finished fourth at 10-8 in the Atlantic Coast Conference, UCLA fourth in the Pacific-10 at 12-6 and, in the Big Ten, Iowa fourth at 10-8 and Purdue third at 11-7.

But those four were a combined 15-1 in the big show. Clemson had won three times before losing to UCLA in the West final.

Louisville coach Denny Crum had issued UCLA storm warnings at the start of the tourney after the Bruins had inserted freshman guards into the lineup at midseason. Lester had returned to Iowa's lineup at the beginning of the NCAA and the Hawks had taken down fourth-seed North Carolina State in State's home territory, No. 1 Syracuse and No. 3 Georgetown. Purdue had ousted third seed St. John's, No. 2 (and Big Ten champ) Indiana and No. 4 Duke as the 7-1 Carroll averaged 27 points and 10 rebounds.

So you had three clubs that had waggled their fingers at doubters and built good-sized momentum. Then you had legitimate U of L, needing overtimes in two games and, finally, a stout second half against Louisiana State.

Or course, thinking back to when the Cardinals' Scooter lost a wheel in December, it was somewhat astounding that they were here, too.

Enough talk. Tip this dude off. There's bound to be at least one worthy of being king. Maybe even four.

Get Your Flu (and Maybe a Ticket) Here

The rain was drumming out a steady beat on the sidewalk when assistant ticket manager Betty Jackson and ticket manager Don Belcher arrived at their office before 8 a.m. on Monday, March 17, 1980.

They weren't the first to get there. Upwards of 400 strong, wrapped in blankets, slickers and garbage bags, under umbrellas, some under nothing, had been there for hours.

They were in a line several hundred feet long. They weren't even hoping to get to the window and buy one or two of the 1,600 Final Four $34 tickets available. They were hoping to get their name on an application form just to have a chance to have it drawn out of a container in a lottery-like deal. The odds of that happening were, well, probably higher than contracting pneumonia.

The names of administrative people, faculty, trustees, donors, legislators and other politicians were dropped into categories under a percentage formula worked out by Belcher. So were priority season-ticket holders and students who had paid their way into the Metro Conference Tournament, then gone to the Midwest Regional sites in Lincoln, Nebraska, and Houston, Texas. Players also got tickets. Families of coaches had to be accommodated.

In addition, between 2,500 and 3,000 students and season-ticket holders who didn't land in the other categories had applied for tickets by the end of the day. Those lines got long enough (and the rain hard enough), Jackson remembers, that dean of students Harold Adams and Tom and Jenny Sawyer, Jenny being an intern in the ticket office, went out and started collecting names. Lottery winners would be notified by phone on Wednesday.

"There were way more people than we had tickets for," Jackson said. "At one point a man named Glenn Gish came running through the door saying, 'Hey, my name got called.' I said, 'No, don't think so,' and he said, 'Oh, I'm sorry, somebody is playing a joke on me.'

"He was probably the only fan who somehow got into the actual office. I told him to come up to Indy. I had the last two tickets for a legislator, went to the arena and the legislator didn't show. I sold them to Glenn and his wife, Paula, at the last minute. I gave my tickets away and sat in the seat for David Olsen [young son of assistant coach Bill] while Sharon (Bill's wife) held David on her lap. It was crazy."

The names were on application forms, which were placed in containers according to their categories, then blind draws were held. Jackson couldn't remember how many were available "to the public," as Belcher designated the majority of the hardy 3,000, and records have been thrown out. But it wasn't a lot.

Back out in the downpour, a man who refused to give his name because he had called into work sick said he and a buddy went to the airport to greet the team coming home from the regional, waited until after 4 a.m., "sipping spirits" as they did, then went straight to the ticket office and dozed off.

It was now 1:30 p.m. "We woke up at 10 a.m. and the line looked like it stretched for miles," he told the *Courier-Journal*. "We've been standing here ever since. I called work. I'll handle the work, but I ain't going to face my wife until I've gotten into that ticket office."

Earlier, in line around the corner, was Kristin Smith, offering soggy doughnuts and lite beer.

"We didn't buy the beer," she told the *Times*. "Some cans just floated by."

Why are you standing in the rain just for a chance at tickets? It'll be on TV.

"You can't say you just saw the game," she said. "You've got to be there."

Griff—the Go-To Media Man, Too

It was Saturday, March 15, the day before Louisville met Louisiana State for the regional title. Darrell Griffith was trying to sleep. He had answered all the journalism questions, then answered them again, and was pretty much talked out.

There was a knock on the door. It was sports information director Joe Yates for one more interview. "C'mon, Darrell, wake up," Yates said. "Aw, let him sleep," protested roomie Tony Branch.

Griffith went. A lot of the national press was on hand now. Yates knew this was a golden opportunity to get Louisville's name out there, and everyone knew the main face on the promo would be Griffith's. He became the pied piper of mediadom.

"He was the coolest guy I'd ever seen," Yates said. "He could have been a pain in the butt to work with but instead was a dream. A consummate pro on that kind of stuff. He made it so much fun for (SID assistant) John Crawley and me."

Yates had already "splurged," he said, and purchased a speaker phone for the SID office. Griffith was locked into a conference call with writers three days a week.

"He appreciated it," Yates said, "because he would not have been able to meet all media demands otherwise."

Crawley looked back in admiration.

"That was the first and last time we did those conference calls," he said. "I think about the demands put on him by us and the university. He never complained. He battled being considered one-dimensional—that he could only jump—for three years, and Iowa (in the national semifinals) was the final stamp of approval that he was more than that."

Said Yates: "He trusted us. He laid his P.R. life in the hands of Crawls and me, and as dumb as we were I think he still reaped some dividends off it. He's not some forgotten person who's drifted off into the sunset. The city and the university will never be able to repay Denny Crum, and they owe a whole lot to that kid."

Don't Even Think About...Hey, How Ya Doin'

The press didn't blitz the other players as much as Darrell Griffith, but it still beat a fairly regular tattoo on the sports information people for non-game-day interviews and such.

"As the season moved along, they [particularly the young guys] became more reluctant," SID Joe Yates said. "It does take time, they're answering the same questions over and over, and you guys could be a pain in the butt."

(However, Kathy Tronzo, Yates' administrative person, said that "Derek Smith came in every single day to complain that he wasn't getting enough press. Every single day.")

To accommodate the ink- and microphone-stained wretches, Yates had trainer Jerry May put a longer cord on his room's phone.

"We'd catch them on the training table, getting taped before practice," Yates said. "We'd take a message, dial the number and hand them the phone. 'Here you are, you're talking to Bob Watkins of the Elizabethtown paper, Curry Kirkpatrick of *Sports Illustrated*.'

"Then we get one of those, 'No, no, no, I'm not going to talk, I am not going to talk . . . hey, how you doing, good to talk to you today.' "

Most of the players made mild (and failed) attempts to protest. Then there was Rodney McCray.

"Rodney was the worst," Yates said. "He just hated to see us walk through that door. He gives you that look—'Ain't talking, ain't talking.' Then he gives you that scowl, the one that's supposed to make you fall down dead.

"We couldn't have cared less. We knew we had Denny [Crum] supporting us. So like we were, 'Okay, whatever you say. Here, he's on the line, talk to him.'"

The truth was that, dissent aside, all the dribblers trusted the media relations guys.

"They knew we were looking out for their best interests and that we were not going to take advantage of them," Yates said. "Nobody ever refused. We [he and John Crawley] were such swell guys that everybody had to like us."

Eaves, the Neglected Point Guard

Jerry Eaves was the guy who beat Tony Branch by a nose in the race for Louisville's fifth starting spot.

Eaves was also the guy who disappeared nearly as much as Branch from daily press coverage, buried beneath Darrell Griffith's escalator, Derek Smith's frenzied rebounding, Wiley Brown's passes, Rodney McCray's blocks, Roger Burkman's floor burns and Poncho Wright's contrail-producing jumpers.

Eaves was the point guard. He was still not thoroughly recovered from an ankle sprained two months earlier. He was averaging 7.8 points, a couple of assists, a couple of rebounds and 26 minutes a game.

First a guard, then a 25-point-scoring forward on three really strong Ballard High School teams in Louisville, he was used to high local expectations. Now a sophomore, he was producing low results. He wanted to do more, get more.

"It's been a rewarding year, but it's been hard on me," he said. "People on the outside want me to score more points, but you can't interrupt the team action. If he [Denny Crum] left me in the whole game, I wouldn't complain. There are times when I can do it, take command. But we've got an All-American guard. Darrell takes over a game. I fill in things.

"I want so bad to get going every game, then I'll miss a couple of shots and Coach Crum will take me out. I know he's subbing at the right time, and Roger Burkman does a great job. But sometimes I want to say, 'Please, take Darrell out.'"

Three games into the NCAA Tournament, though, Eaves was getting his, although not in ways where folks could take notice. He had just two turnovers, plus six assists, in 75 minutes of action, outstanding numbers for the man running the show.

Looking back decades, he smiled at his turnover drought. "That's one of the things I prided myself in," he said. "The whole key to the point guard is that you have to have a value for the ball."

There were two games to go. Maybe there would be other things to value about Jerry Eaves as well.

Keats, Shelley and Wiley

Just before the Metro Conference Tournament, Scooter McCray, that worldly man from the Big Apple, decided it was time for some metrical creativity.

Perhaps harboring a secret desire to become Henry Wadsworth McCray later in life, he cooked up a few lines of rhyme to be delivered at Louisville send-offs or to journalists. But not by his own self.

"Me and Scoot—he being from New York and me this guy from little Georgia," Wiley Brown said. "He'd come to our room, come up with some

rhymes for the next day for interviews or pep rallies, and talk me into saying them."

And Brown would. "A two-minute rhyme—one for each pep rally for
the conference, the start of the NCAAs and the Final Four," McCray said.
"Just something to get them fired up about, that's all."

Remarkably, Brown recalled a lot of the Final Four pep rally poem off
the top of his head nearly a quarter-century later:

> "Hey, all you Big Blue fans
> out there on the floor,
> don't you know the Cards
> are going to the Final Four;
> And all you U of L fans . . .

> "Uh, I can't remember the rest."

The McCray-Brown team would later prepare a bit of not-quite-rhyth-
mic verse for President Jimmy Carter on a White House visit in April.

> "Even though you, president Carter, are the best man in the land;
> Now you'll get a chance to shake the No. 1 Cards' hand."

Something happened to keep Brown from delivering his lines. Perhaps the
enormity of the occasion. But the chief executive was a fellow Georgian, a
peanut farmer, a man the 6-8 sophomore could relate to. So Brown said this:

> "We'd like you to talk to Gov. Brown (Kentucky Gov. John Y. Brown
> Jr.) about getting us a new arena. Ours only holds about 16,000, but we
> need one that'll hold 30,000."

Tongue-tied only to a degree, Wiley Brown was as fearless in the Oval
Office as he was in the paint.

Unavailable Isn't Spelled U-P-T-I-G-H-T

Denny Crum strove to limit the deluge of journalistic requests on his
guys at mid-week and even shockingly closed one practice to outsiders. But
that didn't mean the Louisville coach was suddenly wound too tight . . .

The new arrival: As Tony Branch walked into his office, Crum
announced, "I'm a father."

"You are?" Branch exclaimed. "But Joyce . . . she didn't seem to be . . .

Joyce, Crum's wife then, wasn't. The first calf from the herd of cattle on his nearly two-year-old 55-acre spread in the eastern portion of the county was either born late Tuesday, March 18, or the next morning.

"I went out at 6 o'clock and as usual called my cattle," Crum said. "They always come when I call. One didn't. I checked up the pasture and there was the biggest calf I'd ever seen. It came up to my waist."

In addition, Crum had just spent $15,000 to build a three- to four-acre lake and stock it with bluegill and blue channel cat. On Tuesday, the canine portion of his family grew to four when a new Golden Labrador joined a Black Lab, a Golden retriever and a half-Golden Lab half-Irish Setter.

Is calling cattle what a coach four days away from a national semifinal against Iowa should be doing?

"I've got a few things to do in here, too," he said. "But not at 6 a.m."

TV habits: Crum also found his players studiously viewing game tape. Well, maybe not that studiously.

"I caught these guys living in the past," he said. "They've been watching videotape all week—Kansas State, Texas A&M and LSU. "I said, 'Look, fellas, if you can't afford to go to the movies, watch videotape, but do you mind watching Iowa?'"

Favoritism: Oddsmakers made the Cardinals the choice to win it all.

"If you told me we'd be favored going into the Final Four, I'd have said you were sick," said Crum, thinking back to Scooter McCray's December injury that forced him to a one-senior, three-sophomore, one-freshman lineup.

He told himself then to be happy with 15 victories this season. Now U of L was 31-3 and had won 24 of its last 25 games.

"Damn, we must be good," Crum said, sarcasm dripping from several syllables. "We should be the overwhelming favorite. We should beat everybody by 40 points."

Seriously, does it bother you to be favored?

"It only bothers me when I don't go."

Coach and Player of Year?

The NCAA Tournament's Final Four is a time of national awards as well as national champions.

The Associated Press Coach of the Year, announced on Friday, March 21, was DePaul's Ray Meyer. Louisville's Denny Crum finished seventh. The Rupp Trophy, a dual presentation by AP and a Kentucky organization honoring the Player of the Year, also announced Friday, went to DePaul's Mark Aguirre. Darrell Griffith finished third. And the Kodak Coach of the

Year award, announced Sunday before the title game, was given to Iowa's Lute Olson.

Provincialism was firmly in place, of course, as a protective Louisville press rose up in arms. But *Courier-Journal* columnist Billy Reed had a valid point.

Why not wait until late March before voting instead of late February? Shouldn't these Somebody of the Year people have driven their teams at least to the Final Four, if not the national crown? Meyer and Aguirre, No. 1 during the season, were shocked in their first game of the tourney. Olson's team made the last quartet, but lost eight games during the regular season.

"Lute got it, huh?" Crum said of the Kodak trophy. "I guess that's pretty good for a team with eight losses. If we don't have the team of the year, the coach of the year or the player of the year, I guess we've just been lucky. A toss of a coin got us here, apparently. I even read where we're just lucky because we went into overtime twice (in the first two NCAA games)."

But his words did not have long-standing bitterness attached.

"I don't begrudge Lute or anybody anything," Crum said. "People have said I've done a better job, but I don't know if I have. It does take a lot of luck."

There was still one player honor to be revealed, the Wooden Award in four days. A man called Dunkenstein would grab that.

Scrutinizing the Semis

Iowa-Louisville: The Iowa team that marched into the NCAA Tournament's Final Four resembled the fife and drum folks leading the colonial army out of the American Revolution.

Ronnie Lester, probably the best point guard in America when healthy, had missed two stretches of games because of a sprained knee and then a recurrence. The Hawkeyes were 15-1 with him, 8-7 without him.

Shooting guard Kenny Arnold broke his right thumb. Lester's replacement, freshman Bob Hansen, broke a bone in his left hand. Starting freshman forward Mark Gannon tore a knee ligament and missed 20 games.

And center Steve Krafcisin was wearing a heavy bandage on a thigh during the Hawks' Final Four workout Friday, March 21. "Krafcisin has something wrong with everything," Iowa coach Lute Olson said. "We put tape on his thigh because it was as good a place as any."

"The only nice thing about it all," Olson said, "is that we feel pretty confident that nothing else is going to happen to us for about the next 10 years."

Yet these were the guys (23-8), with Lester playing at 70 to 75 percent, who led the way out of the East Regional, capped by a dandy 81-80 victory over powerful Georgetown after being down 14 points in the second half.

"Lester is the best point guard in the nation when he's healthy," said Louisville's Jerry Eaves, who would try to check him. "He was 70 percent and still went by Georgetown. I hope I get some help on him."

U of L (31-3) hoped the juice it recaptured in the second half against Louisiana State was back permanently and that the Darrell Griffith of those 20 minutes—the Griff of so many games gone by—was firmly entrenched again. If so, Louisville would not be an opponent a Big Ten club had experienced often.

Who impersonated Griffith in practice? "Tommy Grogan," Olson said of a 6-3 freshman. "It was a great imitation. Tommy jumps 14-18 inches (to Griffith's 48)."

Hansen roomed with Lester. On Friday, March 21, Hansen remembered looking out an Indianapolis hotel window.

"Here comes the Louisville contingent going by on the interstate in Greyhounds and with police escorts and red-painted cars," Hansen said. "I say, 'Hey, Ronnie, Louisville's made it to town.' It was like a [wake-up] slap in the face, like, 'Okay, this is the Final Four.'"

UCLA-Purdue: Purdue had the best big man, maybe anywhere, in 7-1 Joe Barry Carroll, and UCLA had a 6-6 sophomore center to oppose him.

But the Bruins (21-9) had handled Ohio State's muscle and Clemson's three 6-10 people, so this figured to be a battle of which style would bend—the stickly zone defense and half-court offense of the Boilermakers (22-9) or UCLA's rapid-fire full-court pressure.

The only unknown element was UCLA's mystique. Was there a mystique?

"I don't know," Purdue coach Lee Rose said. "We share 10 national titles."

UCLA has the majority of those. Ten.

Game 35: Iowa, Saturday, March 22
NCAA National Semifinals

Pregame

Denny Crum walked into the locker room for some last-minute words and did something no one in that family had ever seen before. He danced.

"They had their music on and I did a little foot shuffle," he remembered. "I thought it helped loosen things up. The music made me do it, I guess, although I wouldn't admit it to them. I'm a country-western fan. But I have always enjoyed dancing."

The little snippet got out after the game and the next day Crum was asked about it at the press conference.

"It was just a 1955 shuffle," he said. "They laughed at me. I didn't have a mirror, but I thought it was pretty good."

Guard Jerry Eaves was also asked about it.

"I won't try to describe it," he said. "But he shouldn't ever do it again."

First Half

It didn't seem to be humanly possible—or humanely fair to the opposition—but Darrell Griffith was reaching beyond even his own estimable self. So, too, it seemed, was Ronnie Lester.

With 12:36 left in the first half, U of L led 12-10. Griffith had 10 of Louisville's 12 points, with Rodney McCray following in his only miss. Lester had 10 of Iowa's 10.

With 10:31 left, U of L led 18-17. Griffith had 16 of the 18 points, hitting seven of nine shots from 13 to 22 feet out, plus two free throws; Lester had added an assist to his numbers.

It was as if the Cardinals' senior rocket man was determined to wipe his first two games of the tournament off the map in the blink of an eye. And as if the Hawkeyes' senior Indy racing machine had never done anything bad to his right knee. At this pace, Griffith would outscore Lester approximately 64-40 and U of L would win 72-68.

Sadly, only one would carry on.

With just under eight minutes to go before intermission, Lester scooped up a ball loosened by a careless U of L possession and sped the other way on an apparent breakaway. Louisville's Roger Burkman tore after him, catching up just as Lester reached the goal. Lester rose from the floor on his suspect pins for a layup. Never one to give up on any play, Burkman made contact and jostled Lester a bit as he tried to disrupt the shot.

Burkman was called for a foul. Lester landed awkwardly under the basket, then collapsed. With 7:47 left, he was helped to the locker room. He had messed up the fragile stuff in his knee again. He would watch the rest of the game on a television, his college career over.

Burkman, the aggravating, catalytic reserve who had driven so many opponents up the wall, was instantly an arch-villain in the eyes of Iowa fans. But he did not cause the relapse. The strain on a healthy knee trying to elevate at a high rate of speed in traffic under the basket is severe enough. The stress on one with cartilage damage falls into the high-risk category.

"It was just basketball," said Lester, looking back. "I knew Roger was there, but he was not the reason I hurt my knee. It buckled. It was never the same after I initially hurt it in the season's eighth game."

Lester was actually under strict orders not to take the ball to the basket in Iowa's half-court offense.

"Under no circumstances, because of the concern of someone bumping him," coach Lute Olson recalled. "And he hadn't in any of our other playoff games. But this was a turnover and breakaway. It was not anyone's fault, though. Had Ronnie not already had that injury, the play would not have resulted in that problem."

Burkman felt the same way after the game. "When he sprang it looked like he pulled a muscle, before we made contact," he said.

Kenny Arnold moved to the point. Steve Waite joined fellow 6-10 front-liner Steve Krafcisin. Top defender Kevin Boyle or Hansen, a freshman, filled Arnold's shooting guard slot.

The Hawks regrouped quickly. Louisville led 22-19 at the time but stretched it only to 34-29 at intermission. Griffith had 18 of the 34 points, but Iowa was still right there.

Second Half

Steam was still rising from Darrell Griffith. A 22-footer. A 19-footer from the wing. An eye-popping, 16-foot baseline fadeaway with Kevin Boyle on him like double-stick tape.

But the Lester-less Hawkeyes wouldn't disappear, and the Griffith-more Cardinals wouldn't be backed into an inescapable corner. Like mini-waves surging back and forth, Iowa cut U of L's lead twice to two points and twice later to four.

The last was at 67-63 with 3:54 to go on Hansen's 18-footer from the baseline. "I remember that being a bad shot," he said. But the margin was never narrower than five from then on.

When the seas calmed, U of L had an 80-72 victory and a spot in its first championship game. Mostly, it could thank the man who attacked from out of the clouds.

With seconds left and the Louisville cheering section standing as one for a roaring ovation, Griffith was removed, He headed directly for the Iowa sidelines. He slapped hands with its players, then with Olson.

"I know how their team felt, coming this far and then losing," he said.

Griffith had scored 34 points, four points shy of the record for a national semifinal. His 14 field goals (in 21 shots) was two off Larry Bird's record 16 the year before. If the three-point shot had been in operation then, and the official play-by-play sheets were right, six of Griffith's jumpers would have been threes. He also had six assists, five rebounds, three steals and two blocks, plus four turnovers.

"I took what was given me," Griffith said. "I didn't force anything. It means so much to me to win at this time of the year, but I was sorry to see Ronnie get hurt. He's a heck of a basketball player and I would rather have won with him in there."

Iowa opened with Arnold on Griffith, moved to Hansen and finally to Boyle. Lester even tried for a couple of possessions.

Tony Branch, U of L's other senior, thought he remembered seeing tears in Arnold's eyes during one timeout from the futility of trying to turn Griffith off. Arnold and his teammates said no. But they agreed that Sir Dunkenstein had disappeared from their radar screens.

"I tried to stick my hand in his face as much as I could," said Arnold, outstanding himself with 20 points, five assists and one turnover while wearing a soft cast on his shooting hand for a broken thumb. "But he was on fire. There's nothing you can do."

"He was a great athlete who could jump to the moon," Lester said.

Branch had great respect for the 6-2 Arnold. "Good athlete," he recalled. "Top defensive guy in the Big Ten. And if you've been through the Big Ten, you've been through something. But like we were saying on the bench, when Griffith gets like that—and he got like that too many times in practice—you couldn't do anything with him."

Hansen remembered asking Olson if he could take a shot at Griffith.

"Stupid, youthful exuberance," said Iowa's current radio analyst. "Everybody remembers Darrell for his spectacular dunks. I remember his post-up and strong, sweet jump shot. He had incredible body control to go with the obvious elevation he got. You're up there, all of a sudden gravity pulls on you, and Darrell's still up there, shooting it in your face (or way above your face)."

Afterwards, Curry Kirkpatrick of *Sports Illustrated* asked Hansen what it was like trying to defend someone with 48-inch hops.

Answer: "I've played against a lot of guys who could jump, but they all came down."

Night Falls on Kenny

Iowa's Kenny Arnold was victimized by more than one bird on the wing.

The Hawkeyes were running a play out of their half-court offense, a clear-out for Arnold. He escaped Jerry Eaves, drove for the hoop unmolested and rose for a layup.

Suddenly the sky darkened. Somewhere Jeff Battle of Memphis State was yelling, "Look out!"

It was Rodney McCray, transformed into the human eclipse he had become with Battle on February 4. He stopped the layup near the backboard, slid his fingers around the ball, jerked it away from Arnold and came down with his arms wrapped around it, hunched over in protective mode.

Or, as the *Courier's* Mike Sullivan said on February 5, "squatting over the ball like a mother hen."

McCray remembered the "Kenny Arnold thing because it was a bigger game, the Final Four," he said.

And because, viewing NBC's call of the game on tape, he heard analyst Al McGuire define it as a "squatter" (probably because he'd seen it in Sullivan's game story) and talk about the Cardinals "flying like condors."

Arnold simply remembered something suddenly going terribly wrong.

"I didn't see him," he said. "I went to the basket and Rodney McCray came out of nowhere. I was in the air, and the next thing I knew he had cupped the ball."

UCLA-Purdue

UCLA threw four different people at Joe Barry Carroll on defense. It ran Kiki Vandeweghe at him on offense. And, appropriate in the town of the Indianapolis 500, the Bruins' blurs sped past Purdue 67-62 to earn the improbable right to meet Louisville for the national championship.

The 7-1 Boilermaker pivot scored 17 points, five under his average, and had six turnovers as Purdue couldn't unholster enough long guns to ease the internal pressure and get the big man out of bondage.

"It was difficult because of the outstanding defense UCLA played," Purdue coach Lee Rose said. "We ran through all the offenses we had."

UCLA forward Vandeweghe hit nine of 12 shots and scored 24 points. "I tried to take it right at him," Vandeweghe said, referring to Carroll. "I knew if I slowed and tried to throw up something fancy, he'd block it."

Purdue cut it to 61-60 with 1:31 to play, but the Bruins hit all six of their free throws down the stretch.

Priorities

Darrell Griffith could now reach out and almost touch the promise he had made four years earlier.

One more game, one more victory and a national title would belong to his school, his city and to him.

But, sorrowfully, these landmark moments would have to take a seat a few rows back. Jerry Stringer was in trouble.

Stringer, "J-String" to his family and friends, came upon little Darrell in a park, with a basketball, when they were in grade school. A friendship ensued. They went to DuValle Junior High. Griffith made the basketball team, Stringer didn't. They went to Male High. Griffith became a star and a state champion, Stringer the team's manager.

They went to the University of Louisville. Griffith's star continued, Stringer began work on a communications degree. They lived in adjacent dormitory rooms for three years. When Stringer needed something from Griffith, he beat on the wall. Griffith came.

In early 1979, Stringer had a ruptured disc surgically repaired. It wouldn't heal. A second operation revealed bone cancer in his hip. By March of 1980, he had been fighting it for a year.

Before U of L left for Indianapolis, Griffith went to see Stringer. When he got to Indy, he said publicly he would dedicate his labor and whatever the Cardinals could accomplish in the Final Four to his buddy.

Then he had a game for the ages. At 823 E. Muhammad Ali Blvd. in Louisville, a weakened Stringer watched quietly. "This really has uplifted his spirits," said Christine Washington, Stringer's sister.

At a packed press conference on Sunday, March 23, the day before the championship game, Griffith was asked about his friend.

"Jerry's in the third quarter and he's losing," Griffith said. "But he's a strong individual. I pray to God that he'll win. Hey, Jerry, tomorrow night's for you."

The Sneaky Sneaker Wars

Footwear controversies for basketball players in 1979-80 were laughable next to the ridiculous multimillion-dollar hostilities of today, but they had their moments.

The Metro Conference had a contract with Pro-Keds. All but two of Louisville's players wore them. Darrell Griffith and Jerry Eaves liked adidas. With a nod and a wink from a support team member or two, Griffith and Eaves were able to lace up in adidas, hide the logos with white-out or tape and go play. It never became a public incident.

But the Final Four of the 1980 NCAA Tournament turned out to be the Fort Sumter of shoe wars. When the players went to check into their rooms on Friday, they received surprise welcomes.

"There were brown sacks sitting in front of the doors all folded up so you wouldn't know what was in there," equipment man Bosey Thrasher remembered.

The flim-flam men had arrived. T-shirts. Travel bags. Tennis shoes and more tennis shoes. Nike, Adidas, Pony, Puma, Converse—the representatives all hoping they would be spotting their logos on the Market Square Arena hardwood.

At first no one knew how to deal with this. Wearing them didn't seem to violate NCAA by-laws (as they would years later or, as Thrasher said, "unless there was a $50 bill inside them.") But the Metro would not be happy. Worse, there could be a bunch of upset Cardinals distracted from their national title quest.

"It was small potatoes," sports information director Joe Yates said. "But it could also be mind games. If players are not happy with their shoes, how's that going to affect them? There's too much riding on this. Let's not make a mountain out of a molehill. The coaching staff got it out of the way so they could get on with the real thing."

A minor irritant to some, the shoes were driving manager Randy Bufford and trainer Jerry "Rough House" May up the wall. You didn't want to be driving May up anything.

"They get all these fancy things and they want to wear them," May said, voice rising even at the memory. "They're saying, '____, we can get all this stuff,' and they're putting it in their rooms. I'm saying, 'You can't do this ____!'"

The decision was this: As the contraband arrived, May, Bufford and Thrasher would snatch it up and store it in Thrasher's room. It was especially hard on Derek Smith and Wiley Brown, because they were often blowing out the sides of their Pro-Keds, Thrasher said.

"I had 40 to 50 boxes," Thrasher said. "Everybody and his grandma ended up with shoes. I remember Coach Olsen coming to my room and I showed him. He just shook his head."

Bufford remembered the players (except for Griffith and Eaves) wearing Converse against Iowa, and the Metro calling Crum on Monday before the UCLA final.

"I got nervous and told them they had to go back to the Keds," Bufford said. "They were all complaining. I went to Coach Olsen, and he said, 'Put both pairs in there (the lockers). It's not up to you to tell them which pairs to wear.'"

Bufford said most wore Converse for the final (except the adidas duo, of course). Thrasher's closet was emptied into the trunk of a police car. When the game ended, May and Thrasher climbed into the back seat and the gendarmes escorted the team bus back to Louisville.

The next week the new tennies were passed out to the guys. The next season, the Cardinals were wearing Converse.

A Shoe Fix for Marty and Clarkie, Too

Converse shoe representative Kenny Davis was busy during the season with more than just the top seven or eight Louisville players. Marty Pulliam and Steve Clark, the last two guys to get into games, each had a day on the shoe marquee. At least until coaches noticed.

Pulliam remembered Clark getting a nice pair of leather Converse shoes on a road trip.

"He comes to practice, he's dancing around in them, and it's going to be showtime for Clarkie," Pulliam said. "(Denny) Crum comes in, sees him and says, 'Get those shoes off, boy, and get your Pro-Keds on.'"

That was pretty much how Clark remembered it. "Denny says, 'What are you doing? You can't wear those. Take them off,'" Clark said. "The other guys started teasing me and calling me 'Showtime.' They still do to this day."

Pulliam once asked Davis for a green Converse pair with white stars.

"He wouldn't bring me those," Pulliam said, "but he did bring me a pair of black ones. I wore 'em. Coach (Jerry) Jones said, 'What do you want them for?' I told him they made me look slow. He said, 'You don't need any help in that department.'"

You Guys Look a Lot Like...Louisville

In 1975, after a gasping UCLA had nicked Louisville 75-74 in overtime en route to NCAA crown No. 10, Bruin forward David Meyers said, "It looked like there were two UCLAs out there."

In 1980, with Denny Crum on the astonishingly ironic brink of meeting the school he played for and coached at for the fourth time in nine years in the tourney, it looked like there would be two Louisvilles out there.

It was testament to what Crum had wrought over nearly a decade. This wasn't little Louisville vs. the dreaded Walton Gang in the 1972 semis, nor a good but undersung Louisville vs. the Richard Washington/Meyers bunch in the 1975 semis, nor a wounded Louisville vs. the Marques Johnson/David Greenwood Bruins in the 1977 first round.

A glance in this mirror revealed John Wooden-era UCLA teams wearing Louisville uniforms. U of L was favored. It would be the Bruins' challenge to try to measure up.

The Cardinals ran the high-post offense. The Cardinals manned a full-court press. The Cardinals had the 6-4 to 6-8 leapers who were quick off the line and into the air. They didn't have an Alcindor or a Walton, but there were plenty of flashbacks to Willie Naulls, Gail Goodrich, Walt Hazzard, Mike Warren and Sidney Wicks.

"They remind me of one of the earlier UCLA teams—the smaller ones that Coach Wooden had," Bruins coach Larry Brown said.

Brown was in his first collegiate season after six years in the ABA and NBA. He, too, had become Woodenesque, forced to junk his North Carolina motion offense and call upon old UCLA systems when his team was struggling at 8-6.

But the mirror belonged to Crum. He owned the established program. His team was 32-3. And it was the only one that had Darrell Griffith.

"Now we're on even ground," Crum said. "Those other [UCLA] games we were definite underdogs. No one thought we had a chance to win."

But couldn't some mythological Bruins be flitting around in the arena rafters?

"UCLA's never beaten me," said U of L's sophomore point guard, Jerry Eaves. "I've never played them."

Denny? "Having 'UCLA' on the chest used to be a major factor," he said. "But Coach Wooden is not there anymore. It's not what it was 10-15 years ago. They might think we're in their shadow, but we think they're in ours."

Consensus was the game would be played at warp speed with a score in the 80s or 90s. That seemed logical. Of course, logic hadn't paid much of a visit to the 1980 NCAA Tournament.

UCLA in the Final Two? This UCLA?

The UCLA squad that showed up in Indiana in late March had to be an imposter.

Yeah, it had those cheerleaders with the perfect teeth and the blue and gold pom-pons. It had the big U C L A letters across the uniform fronts.

But this team lost nine games during the season. This team lost six games and finished fourth in a league it had won the previous 13 years and 17 of the last 18. It lost four home games in Pauley Pavilion, where its record in its first 14 seasons was 218-7 (seven!). It lost two straight in Pauley. Never happened before. It lost to in-town rival Southern California for its first time since 1970, snapping an 18-game win streak in that rivalry.

These Bruins weren't just a poor man's version of the UCLA sasquatches that lost five games in seven seasons from 1966-73. They weren't even a shadow of their post-Wooden selves. At least those four Gene Bartow/Gary Cunningham-coached teams had gone 25-3, 28-4, 24-5 and 25-5.

This one was 22-9.

"It was hysterical," Larry Brown said from the safer perch of a head coach's seat with the 2003-04 NBA Detroit Pistons. "I kept kidding my team that we were setting all these records."

It wasn't hysterical, though, to the tens of thousands of John Wooden apostles in Los Angeles who could not take defeat for an answer. Brown, fired by Denver of the NBA a year earlier and in his first college campaign, was probably lucky he didn't wind up in the same fix as Jimmy Hoffa.

"With 40 seconds left in our first game at UCLA, we went into a four-corner (delay) and got booed," he said in Indianapolis. "The next game one of our guards didn't pull up at the free throw line on a fast break, and afterwards a guy jumped on an assistant and said, 'Coach Wooden would never have let that happen.'"

From that low road, things got worse. At midseason the Bruins were 8-6. Out with the motion offense Brown brought with him, in with Wooden's familiar high-post. Out with under-performing veterans, in with two freshman guards and a 6-6 sophomore center. Senior forwards Kiki Vandeweghe and James Wilkes stayed in as the anchors, but there were a lot of times UCLA was operating with four rookies on the court.

UCLA got better, but not much. It was still 15-9 as it reached its last road trip of the season. It beat Stanford and Cal, then waited. In the expanded 48-team field, the NCAA took four teams from the Pacific-10, the fourth (and maybe the 48th) being the Bruins, maybe because of the name on the jersey.

Overlooked schools, to which the UCLA name in the bracket had been a four-letter word for years, were outraged. UCLA fans were outraged, too. 17-9? C'mon. The bar was at an impossible height. When Wooden returned the game to humans, humans naturally were found wanting.

"Expectations of UCLA basketball are a double-edged sword," Vandeweghe said with massive understatement decades later.

So UCLA sneaked in. The Bruins knocked off Old Dominion by 13 points in the first round and inherited the wind. They stunned top-ranked DePaul by six, ousted Ohio State by four, whipped Clemson by 11 and took out Purdue by five.

Now they were on the doorstep.

What? Poncho Worry?

It's 8:20 p.m. on Sunday, March 23. Twenty-five hours before the big game. Do you know where your players are?

Poncho Wright felt a tap on his shoulder. "Want to go get something to eat?" a fan asked.

"Naw, I've had enough to eat," the sophomore forward said. "Coach wants me to lose 10 pounds before next year."

But, as *Louisville Times* writer Dale Moss observed, Wright also had the attention of two young women. They wouldn't mind grabbing a bite.

Wright looked at his watch. Curfew was at 10:30. Otherwise, he and his mates were to police themselves.

"You driving?" Wright asked.

"Yeah," one of them said.

Out the door they went. Anybody think the Louisville Cardinals are feeling the heat of an NCAA championship game?

"I try to hang out with everybody," Wright said before he left. "It's good to know your fans. That way, if you mess up, they don't all get on you."

"You got to get your beauty sleep, Poncho," another fan cautioned.

"I'm already beautiful," Wright said.

Is Fort Knox for Sale?

A few people wondered how many zeroes Darrell Griffith added to his NBA contract with the 34-point, six-assist, five-rebound bust-out against Iowa.

"I'd say about $20,000," ventured forward Daryl Cleveland.

Cleveland may have been a shilling or two low. Guard Greg Deuser may have been closer.

"They've already gotten out of the numbers that I can comprehend," he said.

Derek Couldn't Tie One On

As Louisville edged closer to a time where it might have to attend banquets, ceremonies and dress-up affairs, the Cardinals needed to make sure they had enough wardrobe pieces suitable for such events.

(Although not too many. Denny Crum just asked his teams to be presentable in decent shirts and pants, not to look like they were auditioning for *GQ*.)

Derek Smith got a jump on the fashion police in early March. He decided he would wear a tie to all tournament games (although none in the games—that would be too restrictive).

One problem. He couldn't tie a tie. Some days he couldn't fasten that ornery top button on his dress shirt. Jerry Eaves was his chosen haberdasher.

"When I hear someone stomping down the hall yelling, 'Eaves, Eaves,' I know what's coming," Eaves said.

One More Broken Bus Story

Louisville's season-long hate affair with its transportation was not quite finished.

The university bus, although it did find its way to Indy, had glitches upon arrival. Twice it malfunctioned while the team was practicing. Each time a Louisville dentist named Hal Arnett, staying in his motor home, had been summoned.

The last time was Sunday. He picked up the team after a practice and drove it to the Indianapolis Motor Speedway for a memorable hour or two the day before the final game.

Derek Smith rode a motorcycle. Wiley Brown drove an Indy 500 pace car. Poncho Wright sat in the cockpit of an old A.J. Foyt race winner, and all the Cardinals gathered in and on the sides of another Indy car for a team photo.

A final omen? The last time U of L had severe motorcoach problems it limped out of an Ohio snowbank to win at Cincinnati.

Game 36: UCLA, Monday, March 24
NCAA National Championship

Pregame

As already noted, Wiley Brown never much cared for his artificial right thumb. He didn't appreciate people talking about his thumb first and his game second.

So maybe there was something Freudian about what happened the morning of the biggest game of his life.

The team ate breakfast at a meeting room at the Airport Hilton before heading to Market Square Arena for a shootaround. Steve Donohue was sitting on the bus when a large man loomed over him and said, "Yo, man, I lost my thumb." Donohue looked up at Brown and replied, "Oh, (darn)."

Donohue had been Louisville's student trainer since the 1977-78 school year. He was from New York City. He wanted to be a trainer for a baseball team, the Yankees. He graduated from U of L in the December mid-term and had headed to Florida for spring training, ticketed to join the Yankees' Nashville Sounds Double A farm club when the season began.

But when his Cardinals reached the Final Four, Donohue couldn't stand it. The Yankees brass reluctantly let him off for a couple days. Now he was on a bus next to a guy with one thumb.

Donohue told trainer Jerry May. May told coach Denny Crum. Crum said that when they arrived at Market Square, Donohue and manager Randy Bufford would get in the state troopers' car and hightail it back to the Hilton.

"It was beside the plate to the right," Brown said in 2003. "It was one of those mornings when I was good and hungry and just forgot it. It was not a big deal. I wasn't worried about it."

Speak for yourself, Wiley.

"First we went to the meeting room and asked where the garbage was," Bufford said. "The guy said those memorable words, 'In the dumpster.'"

Bufford climbed into the big green waste can like a detective from today's *Law & Order* and began rummaging. Donohue was led back to the kitchen dishwasher. Piled up there were large gray busboy pans of half-eaten food still waiting to be thrown out.

"Anybody see a thumb?" Donohue asked. The kitchen crew began to snicker. Donohue began his treasure hunt through the pans. Bufford found nothing in the dumpster and came inside. The hotel crew was still chuckling.

Bufford shook his head, remembering the absurdity of the moment.

"I mean, there are people in their kitchen searching for a thumb," he said. "That's probably not something you want to advertise—that a thumb was located in your kitchen."

And it was located. After moving pancakes and syrup and sausage, Donohue said he found it under some eggs.

"We were instantly back in the hero category," Bufford said.

The prosthesis was presented to May who, after spewing a few choice angry-trainer words, got Brown ready for two-thumb action.

Brown appreciated the Donohue/Bufford gesture. "You know, I'm sure it had stuff that had to be wiped off but, by golly, it was in good shape when they got back," he remembered.

The team shot around, went back to the hotel, rested, then returned to Market Square in time to see the final moments of Purdue's 75-58 victory over Iowa for third place. The bright lights were on. A crowd of 16,637, including pockets of red-clad people all over the building, was abuzz with anticipation.

The Cardinals were loose. They warmed up. They went to the locker room for a few last words. They reappeared in the tunnel and stopped, bouncing up and down, slapping hands with bystanders, moments before the 9:15 tipoff.

In a move that today might get a journalist kicked out of arenas for life, I decided to leave my seat, go talk to the guys in the rampway and see if I could get a sense of their readiness.

"I've got an empty spot on this finger," said Greg Deuser, pointing to a digit where a championship ring might fit.

"Now for the pot of gold," an animated Roger Burkman added.

These guys were really loose.

Weren't they?

First Half

Darrell Griffith insisted his compadres were relaxed. They were dancing to their sound in the locker room.

And, true to the good-vibe beginnings of several games during the season, Wiley Brown took and hit the first Louisville shot, a 12-footer 52 seconds in.

But this was one of those rare moments when you'd have to disagree with U of L's leader. Were they tight? Like skin on a drum. Especially the Georgia wingmen.

Derek Smith went one for six from the field in the first half. Brown was zero for four after the initial jumper. In one agonizing, four-minute stretch, beginning with the Cardinals up 14-12, Louisville went zero for eight from the field, zero for three from the line and turned the ball over twice. UCLA wasn't much of a bargain, either, but took an 18-14 lead.

From then on, the conflict became less a struggle of unforced errors, more of strengthening roadblocks. It was the opposite of the predicted duel of vapor trails, but it had become a defense worthy of a championship.

"I tried to sleep, then woke up and was really tight," Eaves said of his night before. "I tried to shake it but I couldn't."

U of L shot 35.5 percent in the half and hit four of nine free throws. The Bruins shot worse, 33.3 percent, but hit eight of eight from the line and led 28-26.

Halftime

Denny Crum marched into the locker room, jumped out of character and evoked the "c" word again, just as he had in the first practice after surviving Kansas State in the NCAA opener. This time he was more specific.

Eyeing the sophomores, he said, "You get a chance to play for the national title and you play like a bunch of dum-dums. You choked. You dinked around. I'd be embarrassed to have played that way in a game like this."

Choke. That's a fightin' word. In the back of the room, Derek Smith and Wiley Brown muttered, in effect, "Aw, shut up."

"It was very tense," remembered manager Randy Bufford. "I didn't get a sense there was a 'choke' atmosphere, other than we played tight and didn't execute well. Were we playing to keep from losing? Were they (UCLA)? Hard to tell. But that team had great athletes. They had talent out the butt."

"He took on just a few of us players," Smith would say afterwards. "He called me that. It's an insult to be called 'choke.' I reacted like I couldn't care what he was saying. It was an insult to my pride."

Jerry Eaves was more forgiving.

"We were, we were choking," he said. "And when Coach Crum talks, we all listen. Coach Crum is not like other coaches. He doesn't demand things and beat your head in."

"But at the end he added, 'Golly gee,'" recalled Marty Pulliam, "and that was pretty rough for Denny."

Moments after his diatribe, Crum felt remorse. For months he had been saying what a delight these guys were to coach. Now he was calling them names 20 minutes before the grandest or most disappointing moment of his and their athletic lives?

"They weren't really choking," Crum said later. "Both teams were just responding to all the pressure. But I wanted to sting them, shake them up. Then just before the second-half tipoff, I apologized for saying it. You don't want to hurt people you care so much about."

Second Half

Although Louisville opened the money portion of the game by having its first two passes stolen, tenseness had been replaced by intensity.

But a fierce battle had been joined by both sides. The struggle lurched back and forth, U of L down two, up four, down one, for the first 12 grinding minutes of the half.

Each decision a player made became more critical than the one before it. The blue and gold of UCLA, the school that shouldn't have been there, was becoming bluer and more golden. For those who could visualize John Wooden's face hovering over the proceedings, the image was rapidly expanding.

In a 1:47 stretch that reduced the game clock to 6:28, the Bruins got three field goals while the Cardinals went 0 for five, moving UCLA on top 50-45.

There was big trouble in Cardinal land now. No one had managed a five-point lead in the first 33 minutes. In this kind of tug of war, five looked like 15. Crum called one of his favorite plays, Guard Cut Center Out with an eye on Griffith posting up somebody on the low weak-side block.

"Michael Holton was fronting Darrell (Griffith)," Crum recalled. "Rodney (McCray) threw the ball to Wiley (Brown) at the high post. Darrell had Holton pinned, Wiley made a perfect lob, Darrell caught it and stuck it in off the backboard, Holton fouled him, and Darrell made the free throw. To me, that was the key play, one that kind of turned things around."

But at 50-48, it was not a momentum shifter. Mike Sanders hit two free throws. Griffith countered with an 18-footer. Kiki Vandeweghe's driving layup stretched UCLA's edge to 54-50 at 4:32.

Brown received an in-bounds pass and dribbled up the left side. Jerry Eaves, the point guard, was in the middle of the court hollering, "Brown, throw the ball, throw the ball." At about mid-court, Brown did.

Vandeweghe deflected the pass, collected the ball and thundered the other way on an apparent breakaway.

If he scored, it would be 56-50. As precious as each point had become, it was probably fatal to U of L.

Eaves remembered thinking exactly that. "Now it's nothing but a footrace," he said. "My goodness, if Kiki dunks the ball, it's over."

A desperate Eaves tromped on his accelerator, running like he'd never run before, hoping for personal or divine intervention.

Brown also remembers an awful feeling in the pit of his stomach. "I thought, 'Man, I've lost this game,'" he said. "I told myself, 'You threw it away. Get down there and rebound.'"

Vandeweghe was thinking dunk.

"He had big hands," recalled Eaves. "He picked it up in one hand, his right. I caught up and got in front of him, making him pull back a bit and bobble the ball."

Eaves had brushed him and jiggled the grip just enough. Vandeweghe tried to reclutch and shoot a layup, but he was too far under the backboard. The ball smacked off the glass and skimmed the rim. Eaves flew out of bounds one way, Vandeweghe the other.

"Wiley snatched the rebound because he was hauling butt down there," Eaves said. "I came back in bounds. I told Wiley, 'Give me the ball.'"

Then-UCLA coach Larry Brown relived the moment years later. "He ran right across him and got a little piece, just a tiny thing," Brown said. "I don't think people realize that, one, Kiki has the biggest pair of hands you've ever seen and, two, he's an amazing leaper. Ninety-nine out of 100 times, that's a dunk."

At the time, Vandeweghe graciously gave Eaves the nod. "He cut under me and I tried to change direction," he said. "I would have attempted a dunk, but he made a super defensive play."

The general manager of the Denver Nuggets remains gracious now, but says, "There was definitely contact. They could have given me a foul, but they didn't. Big turning point."

Suddenly the spotlight beamed in the face of one of the overlooked Cardinals.

With under four minutes to go, Larry Brown changed up to something he disliked, a zone, for one defensive trip because Louisville was having trouble scoring.

"We got the right guy to take the shot, a quick shot," Larry Brown said.

That guy was Eaves, but he buried the jumper, an angled 16-footer, and U of L was down 54-52 with 3:26 left. UCLA missed, and it was Eaves once more, burrowing down the lane for a half-hook, half-layup to tie it 54-54.

At the other end, UCLA tried to respond rapidly. Guard Rod Foster rose for a 20-footer. It was in. "Three-quarters of the way down," Larry Brown recalled. It swirled around halfway below the iron once, then mystifyingly climbed back out.

Griffith pumped home an 18-footer. At 56-54 Louisville had its first lead in seven minutes. A UCLA turnover. A Louisville delay game. Sanders fouled Smith at 0:52. The Cardinals had hit just eight of 15 free throws. Smith made both, making the score 58-54.

Vandeweghe missed a jumper at 0:29. McCray hit one of two free throws at 0:14. UCLA's Cliff Pruitt missed at 0:04.

Scoring the last nine points, shooting 59 percent in the second half, Louisville won 59-54, capping a record 33-3 journey with its first national championship.

Griffith leaped and banged both fists on the backboard. Crum smiled in relief and let out a deep breath. No more "can't win the big one" talk.

Wiley Brown held up a "newspaper" called *The Indiana Journal*, concocted by an aunt, that screamed in wartime headlines, "WILEY AND DEREK WINS NCAA!" Grammar bad. Thought good. The castigated Georgians had made five of 10 second-half shots and two monster free throws.

Poncho Wright, the Ville-Nap fortuneteller, was again peering into his crystal ball and reporting that "The Ville is going to the Phil (the 1981 Final Four would be in Philadelphia)."

Wiley Brown announced that "Ooeyville-lay is-yay Umber-nay Un-way (Louisville is No. 1)" to his pig-latin fans.

Back in the empty locker room, in the wee hours of Tuesday, March 26, a man looked into a cubicle and saw the last rubber glove used to keep Brown's bionic thumb in place. It had no traces of eggs or syrup on it. Just sweat.

A Kenny Loggins song, "This Is It," one Cardinal fans had used as a season-long theme, could be heard faintly in the background. The man reached down and picked up the glove. He took it home.

He realized that, song or no song, if there ever was a perfect keepsake from 1979-80, this was it.

Stepping into the Biggest Searchlight

The magic carpet Louisville had been flying for six months had seemed to yield an omen or irony with every dribble. Here was one more.

Sitting on the dias at the press conference after the victory, Darrell Griffith and Jerry Eaves were being asked about the Vandeweghe play and subsequent 9-0 finishing rally begun by Eaves' 16-foot wing jumper.

"Griff's at the point talking about where he threw me the ball, and I hit that little shot," Eaves recalled. "The thing was, usually I'm on the top (of the circle as the point guard) and Griff's on the wing. But they were playing him so hard there, and I'm reluctant to take the shot from the top, so Denny flip-flopped us. It made UCLA come out farther and opened the wings up more."

A voice interrupted Eaves' description. "I thought you were just going to stay out of Griff's way," it asked.

Eaves chuckled. Questioned the day before where he fits into the scheme of things, Eaves said then, "I got the easy role. I watch Darrell play." This night he answered, "Well, he just needed a little help."

Overlooked, underpublicized, often ignored, Jerry Eaves went four for four in the second half for eight points with three assists. In the five NCAA Tournament games, challenged by some of the country's most talented backcourts, he had six turnovers in 127 minutes. After a zero for three NCAA opener, Eaves hit 13 of 21 shots.

"Down the stretch, Jerry told me, 'I want that ball,'" Rodney McCray said. "I thought to myself, 'Hmmm, the man wants the ball that bad, I'll try to see that he gets it.'"

U of L doesn't win the title without Eaves. Or course, it doesn't win it without a lot of others, either.

Here's a Real Wake-Up Call

Two of Louisville manager Randy Bufford's duties were to have Denny Crum's clipboard at the ready when the coach called a timeout and to quickly scoop up a player's warmups when he was motioned into the game.

At one point against UCLA, Crum called for Roger Burkman.

"I was in the first seat," remembered Bufford. "When Coach Crum called a player, I'd stand up to get the warmup and put it down at the end of the bench. He called for Roger and sent him scurrying my way right as I got up.

"My left hand had the clipboard. It nailed him right in the mouth and cut his lip. He was down there at the scorer's table, bleeding, looking back at me and saying, 'Damn, Buff.' It quit bleeding on its own, and he didn't need stitches, but it was enough to startle him."

Burkman went on to play 11 minutes. Bufford forgot about it. Decades passed. Not long ago Bufford enrolled his son in Burkman's basketball camp in Louisville.

"He called my kid out, said his dad smacked him in the mouth in the championship game and told them the whole story," Bufford said. "My kid came home, embarrassed, and said, 'Dad, did you slam Roger?'"

"Of course I'm spinning it differently these days, telling people I was just trying to shake him up and get him ready to go."

Big Finish for Griff, Big Start for Rodney

Louisville's Darrell Griffith was named Most Outstanding Player of the Final Four, beating Purdue's Joe Barry Carroll 140 votes to five.

Not a bad choice. He hit nine of 16 shots in the championship game, scored 23 points and had three assists. In Indianapolis he went 23 for 37, 11 for 16 from the free throw line, averaged 28.5 points and added seven rebounds and nine assists.

In separate balloting, Griffith only edged worthy adversary Kiki Vandeweghe of UCLA 151 votes to 145 to lead the all-tournament team. Vandeweghe hit 13 of 21 shots, went 12 for 12 from the line and grabbed 12 rebounds in his two games.

Rodney McCray got the fifth most votes on the five-man squad and four other Cardinals also were mentioned.

Like Griffith, McCray was not a bad choice, either. His 11-rebound, seven-point contribution against the Bruins was critical and followed a 14-point, nine-rebound job against Iowa. And the second worst free throw percentage shooter on the club went seven for eight in two games.

"I wasn't tentative," said the freshman. "Biggest game of the season. No time for jitters."

A Singular Triplicate

Louisville's NCAA championship put it in a private club with only itself as a member.

The Cardinals had now captured the NCAA, National Invitation Tournament and National Association of Intercollegiate Basketball (now NAIA) crowns. Nobody else could say the same.

U of L won the 1948 NAIB with an 82-70 victory over Indiana State in Bernard "Peck" Hickman's fourth season. Eight years later the Cardinals had moved to NCAA Division I and grabbed the 1956 NIT 93-80 over Dayton with All-American Charlie Tyra averaging 23.8 points and 22.2 (no typo) rebounds for the season. Hickman was in the 12th of his 23 campaigns, and the NIT was still nearly as big as the NCAA.

A Net for J-String

Darrell Griffith, a Metro Conference cap askew on his head, cut the final strands of the net at Market Square Arena and waved it at delirious Louisville fans.

As promised long before, he had delivered a national championship. As promised to a friend only days before, he had delivered two victories in the Final Four.

Now, also as promised, he would deliver the net to Jerry "J-String" Stringer.

Stricken with bone cancer, weakening steadily, his weight down from 150 pounds to 89, Stringer watched the title game in his bed surrounded by 18 friends and *Louisville Times* reporter Andrew Wolfson. Just before tipoff, he whispered, "If Darrell wins this game, I'll know everybody around the world knows he won it for me."

Stringer was 22, president of the U of L student government, president of his fraternity, Griffith's close buddy since grade school.

Stringer's eyes closed as Louisville fell behind by five points. Stringer's eyes opened. "You can't lose, you can't," he said in a voice heard away from the bed for the first time.

Louisville came back. "They brought it home to you, Jerry, they brought it home," someone said.

A day later Griffith gave the championship net to his friend. Hopes and prayers, however, were not enough. On April 30, 37 days after Jerry's Game, Stringer died. On May 3, Kentucky Derby day, Griffith was a pall-bearer at his funeral. On May 4, Louisville's national champions played a softball game against the city's professional softball team, the Kentucky Bourbons.

The game raised $1,500 to help defray the Stringer family's medical expenses.

"This means a whole lot to me," Darrell Griffith said.

Thanks for Your Support

UCLA's Larry Brown eased his way off the Market Square Arena court after the buzzer sounded.

He was disappointed, severely disappointed, but he was feeling mighty good about his guys. They could have packed it in by January. They could have buckled in the face of UCLA expectations.

"I'm walking off so very proud of my team, how we gave ourselves a chance to win the final game, and this alum comes up and says, 'Congratulations, Larry, you did it again.'

"I say, 'Thank you.' He says, 'Yeah, you're the first coach to ever lose a final game at UCLA.'"

Brown didn't get mad or even look at the guy as a numbskull.

"I just went on," he said. "It kind of tickled me. I don't think he understood what it meant to get there. I look at Ray Meyer (ex-DePaul) and so many coaches who run great programs that never get there, so that guy didn't do anything to affect me. You have to be pretty dumb not to understand what these kids accomplished."

A Congratulatory Gesture Above and Beyond

Awash in the warmest of feelings, the majority of Louisville's players boarded the university bus in the wee hours of Tuesday, March 25, for the two-hour-plus police-led ride back to campus.

The coaches had other transportation. So did Darrell Griffith, Tony Branch and Wiley Brown. Trainer Jerry May and student trainer Steve Donohue rode with the troopers.

The rest were on the bus and settling in when a surprise visitor boarded. It was Larry Brown. How many coaches who just lost a national championship would made this kind of sportsmanship effort?

"I admired Denny (Crum), loved their team and thought the whole scene was neat," Brown said years later. "I never had a clue that Louisville, Purdue and Iowa were so close to Market Square Arena, and all those buses and cars were getting ready to go.

"I just wanted to say something. I didn't have a chance to go in the locker room. There was such craziness after the game, people picking Darrell up. The only person I had a chance to say something to was Denny, and he was kind of in a state of shock. I felt it was such an accomplishment and was just proud to be a part of it. I wanted to explain that."

So Brown went down the rows shaking hands with some wide-eyed players.

"I've always been a Larry Brown fan just because of that," Roger Burkman said.

"He called my name," said Marty Pulliam, who played two minutes in the five tourney games, none against UCLA. "He shook my hand. He said, 'Good job, Marty.' I was impressed by that. How did the man know who I was?"

"Hey, Larry Brown has class," Poncho Wright said. "I mean class."

CHAPTER ELEVEN

The Aftermath:
March 24, 1980
and Beyond

A Full-Blown Barnstorming Tour

As the Louisville Cardinals' grip on the 1980 national championship became vise-like, one could almost hear a unified countdown of the final seconds rise up from people in all parts of the city south of Indianapolis.

When the title became reality, they poured one more beverage into their mouths and poured themselves into the streets. The town of bourbon makers and horse racers was suddenly a part of the university instead of the other way around.

They swarmed and swirled and shouted and hugged in their revelry. At the Red Barn, the campus hangout/beer and dance hall stuck between the team's practice facility and athletic administration on Brook Street, it was more like rebelry.

Inside, under perhaps the dual intoxicants of alcohol and that enticing female, maryjane, they sprayed beer on each other as empty bottles and cans and broken coolers littered the floor. Outside, they climbed atop buildings. The shinnied up light poles. They tore down street signs. They lit a bonfire. They were out there by the thousands, and a couple may haveeven been sober, but that was only a guess.

Cars with red streamers took over Louisville's main drag, Broadway. Police had to rein in partiers on 32nd Street. Joe's Palm Room patrons gave their television a standing ovation. At Dutch's Tavern, guys banged mugs until some broke, and bartender Ross Uhl declared, "It's a madhouse. Best night we've ever had by far."

Back at the Red Barn, Cindy Crum, Denny's daughter, had missed the trip to Indianapolis because of spring break in Florida, but was happy to be where she was "because all my friends are here." She picked U of L by 10. The margin was five, but she had the right side.

Meanwhile, on the street and up the poles, the degree of lunacy was rising steadily.

One Last Fateful Bus Ride

The Louisville players poured Sprite, not champagne, on each other in triumph, they mostly being non-drinkers of non-drinking age.

The majority of them climbed aboard the university bus. Derek Smith pulled his new watch out of the box, put it on and stuck an unlit cigar in his mouth.

"Let's get the Ville to the Ville," ordered Greg Deuser, and the vehicle lurched away from Market Square Arena, onto Interstate 65 and headed home.

Louisville Times sports editor Lou Younkin was given permission to ride back with the guys, a good move for the newspaper.

The bus rolled merrily along. It was hard to imagine after a season of transportation potholes, but the last and most important trip might actually be pretty terrific.

Not so fast.

Louisville patrol cars joined the escort service about 20 miles north of the Ohio River and the police brought the team to the city. They blocked off an intersection at Arthur Street. The bus turned right, went under a viaduct and turned left on Brook, planning to ease past the Red Barn and deposit the players at their Crawford Gym facility.

Not so fast.

"All those people, all of them drunk, on top of buildings, on top of telephone poles," recalled equipment coordinator Robert "Bosey" Thrasher. "And we were going incredibly slow."

"At first, close to campus, we had rolled down the windows, shaking hands and kissing babies like a politician," remembered Roger Burkman. "It was really fun. Until we got to the center of campus. The closer we got, the drunker the people. They wanted memorabilia—a lock of your hair, a piece of your shirt. We rolled the windows back up. We moved away from the windows."

People climbed on the police cars. Then they climbed on the bus roof. The roof began to creak. And slope downward. Marty Pulliam, 6-9, stood and put his hands on the ceiling.

"I just wanted to help hold it up," Pulliam recalled. "I don't think it would have given way, but . . ."

"It was crazy, scary until they got them off the roof," remembered Jerry Eaves.

"The bus was rocking," Burkman said. "The roof was caving in, a foot down. It was not fun now."

The roof held. Trainer Jerry May got out of a trooper's car up ahead and got on the bus. A couple of players wanted to get off right then and make a mad dash to Crawford.

"Jerry was cussing like a sailor," Thrasher said. "He said, 'We ain't getting off,' and made a decision to get it out of there."

It was now closing on 4 a.m. The bus started inching forward, "bumping a few of the people out of the way," Thrasher said. Pulliam remembered lumbering into a nearby fenced lot by the not-aptly-named Dept. of Public Safety. A fence was toppled.

The bus wiggled out of there, got back on I-65 and headed for the U of L football office at the State Fairgrounds, about a mile away. They arrived. No one had a key.

About six cars were left in the motorcade, one of them containing Louisville Mayor William Stansbury. He conferred with May and assistant athletic director Jack Tennant (who set a record in '79-80 for most beleaguered travel coordinator) and they decided to go to the Executive Inn, a hotel just outside the Fairgrounds, for what little was left of the night.

The team was due in Stansbury's office in five hours to be named honorary mayors. It was to appear before the state legislature in Frankfort that afternoon. It was to be welcomed by an expected gigantic pep rally at Freedom Hall that night. But only if the players were still alive.

"If the crowd (at the pep rally) is anything like the one here tonight," Eaves said, "I don't think I want to go."

"I don't think a lot of these people will be up by then," Pulliam said.

So most of the emotionally and physically spent Cardinals got a couple hours of shuteye at the hotel, then prepared to crank themselves up again.

"We thought we were on top of the world," Thrasher said. "Then we thought we were going to get stomped. Then we thought we were going to get killed."

A quarter-century later, Burkman looked back and said, "I thank the good Lord I'm still here."

A Trophy Is Worth a Thousand Pictures

As the Louisville players dragged themselves into the Executive Inn, tired, nervous, much of the joy of the most joyous occasion having left, trainer Jerry May left his police ride and decided to stay with the team.

Equipment man Bosey Thrasher got a lift back to the U of L football complex, where his car was parked, and gathered his belongings. And one belonging that didn't belong.

The national championship trophy.

"There I stood with my suitcase over my shoulder and the trophy in my hand," he said. "It had been forgotten in the chaos. The next day there was so much confusion with all the places everybody had to go that nobody wondered where it was at."

It was at Thrasher's home in Valley Station, south of the city. For a week.

"Every kid in the neighborhood touched that trophy," he said. "They all knew I had it. They couldn't believe it. They loved it. They all wanted their pictures taken with it. I could have made a fortune."

Class First, Tributes Second

Approximately 13 hours after winning a championship, between the time he would become one of the "mayors" for a day and honored by Kentucky legislators, Derek Smith had to do something that was really important.

The March NCAA run had forced him to miss a lot of work in Prof. Marilyn Wilson's phonetics class of his public speaking curriculum. Having already come miles in articulation from the reluctant, hard-to-understand rural Georgian who had arrived at Louisville in 1978, he had no plans to stop now.

U of L had canceled classes for the day. In the early afternoon of Tuesday, March 25, Tim Hynes, dean of the theatre arts department, and Prof. Michael Holtois were in the theatre annex building (since razed) watching a replay of the UCLA game with a few others.

"It was fair to say we were ardent basketball fans," Hynes remembered. "We were at a part of the game (Louisville leading 56-54, 52 seconds left) where Derek is at the free throw line. Probably the difference between winning and losing."

Who walks in? Derek Smith. He was looking for Wilson to find out what he had missed and needed to make up in her class. He walked over to the Hynes group.

"I asked him what he was thinking (on the court)," Hynes said. "It was the usual Derek response. He thought 'it would be a good idea if I made the free throws.'"

He did, putting the Cardinals up 58-54 en route to the 59-54 victory.

Was it startling to see Smith walk in seeking class assignments instead of conquering hero status? "No shock," Hynes said. "Students—even athletes—are trying to do the best they can. He was a solid B-C student and a man with a sense of direction. U of L helped put some texture to that direction, but he had a full sense of it."

Assistant coach Bill Olsen knew of examples of athlete-class relationships in other years that went in the opposite direction.

"This one," Olsen said, "almost brings tears to your eyes."

Getting up for the Political Game

On March 25 a bus-lagged Louisville basketball team was as fearless on various political courts as it was on ones with hard wood.

In Louisville's city hall, Mayor William Stansbury declared 1980 the "Year of the Cardinals" and asked his citizens to wear red and black the next week.

In the Fiscal Court building, County Judge Mitch McConnell asked the court to approve putting up 11 five-foot-by-four-foot signs on highways in his jurisdiction that would read: Welcome to Jefferson County, Home of the University of Louisville, 1980 NCAA basketball champions." There was no dissent.

In Henderson, Kentucky, a top Kentucky political contact of president Jimmy Carter's, banker Dale Sights was trying to arrange a trip to the White House, and it looked promising.

In Washington, D.C., Kentucky senators Wendell Ford and Walter Huddleston and U.S. Rep. Romano Mazzoli presented resolutions to each congressional chamber.

And in Frankfort, Kentucky's capital, the Cardinals, many still in their warmups, ran their 2-2-1 press at the state legislature.

Darrell Griffith, who had worked on the successful campaign of State Rep. Aubrey Williams years earlier, walked to the speaker's rostrum in the House, gazed over the assembly and asked, "Will you please give us an arena? A 25,000-seat arena would solve everything."

Tony Branch, the other senior, told the House he would like to introduce a resolution that Griffith's No. 35 be retired.

"If ever in the history of a university a number should be retired, it should be Darrell Griffith's," said Branch, although Griffith probably thought after the NCAA opener the number should be TB's 23. The school promptly removed 35, one of four to be so honored.

Branch then retired to the governor's office, where he sat in John Y. Brown Jr.'s chair and put his legs up on the desk. Brown gave the whole team the honorary title of Kentucky Colonel and presented Denny Crum with the Governor's Distinguished Service Medallion. Only 43 of those had been awarded in the previous 23 years, and Brown said the only other coach to receive it was Adolph Rupp.

Brown and then-wife Ellie owned the old ABA Kentucky Colonels before disbanding it rather than pay the NBA entry fee a few years earlier. Now he looked at Griffith and rued the day.

"I wish I still had them," he said. "Darrell, we sure could have used you."

An Exchange of Valentines

Tuesday night, March 25, 19,400 people ushered the Louisville squad into a victory celebration at Freedom Hall. Another 5,000 had to be turned away.

Gov. John Y. Brown Jr., an apparent glutton for punishment, and wife Phyllis came to this rally, too.

Denny Crum introduced him with: "It gives me great pleasure to introduce to you the man who is going to bring us our own arena, Governor Brown."

The crowd welcomed him with some boos, some cheers and the chant, "Where's Our Arena?"

Brown pacified them with: "Why do we have to have this meeting in this old gymnasium?"

Cheers.

"I get your message."

Cheers again.

The U of L coaches spoke, respect from another state school and its fans on their mind.

"I want you to repeat after me, 'We Are Somebody,'" Wade Houston said.

"I promised my wife I'd be humble and not mention anything about a little school outside of Jefferson County," Jerry Jones said. "But now they've got to look at us eyeball to eyeball."

And Crum said, "At least for this year, and maybe for evermore, we are the university of Kentucky."

Yet assertions of equality and things that could be accomplished with basketball facilites took a distant back seat to the reason this many people had come: To salute the fellowship of the '79-80 Cardinals and the bond that developed between them and their fans.

Wiley Brown, probably with help from ghostwriter Scooter McCray, offered another poem:

All of you who didn't have any faith,
The Cards have won the NCAA;
The Cards are known all over the land,
We couldn't have done it without you wonderful fans.

To which his buddy, Derek Smith, unintentionally added a postscript:

To make that victory more meaner,
We would like to have had it in Rupp Arener.

Jones and Tony Branch made even deeper penetrations with the multitudes.

"We knew all along what kind of team and kids we had," Jones said. "This is their moment. The city's moment."

"Diana Ross sings, 'Reach out and touch somebody,'" Branch said. "If basketball can bring this many people closer together, if the Louisville Cardinals can bring this city and this state closer together, then basketball is worthwhile. Let's not let it stop today."

A Campus Reinvented

A 1980 University of Louisville senior returning today to the campus for the first time since he graduated would probably think it had been moved.

New academic buildings are sprinkled throughout. Some old academic buildings are gone. Parts of streets are gone. And the portion facilitating athletics at the school is unrecognizable.

How much of this is due to the 1980 national championship? Conversations with several administrators couldn't pinpoint one dwelling as being entirely constructed with money pledged as a direct result of the title. But not one of them doubted that pieces, usually large pieces, of everything that changed at U of L happened because of respect and recognition gained from that accomplishment.

After pushing so hard for a new arena, a university delegation met with Gov. John Y. Brown and proposed that if the state would absorb most of the cost of a Student Activities Center, U of L would have Freedom Hall renovated, pay for it, and stay in it.

The new $13.3 million Freedom Hall, capacity increased from 16,613 to an official 18,865 (but with some games drawing over 20,000) opened with 24 luxury boxes for the 1984-85 season. The $23 million SAC was built over a railroad track and wiped out the infamous Brook-Brandeis corner where the bus was attacked in the wee hours of March 25. It opened in 1990. The Red Barn was saved.

"The state got off with $15 million or so (instead of footing a possible $30 million bill for a downtown arena)," Bill Olsen said. "The athletic department contributed five million dollars to the SAC and another five million dollars to buy land for the Cardinal Sports Park (softball, soccer, field hockey) across the street. Denny Crum should get a lot of credit for that."

Olsen was the '79-80 team's assistant head coach. Three months after the championship, he became the school's athletic director. He and Crum immediately set about taking advantage of opportunities.

Crum was lucky that the crown coincided with a governor who was a former basketball team owner and golfer.

"John Y. knew we had a legitimate gripe," Crum recalled. "He was a big basketball fan, he felt we were deserving of it and felt that Louisville and Kentucky should have been playing year. The championship established us as one of the premier basketball programs in the country. It helped open the door to recruiting, and I think helped the university with people in Frankfort.

"President [James] Miller had a need for four or five academic buildings if we were going to be reaccredited [as part of the state educational system]. But the government was not responsive. Steve Bing [a vice-president and liaison between athletics and administration] asked me to talk to John Y. I said I'd be happy to. We talked, he made a commitment and they were built."

Bing remembered responses to the name "Louisville" taking a quantum leap in a variety of areas.

"It totally changed the perception of the University of Louisville," said Bing, now a partner in an investment company. "Student applications for enrollments from the eastern part of Jefferson County increased dramatically. Fund-raising increased dramatically. It became more than accepted, it became fashionable, to be associated with U of L."

Olsen, meanwhile, started building a money tree with tickets and television.

"The championship created a supply and demand for tickets," he said. "Before 1980 people were able to cherry-pick the schedule and just buy for big games. After 1980 they had to be season-ticket holders to see the big ones. For the first time we were able to sell out Freedom Hall on a season-ticket basis. We created a waiting list.

"After that, almost every seat required participation in the Cardinal Athletic Fund [meaning one had to contribute to a fund just for the right to buy game tickets]. But the real benefit came after we expanded Freedom Hall and were able to leverage basketball interest into support for the football program."

How much flak did that bring on?

"Some," Olsen said. "It was hard to tell if it was serious or good-natured. Some people would smile and say it was extortion. I'd smile back and say it was the opportunity to be entertained in the fall of the year and support your favorite local university."

At the same time Olsen was becoming a TV mogul dressed in an AD's suit.

"We were able to get national TV contracts we didn't have before," he said. "We generated more dollars from national TV (because of 1980 and the teams that immediately followed) for a three-, four- or five-year period than maybe anybody else. It was over one million dollars a year in TV contracts."

In 1980 the athletic budget was three million dollars with two-thirds of that subsidized by university general funds, Olsen said. Two years later the budget was five million dollars and athletics was self-sufficient.

"When I retired in 1997, we had $50 million in a reserve fund," Olsen said. "The 1980 championship was probably the pivotal event in the history of the athletic department."

Greeting the Commander-In-Chief

By the time the Louisville Cardinals concluded their triumphal tour of Kentucky's political houses, March had ended and a visit to Washington had been arranged.

The team flew to D.C. on Thursday, April 3, to see Daryl, Derek and Wiley's "peanut man" and assorted other dignitaries.

Wiley Brown, Derek Smith and Daryl Cleveland presented president Jimmy Carter, their state surrogate, with an autographed basketball and U of L T-shirts for the chief executive, the first lady and daughter Amy.

Denny Crum gave the president an NCAA championship watch and complimented him on his taste in clothes (their suits looked like they came off the same rack).

The president said the players were "a credit to the nation" and that he was honored to meet them. "When the pressure was on, you came through," he said. "That's the kind of leadership we admire."

No one mentioned to Carter that they had named one of their dunks "Free the Hostages" in recognition of those held captive by Iran's Ayatollah. Perhaps the timing wasn't right.

At lunch, such senators as Strom Thurmond, R-South Carolina, John Culver, D-Iowa, and Alan Simpson, R-Wyoming, congratulated the champs and asked for autographs. The lead dignitary in that line was, of course, Darrell Griffith. Tieless and open-collared, he wasn't being confused with, say, the president of France, but he comported himself as the head of some state.

Probably the state of basketball.

Tight Security, Tighter Security

Visiting the White House was one of life's greater thrills for Steve Clark, the non-scholarship freshman guard from Louisville.

"I was like Gomer Pyle—'Goll-ee, look at this!'" Clark recalled.

First he remembered the precautionary checklists.

"We had given our social security numbers to Collette Zwicker (Denny Crum's secretary) so they could do background checks," Clark said. "Same with a bunch of reporters who went with us. Getting into the White House was difficult then, even before all the terrorist stuff."

One of the journalists apparently hadn't provided enough information.

"We flew to Washington and took a bus to the White House," Clark said. "Before we went in, a Secret Service man at the gate walked onto the bus, walked straight up to a certain individual, one of the reporters, and said, 'You have to give us your driver's license.'

"That just blew my mind. How they knew out of 100 people who hadn't even gotten off the bus yet or checked in, I don't know."

Later the group was on the White House lawn. Clark, Roger Burkman and Daryl Cleveland stepped back away from the others to take pictures. The Secret Service was there to intercept. Clark recalls the exchange thusly:

Secret Service: "You need to get back with your group."
Players: "We just want to get a picture."
Secret Service: "No, no, you need to get back to your group."
Players: "We're just going to get a picture right here."
Secret Service: "You're making all these people nervous."
Players: "We're going to get this picture and then go back."
Secret Service: "I'm insisting that you go back now!"

The security man pulled them back to the group, but not before Clark snapped a photo on the move that managed to get the White House but not the people.

1975-84: Annual Sequels of
Hitchcock's *The Birds*?

It would be blasphemy to suggest, even whisper, that another program could immediately follow UCLA's unthinkable 1964-75 annihilation of college basketball with a surge that would remind anyone of the Bruins' 10 national titles in 12 years.

Yet the Louisville Cardinals' 10-year ride from 1975 to 1984, ending when a wounded 1984-85 squad finished 19-18—and excluding the 1986 championship—bubbled with potential glory, what-ifs and oh-so-closes. If late-1970 guard Phillip Bond, who authored the "Doctors of Dunk" call to battle, could have loaned his last name to a few other U of L clubs besides those of 1974-75 and '79-80, who knows?

UCLA should rightly throw up an enormous roadblock at even the hint of such a possibility. No one will ever smother a sport the way the Woodens did. And all the other teams that impacted the '75-84 period could make good cases of their own.

Kentucky: What if Sam Bowie had an injury-free career? What if Duke's Vince Taylor had been called for a foul instead of a good play on Kyle Macy's last-second shot in the 1980 Mideast semifinal? What if UK had not totally lost its ability to accurately shoot a basketball in the second half of the 1984 national semis?

Indiana: What if it had a healthy Scott May in the 1975 Mideast Regional? What if Isiah Thomas had stuck around for 1981-82 and '82-83?

North Carolina: What if Michael Jordan and James Worthy had stayed four years, too?

Georgetown: What if Iowa hadn't made up a 14-point deficit in the 1980 East final? What if the Tigers hadn't thrown a backcourt pass away in the 1982 national final?

UCLA: What if John Wooden hadn't retired in 1975?

Those of us who were there for most of Louisville's 10 seasons in that era have reason to play the speculation game, too, regardless of how far off the national marquee the Cardinals then seemed to be in the minds of fans, press and elitists.

1974-75: 28-3. One of a half-dozen little things could have stopped Wooden's final team in the national semis. A 75-74 overtime loss prevented ed a cataclysmic match with Kentucky for the title. "That team was very similar to the 1980 team in terms of its personalities and how it got along," assistant Jerry Jones said.

1975-76: 20-8. Started off 18-4 and needed only to beat Memphis State at home in the semis of the Metro Conference tourney to make the 32-team NCAA field, but couldn't.

1976-77: 21-7. Was 18-2, had won 15 in a row, nearly made it 16 at Nevada-Las Vegas before forward Larry Williams broke his foot in the next game. Squeezed into NCAAs and gave UCLA a reasonable battle with Williams playing on little more than one leg, but lost 87-79. "We had the best team in the country at that time, no question," coach Denny Crum said.

1977-78: 23-7. Started 16-3, lost three on the road, then was back in powerful gear by the time it met DePaul in Midwest Regional semifinal. Center Dave Corzine scored 46 points as DePaul won 90-89 in two overtimes. Crum and assistant Bill Olsen argued (some say raged) about whether to half-front or play behind Corzine instead of fronting him with hope for weak-side help.

"It was hard to watch Corzine shoot layup after layup," Olsen recalled. "We did have a discussion. But only one person would make the final decision."

The subject still gets Crum's hackles up. "It wasn't Corzine," he says. "Look at our free throw shooting (five big misses down the stretch). We didn't have anybody to stop Corzine but did a great job on everybody else." Darrell Griffith missed two of the free throws. In 1980 he said, "I felt nothing could have stopped us if we had gotten past that one."

1978-79: 24-8. Started 21-3, backslid, then staged an all-out rally in the second half that caught Arkansas before exhaustion signaled an Arkansas victory in the regional semifinal. U of L's effort has been given some credit as a catalytic force for the next season.

1979-80: 33-3. Exceptional personal ties, respect and that rarest of things for a coach, a trouble-free season, yielded the best team in Louisville history and one that threw down the ethical gauntlet for those that followed. NCAA champions.

1980-81: 21-9. Started out 2-7, leading to the unforgettable remark by new assistant Bobby Dotson, "I always wanted to come to a program and turn it around." Reconstructed its egos, directions it was heading and reason for playing the game, inserted freshmen into a couple of spots, then won 18 of its next 19. Beaten in its first NCAA game 74-73 on a 45-foot shot at the buzzer by U.S. Reed, who quickly became Unbelievable Shot Reed who authored the Cardinals' Unconditional Surrender.

"If U.S. Reed had not hit that shot, we felt it would have been another Final Four, possibly a national championship," Scooter McCray said. "That was the deepest team I think I've ever been on."

Indiana won it all in 1981. The center on that squad was Landon Turner, a close friend of U of L forward Poncho Wright. An auto accident would later paralyze Turner and put him in a wheelchair. Wright's jingle after Louisville's 1980 crown was "The Ville is going to the Phil." IU grabbed the title in Philadelphia's Spectrum.

"I tell my buddy Landon all the time, 'You're lucky U.S. Reed hit that shot, because if he didn't, you guys wouldn't have a championship,'" Wright said.

Had Louisville beaten Arkansas, Louisiana State would have been next. "I had a sigh of relief when Arkansas won," then-LSU coach Dale Brown said recently. "I thought Louisville was probably too gifted for us."

1981-82: 23-10. Lost four straight in January, then became the familiar high-heat never-ease-up Cardinals to gain another Final Four. Lost to Georgetown and freshman Patrick Ewing 50-46 in the semifinals at New Orleans. "Milt Wagner (an important freshman guard) got a skin infection that was so sensitive he couldn't hold, catch or dribble the ball," Crum said. "Weird thing. He had to wear golf gloves to play."

1982-83: 32-4. Beat Kentucky in overtime in landmark Mideast Regional final to make third Final Four in four years. Semifinal match with Houston's Phi Slamma Jamma aerial act expected to be real national title game and one of the best NCAA games ever. It didn't disappoint. Cardinals led by eight in the second half, were buried 21-1 by an absurd ram-bam spurt, then trimmed a 13-point Houston lead to six before losing 94-81. Houston then was shockingly deprived of the title by North Carolina State.

"In 1981 we struggled on court after Griff (Darrell Griffith) was gone until we found our identity," Scooter McCray said. "But everything that had been instilled in us by the '80 championship team—that will, that desire—was still there. It helped get us to two more Final Fours."

1983-84: 24-11. The U of L-UK match made in NCAA heaven finally forced the schools to set regular-season dates. The first was the opener for both schools in Lexington on November 26, when Crum's teams were annually at their worst. Kentucky won 65-44. It seemed a lot of pain was involved with each point the Cardinals managed to scrape up. Four months later they met again, in Rupp Arena again, in the Mideast semifinal. U of L led by four at the half. It was down just two with three minutes to go. Undersized center Charles Jones had somehow neutralized UK's dreaded Twin Towers of Sam Bowie and Melvin Turpin. Dickey Beal, a 5-11 guard, stopped the team in red 72-67.

So, were these 10 Louisville squads among the most respected and feared by insiders? "No question about it," said Arizona coach Lute Olson, boss of Iowa in 1980. "They were well recognized nationally."

"I'd tell my assistants, go find athletic kids who can play more than one position, kids that have no necks but long arms and are split high," then-UCLA coach Larry Brown said. "If you look at Louisville, that was Denny's thing."

"Looking back now you realize how hard it was, but at the time you thought that every year you were one of 10 teams that had a chance to be national champs," said Bill Olsen, Crum's assistant for the first six and athletic director for the last four from '75-84. "Every year. Not many schools today can say they're one of 10."

A chart showing the performances of the 10 NCAA Tournament champions, plus other notables, from 1975 through 1984 is on the following page.

A Game Whose Time Was About to Come

The newspaper cry started two or three seconds after the buzzer sounded ending the 1980 national championship contest.

It's time. Bring it on. Get it on. Start a network bidding war. Play the nation's best and fiercest rivalry (possible apologies: North Carolina-Duke, Indiana-Purdue, maybe a couple others) that has never been played as an in-season game in the modern era.

Louisville versus. Kentucky.

The local guys, mainly the *Courier-Journal's* Billy Reed, went after it first. Reed asked the state legislature to adopt a resolution demanding the game.

New York Times columnist Dave Anderson weighed in next with a yarn about the deadly seriousness of Kentucky's program vs. the laid-backness of Louisville's, and racial tinges that had attached themselves to the teams for years.

A few weeks earlier, before the Final Four, UK president Dr. Otis Singletary said that no one in the Kentucky program "feels UK has anything to gain and possibly has something to lose" by playing Louisville. "The fact is," Singletary said, "we have a pretty good schedule that we worked up over the years—let U of L go build their own program."

D.G. FitzMaurice, sports columnist in the UK heartland, reminded his *Lexington Herald* readers of Singletary's words.

Fitz said this: "It's a game that begs to be played. But Dr. James G. Miller (U of L's president) may feel U of L has nothing to gain and possi-

NCAA TOURNAMENT POWERS 1975-84

Team	A	W-L	CH	RU	T3rd	3rd	4th	RF	RSF	2nd	1st
Louisville	9	19-8	1	0	2	1	0	0	3	1*	1
Kentucky	8	17-7	1	1	1	0	0	2	1	1*	1
Indiana	8	18-6	2	0	0	0	0	2	3	1	0
UCLA	8	18-7	1	1	0	1	0	1	2	2**	0
North Carolina	10	18-9	1	2	0	0	0	1	2	2**	0

(selected others, in alphabetical order)

Team	A	W-L	CH	RU	T3rd	3rd	4th	RF	RSF	2nd	1st
Arkansas	8	9-8	0	0	0	1	0	1	2	2**	2
DePaul	7	8-7	0	0	0	1	0	1	2	3***	0
Georgetown	8	12-7	1	1	0	0	0	1	0	2*	3
Houston	5	12-5	0	2	1	0	0	0	0	0	2
Marquette	8	9-7	1	0	0	0	0	1	1	1	4
Michigan State	2	7-1	1	0	0	0	0	1	0	0	0
No. Caro. State	3	6-2	1	0	0	0	0	0	0	1*	1
Notre Dame	7	9-9	0	0	0	0	1	1	4	1*	0
St. John's	8	5-8	0	0	0	0	0	1	1	2*	4
Syracuse	8	8-9	0	0	0	0	1	0	4	1	2
Villanova	6	9-6	0	0	0	0	0	3	3	0	0
Virginia	5	11-5	0	0	1	1	0	1	1	0	1

Legend: A – NCAA Tournament appearances during 1975-84 period;

W-L – Won-loss record in NCAA Tournament;

CH – National championships;

RU – National runnersup;

T3rd – Tie for national third place (games to decide third and fourth places were discontinued after 1981);

3rd – National third-place finish;

4th – National fourth-place finish;

RF – Lost in regional final;

RSF – Lost in regional semifinal;

2nd– Lost in second round (asterisk indicates team had drawn bye and was playing its first game);

1st – Lost in first round.

bly has something to lose by playing Kentucky." And he added this: "Surely Dr. Miller wouldn't be caught saying, 'The fact is that we have a pretty good schedule that we worked up over the years—let UK go build their own program.' Or would he?"

It took three more years before somebody took someone seriously. When they did, it was worth it. A series was scheduled that was worth playing, worth playing in, worth watching and worth a princely dollar or two to each school's money chest.

No Palace Intrigue on
U of L vs. UK (Some Say)

The Louisville and Kentucky sides yakked and yakked and yanked each other's chain during the 1980 NCAA Tournament.

It was all harsh enough to redefine the word "acrimony" as the Cardinals advanced farther than the Wildcats, got past Louisiana State and headed toward the big prize.

Anybody with half an ear cocked toward the tourney could hear it. Certainly that included NCAA selection committee members, a couple of them maybe devious enough to use their pencils to give this arch non-rivalry a nudge.

For the 1982 show, the boys from Shawnee Mission, Kansas, all but said, "You shall play." They dropped both U of L and UK into the Mideast Regional. Louisville got a No. 3 seed and a first-round bye at Nashville, Tennessee. The Cardinals would meet the winner of Middle Tennessee State and . . . Kentucky! But playing so tight it appeared rigor mortis was setting in, UK was stunned 50-44.

The NCAA was less obvious in 1983. If the schools could each win twice, they'd face off in the Mideast final in Knoxville. In the semifinals, U of L had to squeeze past Arkansas by two points, and UK had to edge Indiana by five, but it happened.

So, did the NCAA, maybe in cahoots with new TV partner CBS (1982), scheme to hook the Cards and Cats into the meeting that has become such a highly anticipated annual regular-season game?

Don't make Denny Crum or Bill Olsen laugh.

"I know the process the selection committee uses does not include input from television," Crum said. "I know all kinds of people on the committee and all will tell you that was never the case. We lived in the same region, and it was logical to play in the same region."

(However, it was logical only after the event was expanded to 48 teams in 1980 and the committee given the ability to seed and move squads around. Prior to that, UK's Southeastern Conference home automatically fed the Mideast Regional and Louisville's Missouri Valley and Metro leagues fed the Midwest.)

But didn't 1982 look suspicious, when CBS signed its first three-year contract and the "selection show" was on live TV for the first time?

"Nope," Crum insisted. "Television had no say-so."

Olsen was U of L's athletic director by 1982.

"Just a quirk," he said. "I don't know how you can prove or disprove that one."

Comics, Critics and Combatants

Where appropriate, we have tried to leave a trail of breadcrumbs attempting to unmask the Louisville Cardinals as humorists, identify how honest they were as self-evaluators and view their worth through the eyes of the enemy. Here's a final lump-sum look at those categories.

The Joke's on Everybody

Not one U of L player was auditioning to become the next Johnny Carson. Their funny stuff wasn't thought up, written into a monologue, practiced and executed. It just sort of fell out of their mouths.

Tony Branch, repeating a Wiley Brownism during the hard-running preseason conditioning drills to shape up the full-court press: "Coach ran us so hard my toenails came off."

Derek Smith, on his battle with newcomer Poncho Wright for the starting small forward spot: "They'll have to roll Poncho into games in a chair with one leg sticking straight out, because I'm going to break it."

Darrell Griffith, answering Roger Burkman's question on whether there's room for one more on a hotel elevator: "It carries 2,000 pounds. Room for 10 people and a roach. Crawl on in, Roger."

Trainer Jerry May, announcing rules for the rental van he is about to drive: "This is your captain. We will be maintaining an altitude of 20 feet. There will be smoking in the first two rows only."

At practice in January, the day after Smith had a shot blocked hard by Kansas State, Marty Pulliam approached with a glass of water. Smith: "What's that for?" Pulliam: "Thought you might still have some leather stuck in your throat."

Griffith, discussing the mistakes people made in the narrow overtime NCAA Tournament escape from Kansas State: "What matters is that we're going to Houston (for the next regional round)." Brown, overhearing: "For a few seconds I was sure you were heading for Dallas." Griffith: "Dallas?" Brown: "Yeah, to that new pro team."

Branch to Griffith, after watching the vertically challenged fellow misfire on a flying dunk in practice (he was 40 for 40 in the season's first 34 games): "If you can't dunk, don't try."

My Fault! No, My Fault!

The Cardinals blamed themselves for things that went wrong. Or they blamed no one. Unless, of course, there was a good opportunity to stick a needle into someone's arm and twist it.

They enjoyed doing that. The recipient was smart enough to know when it was being done with tease instead of malice aforethought. Everyone was man enough to shoulder the load when it came his way. And mad enough to do something about it.

Poncho Wright, coming out of a slump with a five-for-10, 11-point second half against Tulsa: "Coach (Denny Crum) told me to stop worrying about missing a shot or making a mistake. I don't know what's been wrong with me lately."

Darrell Griffith, after contributing to U of L's 17-of-32 free throw demonstration in January against Florida State by hitting three of eight: "I thought it was National Miss Your Free Throw Day."

Wright, after adding eight of eight free throws and 16 points to a third victory over Florida State in March: "That's the best I've ever done at the line. But the guys aren't too happy with me. They were getting me the ball in good shooting position. I should have been taking the ball up more strongly and getting three-point plays. I was costing my buddies an assist each time."

McCray, discussing his in-bounds pass on the magical final play and shot by Tony Branch in the 71-69 OT victory over Kansas State in the Midwest Regional: "I was going to call a timeout if I hadn't seen Wiley." Fourteen seconds remained in overtime, but McCray was very close to a five-second count when he spotted Wiley Brown. McCray was told that Louisville had no timeouts left. "Oh, NO," he said, practically terrified. "I would have given them a technical foul shot!"

Derek Smith, assessing his first half work (two points, two rebounds, two turnovers) and ignoring his 13 points and 10 rebounds overall after beating LSU for a trip to the Final Four: "Wiley and Rod played extremely well. I didn't play worth a daggone."

Eaves, on his combat with LSU big-time point guard Ethan Martin (one for 11 shooting, five turnovers to Eaves' three of three, nine points and zero cough-ups): "It's not like I stopped him. He's too good for that. He just didn't get going."

Six-nine center Marty Pulliam, years later on his role after averaging 2.3 minutes in 12 games: "It was fine with me. I was just along for the ride. Nobody had to tell me that talent-wise I had no business on that team. I faced Rodney McCray every day in practice and got killed every day. But people would rag on me, saying how I got more ink (in the papers) per minute played than anybody in the country. Might be right. We came in for one reunion and I got my picture in the paper. I'm no fool. I got next to Griff and didn't move."

Batten Down the Hatches, Mateys, Here They Come

As early as the first exhibition game, opposing coaches and players were startled by the depths and lengths to which Louisville was willing to go to win games. Especially those who had seen the Cardinals go through patches in the past when it seemed they had just left a hypnotist with a swinging watch.

Sure, Darrell Griffith's elevator still went all the way to the top for stuff(s) that might have been a bit over the top to some. Others had showy moves, too. But this season, power surges, convulsive fast breaks and other things were nailed into place with one thought in mind—the numbers on the scoreboard. Individualism had a seat on the end of the bench. And when the spectacular did happen to erupt, you didn't see a Cardinal banging his fist on his chest or screaming in somebody's face about it.

Marathon AAU guard Floyd Smith, after a 111-72 U of L exhibition victory in November: "They work together, they rebound, they play defense. They have a couple of weaknesses, but you can't notice them the way they hustle. They're very awesome."

Marathon coach Scotty Baesler: "Their press just devastated us. I'd never hold the ball, of course. I'm not sure we could have held it if we'd wanted to."

Marquette coach Hank Raymonds, after a 13-point defeat: "Their defense is what makes them good this year. They're working at it. They're hustling. They're covering up for each other. That's something they didn't do last year. He (Denny Crum) is playing a little bit like John Wooden's teams. He was out there in the glory years, and this looked like the UCLA-type situation."

St. Louis coach Ron Ekker, on U of L's press: "Even when their press doesn't turn the ball loose, it affects the other team physically and emotionally as the game goes on. You lose your persistence, your zest. Louisville's quickness might be its chief asset, or it might be a draw between that and their jumping and shooting ability. But they win on that defense of theirs."

Florida State guard Mickey Dillard, on relentlessness: "Their tempo never changes. Nobody on that team seems to get tired."

Memphis State coach Dana Kirk, on time bombs: "Louisville explodes and intimidates. They do things you don't see every time you walk on the court."

Providence coach Gary Walters, sizing up his team's problem before meeting the Cardinals: "They're the quickest sons of guns in the country. Their offensive rebounding is something else. Lack of passing has been a weakness of theirs in the past. Now it's a strength. We'll try to hold on as long as we can."

Virginia Tech coach Charlie Moir, on his work as a guest analyst for U of L's 88-60 victory over Memphis State: "I'm afraid I wasn't much of a commentator. I got caught up in watching what was going on and enjoying some of the great plays. Louisville can put you completely out of business in a three-minute period."

Cincinnati coach Ed Badger, on U of L's buoyancy in troubled seas: "They have six or seven kids who can beat you. Griffith is their finest player, maybe the finest in the land, but if you hold him down, Smith and Brown will kill you. They can muscle with anybody, no matter the size. On the tough nights, after the tough trips, they win. Somehow, they win."

You Don't Mean *That* Rodney, Do You?

Rodney McCray didn't believe too much in smiling. During his four years in Louisville, if anyone managed to snap a picture of the 6-7 center with the corners of his mouth upturned, and saved it, it would be a rare artifact that could bring high dollar on E-bay.

Walking up to Rod, staring at the scowl, you always asked yourself the question, "Is he really this mad at me?" before you started a conversation. Usually he wasn't. Emphasis on the "usually."

So it must have seemed like an out-of-body experience not too long ago when McCray, who lives in Houston, returned to Louisville for induction into the Kentucky Hall of Fame.

"They had a film with Griff and Wiley talking," he recalled. "When we played, you felt things, but nobody ever talked about them."

Here, on a big screen before a big audience, was Darrell Griffith saying, "If you had to start a team and pick one player to start it, it'd be Rodney McCray." And here was Wiley Brown saying, "Rodney made everybody a whole lot better because he was unselfish and not worried about stats."

"I would like to get a copy of that tape because I was like, 'Who are these guys talking about?'" McCray said. "I felt I did what I was supposed to do—get a good education and help the team win as best I could. We had a lot of love for each other but never discussed it. To hear them say those things made me emotional."

Unbroken Links

One of the true measures of a person's "realness" is what comes later.

Perhaps you were greeted by a big backslap, a "Hey, how ya doing" and an invitation to join the with-it crowd when you were in a position to be useful. Perhaps you were ignored in a "I've never seen this guy before" kind of way five years later when you had become irrelevant.

Athletes and the high, medium or low strobe light cast in their direction makes them susceptible—maybe more so than others—to such critique of their humanity. Were the 1979-80 Cardinals really fused together at the heart, or was their great big season one great big act that dissipated as time moved on?

"Every so often I'd be asked to help carry some of our stuff around," recalled Steve Clark, the walk-on who played in six of 36 games for a total of 11 minutes. "Because I wasn't a scholarship player, I took it that I'd have to help as a 'player-manager.' That kind of bothered me, but I didn't say anything.

"But I remember Darrell (Griffith) saying to me, 'Steve, you need to talk to Coach Crum about that. You're either a player or a manager, but you're not both. I respected Darrell for saying that. I don't remember saying anything to Denny, but Darrell may have said something to somebody, because I don't remember having to do much more after that."

Sports information director Joe Yates remembers coming upon Derek Smith when he was a pro and, with typical Yates wit, blurting out, "Sure wish I had a sweatshirt like that."

Remembers Yates: " 'Here,' he says. Yank. Here it comes. He gave me the shirt off his back."

Greg Deuser played minimally for the Cardinals, too—161 minutes in 22 games.

"As a very minor component of that team, with us being at opposite ends of the spectrum, Griff will always acknowledge me in a crowd," Deuser said. "It gives me some sense of pride that the day-to-day fighting in practice, he appreciated that."

"My stepdad used to work for TWA in Louisville," Clark said. "Whenever Griff flew into town, he always made it a point to find him (in the airport), talk to him and have him tell me he said, 'Hey.' I thought that was a great quality for a guy of his stature."

Clark went to visit his sister in Denver in the mid-'80s. He knew the San Diego Clippers would be in town to play the Nuggets and Smith, a Clipper, should be along. They went to the game.

"I remember yelling down to Derek," Clark said. "He turned around and looked, and I can still remember the smile on his face. It was like his best friend that he hadn't seen in years had just said 'hi' to him.

"He motioned me to meet him after the game. We went out and had a great time. Here he was out of his town, on a hectic schedule, and he found time. And he gave me one of his practice shirts."

Bob Hansen, the Iowa forward beaten by Louisville in the 1980 national semifinals, was drafted by the Utah Jazz four years later. There he found himself on the same team with Griffith and Jerry Eaves. His locker was next to Griffith's.

"These guys were not, you know, clowns," said Hansen, now an Iowa radio analyst. "They were men. They were respectful. They were dedicated. I competed against Darrell every day in practice, and he never mentioned the Final Four games, not once. I have to pinch myself over the years to just have been around him. Darrell, Jerry, their families, they were absolutely the best."

One could almost see Steve Clark's smile widening over the phone as he melted away the years and returned to the teenagers from 1979-80 and geezers Griffith and Branch who led them.

"People come over to the house (in Knoxville, Tennessee) and see all this memorabilia," he said, "and next thing you know friends are going around telling folks I was a star at Louisville. It (the title) is really big to people, bigger than I thought.

"Some had the role of a practice player, some the role of being the one everybody went to at crunch time. My role may have been for other guys to make fun of me.

"But the whole team remembers everybody. There are teams with all the talent in the world who can't pull it together because 'it's all about me.' With us, it wasn't 'all about me.' I couldn't be happier. It was a lifetime experience. I could have gone to a small school and done okay. But there are a lot of players, great players, who have never won a national championship."

Wedging Your Way into a Mindset

Debbie Young, the Louisville athletic director's administrative aide, was at a house for a cookout in 1983 or '84. It began to rain, and the 10 or so people retired to shelter and pulled out a version of Trivial Pursuit.

Young was partnered with Patti Anderson-Turner, who had subbed in the sports information office while Kathy Tronzo was on maternity leave in 1980. The pair landed on a "sports" square, where they could win a wedge of the pie with the correct answer.

The question: "In 1980 who was called Dr. Dunkenstein and led the University of Louisville to the national basketball championship?"

"I said, 'Well, I can answer this,'" Young said.

Another voice argued, "You cannot get a wedge for that question."

Young answered, got the wedge, and had one more thought:

"We're in Trivial Pursuit. We've arrived."

CHAPTER TWELVE

The Season in 3-D:

Denny, Darrell and Derek

DENNY CRUM

After a 30-year turn at the helm of the Louisville Cardinals, Denny Crum resigned in 2001.

It was the only captain's chair he had ever occupied, remarkable for a man who figured to use U of L as a pony express stop on his way back to UCLA when he first arrived in 1971.

He had lived with many unpleasant moments in his last few coaching seasons—investigations, probations, three losing records—and in the final months there were verbal volleys fired from separate offices in the Student Activities Center harsh enough to singe an ear.

It was uncomfortable to watch someone with two national titles, six Final Fours, 675 victories and a 42-23 NCAA Tournament record reach such a strained sporting denouement, but in the end Crum announced his retirement with his head up and a smile on his face.

He had raised the bar to an extreme height in his first 15 years, and his second 15 couldn't get to it. But many of his second generation of players couldn't match the physical and personal standards set by the majority of guys in the first era, either. Plus, the behemoth he was most responsible for constructing—a 19,000-plus following with a waiting list and a multi million dollar operation—had a voracious appetite of demands.

There were plenty of anonymous critics questioning his philosophies, strategies and coaching ability through the 1990s. But any who dared to unmask themselves could expect to be challenged by a large contingent of former players, led by a 1979-80 team wearing armor, brandishing weapons and spoiling for a fight.

Crum had three rules: Be on time, go to class, don't do anything that was not in the best interest of your team. If you wanted to become an adult, fine, go ahead, that was up to you. The '79-80 squad said thank you.

"My parents had raised me to that level," Scooter McCray said. "Now it was time for me to become a man. I have a father. I don't want anybody telling me who to be. I want to make my own mistakes, learn from them and grow."

Reserves Poncho Wright and Daryl Cleveland, for one reason or another, could have groaned at the mention of their head guy. Instead, Cleveland said, "He was straight with you. He treated you like a man. I liked Coach Crum." And Wright said, "He didn't treat you like some little-bitty kid."

The players, the assistants (and most of all, the wretches with pens and cameras) also knew they were not going to win any debates with this smart, quick-thinking, mathematical problem-solving CEO over something in his own company.

Tony Branch remembered Crum trying to get him in shoot-from-the-corner contests, a deadly spot for the coach.

"I'd say, 'Let's play one on one,' " Branch said. "He'd never play one on one and I'd never shoot from the corner."

It was maddening to get in the most miniscule of disagreements with him, because you would always lose. But his supreme belief in his own supremacy gave Crum a unique calmness in an agitated profession. He was relentless in teaching specifics. He was eerily successful on play calls at the ends of games. It must have led to extra frayed nerves for the guy on the opposing bench.

"I wish someone had the ability to go back and look at statistics after a game decided by five points or less and figure out our conversion rate percentage," Greg Deuser said. "I'll bet it was tremendously high."

Roger Burkman: "Any time we needed a stop or a basket, he'd call something the opponent hadn't seen. Nine out of 10 times it'd work. Great game coach. Best I've ever seen."

Branch: "If we were up one, down one or tied, and he'd say, 'If you do what I tell you to do, this is going to work,' we believed."

He tried to build each team slowly and deliberately, so it would become a crescendo in February and March. That didn't always happen but, as one example, he was 7-7 in his first 14 season openers and 36-2 in the Februarys of 1980-81-82-83.

"Denny's recruits were always really athletic and had the kind of good size where he could switch everything defensively," Arizona coach Lute

Olson said in 2004. "His defenses created a lot of problems for everyone they played. He was the guy, Mr. March or whatever, because his teams always seemed to be there when they needed to be for the playoffs."

Crum experimented with various combinations, discovering who did what best and who fit best with whom. When the Cardinals reached the business portion of the schedule, pieces were in place, the system was installed and the players could generally execute from a position of strength and confidence.

He did it with the calm and precision of a teacher and with hardly a vulgarity ever leaving his lips. An occasional "hell" or "damn." Anything stronger took something like an incident at Cincinnati in the early '70s, when someone poured a soft drink on his head while he stood in a rampway conducting an impromptu press conference.

"He never cussed, at least never around me in any of the practices," said Steve Clark, a freshman walk-on in 1979-80. "You knew you were in trouble if he called you 'Buster,' something like, 'You got out of control, Buster.' He didn't have to use tirades or cusswords to get people to perform. I think that's a trait anyone would like to have."

"I don't remember him having a temper tantrum," equipment manager Bosey Thrasher said. "For him not to do that is amazing."

Bill Olsen, then the assistant head coach, had his share of contentious exchanges with the head man through the '70s. He never won one as far as anyone knew. That may not have set well with the ex-Marine then, but he was okay with it later.

"One person makes the final decision," Olsen said. "That's why we won. I don't think there was anyone in coaching, maybe not to this day, who was able to play the percentages, think clearly and stick to the gameplan like Denny."

How deeply were Crum's fingerprints embedded in the 1980 championship? Deeply. But the fiery defense he'll offer on most subjects was the opposite of his response if you tried to give him credit for the title. He was mostly happy to see Darrell Griffith and Branch get some dessert, win 15 games and muzzle critics—for a few months, anyway.

He mentioned contributions of about everybody on the squad, and said, "I had two seniors (Griff and Branch) in different roles who provided leadership I don't know that I had on any other team. Those two were amazing."

Mention Denny Crum and most will have the same vision Iowa guard Bob Hansen still does.

"That rolled-up program, the red sport coat, calmness on the court," Hansen said. "Not an in-your-face-type guy. Not one to intimidate the opposition. Not one to rant and rave. He seemed to be a man of few words, and maybe that comes from the John Wooden tree. But that year Denny knew what he had—men who could handle it."

Mid-October 1979 to mid-April 1980 was a life experience so exceptionally rich and fulfilling it should be preserved in a time capsule, a pain pill to be taken for relief on a sick day. Then the Cardinals went and won a national championship to boot. Man! They didn't have to do that. Watching them play and getting to know them as plain folk made the ticket to ride on this caravan impossibly cheap.

They were, indeed, "men who could handle it." Coaches who could handle it. Support people, too. Credit goes to all of them. Equally. That's why they call it team.

DARRELL GRIFFITH

Darrell Griffith spent three years walking around a University of Louisville campus filled with snipers in trees.

Can't play fundamental basketball. Careless. Doesn't play defense. Won't focus on free throws. Can't dribble. Won't play team basketball. Hot dog.

The shots came from all directions. Some came so close he heard them whine by. But he was never wounded.

"My father always said, 'As long as you're doing the right thing, let things people say hit your shoulder and bounce off,'" Griffith said. "I let my game do my talking."

Whether his game was talking clearly or its voice was hoarse, Griffith was often in line to be tarred and feathered if the team went bad, too.

"He was always looked at as an underachiever until his senior year," sports information director Joe Yates said. "The prominent booster types were always looking for some kind of reason Louisville didn't win. If Griff got 24 points, he should have had 36, that type of stuff."

Some of the shots also came from people who practiced in the same gym he did.

Ballhog. Selfish. Not a team player. My time in the limelight, not his.

"College sports is a life's lessons experience," Griffith said. "and there are going to be times when you run across all the things you heard about prior—dissension, whatever. If you shined, there was always going to be someone wanting to take the glare off that shine.

"I was a team player. God gave me a special talent to do certain things. Some people might not be able to deal with that, and you needed to prepare yourself for that. It (what they said) didn't bother me. My job was to win."

Some of the criticisms were far from the truth. Some, not that far. But what do you do with a 48-inch vertical and a simon-pure jump shot? Do you say, "Make sure you're always in good defensive position and don't jump so high?"

Wade Houston, the U of L assistant who was Griffith's high school coach at Male, addressed the internal sniping.

"It's a testament to his character that he didn't allow himself to be influenced by some of the older guys and was able to stay focused on what he needed to do," Houston said.

Houston also took a swat at the fundamentalists.

"The players that are great fundamentally are the ones that don't have that much talent," Houston said. "Darrell's problem was that he was so gifted he could do things just on talent."

The coaching staff understood, but still had its maddening episodes.

"Denny (Crum) was very strong with him on many occasions," assistant Bill Olsen said. "Because of his great ability, he had a tendency not to play defense fundamentally the way he could and should. He'd take chances, gamble, get overcommitted, and in games where he got in foul trouble he'd be taken out because he wasn't playing any defense.

"But I never remember him arguing with Coach Crum or even showing any facial expressions that he was upset in any way."

That was also Griff. If he'd made someone mad, whether he knew why or not, well, hey, Coach, here's a hug.

Houston smiled.

"If he's back defensively against the break, instead of breaking his body down, sliding his feet and doing the things fundamentally correctly, he might let a guy go by him, then go up and pin the shot on the glass," Houston said. "Was that good fundamental basketball? No. Did people enjoy seeing it and did he enjoy doing it? Yeah.

"I don't think Denny was enamored of some of the things he did, but Darrell was the kind of guy who would come up, pat you on the butt as you were chewing him out, and you'd end up hugging him back."

Houston's smile turned into a chuckle. He had thought of a pretty good example.

"In my first year at Male (1973-74) we're playing Jack Givens and (Lexington) Bryan Station in the quarterfinals of the State Tournament at Freedom Hall," he said. "We're down 10-12 points in the first half (to one of the tourney favorites). We're playing tight, not getting anything done.

"We're walking to the locker room at halftime and Darrell (then a sophomore) and I happen to be walking together. I'm saying, 'Griff, you've got to stop letting (future University of Kentucky star) Givens go (drive along the) baseline. He likes to go baseline. He's left-handed.'

"He kind of smiles at me, like everything I've just said has gone right over his head. He whacks me on the butt and says, 'Coach, we got this one. Don't even worry about it.' We come out in the second half and it was like he had a vision, like the first half was just toys to him (and Male won 84-75)."

But the pieces of Griff that people ignored or didn't know about—work ethic, intelligence on court and in classroom, a strength of character that kept mind-altering agents out of his life, kindness to others, determination to succeed and ability to lead—would all surface eventually.

Rodney McCray had only heard stories about Griffith.

"All I knew was that he could jump over people," McCray recalled. "They ain't telling me he can shoot jump shots like he did and defend and . . . that he's got a 48-inch vertical. Then you see him work as hard as he worked. This guy is no joke. And he always talked positive—'Let's take care of business,' 'Let's go, we're going to win this one.' That's the kind of guy you want to fall in step behind."

Tony Branch was Griffith's teammate for four years.

"He only knew one speed in practice—full," Branch said. "He was Reckless Abandon. Someone who could jump like that, you had to protect him. He was not from this planet."

Griffith knew he could be a one-man S.W.A.T. unit if he wanted. He didn't want. Winning was more comforting than leaping. But as a subtle reminder his senior year, Greg Deuser remembered a ritual performed by Olsen before most tipoffs.

"I believe I recall Bill saying to Griff, 'Go ahead and make your impact on the game, but get everybody involved,'" Deuser said. "It got to be a habit, even though Griff was very much oriented toward getting the whole team involved."

"Deuser was pretty observant," Olsen said. "I don't remember exactly how I'd say it to him, but it was just a friendly reminder. It seemed to take some pressure off him."

Griffith, 46 in June of 2004, doesn't play basketball anymore. The foot he broke late in his 10-year stand with the Utah Jazz that led to the end of his pro career has healed, but the springs that were constructed on a celestial plain and loaded into his legs have gathered rust.

"I've got knee problems from the jumping, the wear and tear," he said. "Don't check my vertical now."

He's done well, though. Nice house. Own charitable foundation. Partner in a telecommunications company.

Asked about playing at current NBA prices, he said, "Oh, man, rewind the clock. Let me be a second (overall) pick (as he was in 1980) coming out now."

But he also said, "You've got to look at the time period you served. Charles Barkley came up to me at an All-Star game, hugged me and said,

'I just want to thank you guys. You're the ones who have enabled me to do what I'm doing now.' I could go back and hug the Walt Fraziers and Elgin Baylors. I've been blessed."

Blessed? Jack Lengyel, the 1980 Louisville interim athletic director who went on to a longtime AD post at Navy, was asked his most memorable impression from that season. He spoke for many.

"Darrell Griffith's leadership on and off the court," he said. "He signed autographs after games until he was the last person left. He was the most humble, gracious person. In my 40-some years as a coach or AD, one of the best role models, student-athletes, gentlemen, outstanding performers and public relations persons would be Darrell Griffith. He is cast in the mold of (Navy sports heroes) Roger Staubach, David Robinson and Joe Bellino."

So let us raise a Stein to His Griffness, and then cast it fiercely downward through an iron hoop.

DEREK SMITH

At the 1979-80 Louisville Cardinals' 15-year reunion in 1995, Marty Pulliam walked up to Derek Smith and stuck out his hand.

"Instead he gave me a hug," Pulliam remembered, "and said, 'You have to hug people because you never know who's not going to be here next time.'"

Smith had made a special effort to get to that gathering. It was in February, he was in his first season as an assistant coach for the Washington Bullets, and he had taken the occasion of the NBA's All-Star break for a quickie Florida vacation with Monica, daughter Sydney and son Nolan.

On the radio he heard "This Is It," the Kenny Loggins song that became U of L's anthem in 1980, jumped on a plane, attended the reunion and flew back to Florida the next day.

The next reunion was in 2000.

"It was Derek who wasn't there," Pulliam said. "I spent most of three days avoiding Monica because I didn't know what to say. Finally I went up to her, hugged her and said, 'I'm sorry I didn't come up before, but I just couldn't think of anything to say. I still can't find any words.' She nodded, like she understood."

The Smiths were on a cruise with a large portion of the Bullets organization in August of 1996. The ship was returning from Bermuda when Derek sat down to dinner on the 9th. After eating, he suddenly collapsed. In minutes, he was gone.

"There was a chair left empty on the stage where we were sitting," Pulliam said of the 2000 reunion. "I don't know if it was on purpose, just extra or what. Griff (Darrell Griffith) asked Derek's boy to come up and sit with us. He hung out with us the rest of the week, signing autographs and everything."

"It was like Nolan took his father's place," Daryl Cleveland said. "It made a world of difference to us."

Derek Smith was 34. He had energized the lives of more kids, enlightened the understanding of more adults and pulled himself through more stages of worldliness in less than half a lifetime than most of us could have accomplished in two.

Chasing Degrees, Rebounds and Recognition

Derek Smith walked around with chips of various shapes, sizes and types on his shoulder. No wonder.

As a basketball player, he was first a "sleeper," basically unknown, and then a "tweener," at 6-6 caught in the NBA abyss between big guard and small forward.

As a person, he came from little money with a mom working hard to run a family of five sons and a daughter by herself. His life experiences were, to be generous, constrained.

As a student, he had diction problems, lacked good study habits and was awestruck by the challenge of college courses.

Combined, this was a recipe for failure. Except that his enormous hands that swallowed basketballs were matched by an enormous heart. And by an enormously rare personality trait—his word was golden. Whether you liked what you heard or not, it came straight and honestly from the big ticker.

The Student

Smith was 16 when he arrived on campus for his freshman year. Basketball camps were going on. He was interviewed by a local TV crew. Later he was in the lounge when the interview aired. He stammered and was hard to understand. Some campers began to laugh.

"I saw this guy who looked like me and was talking but didn't sound the way I talked," Smith told assistant coach Bill Olsen. "I went up to my room and cried."

"I was told he was so embarrassed he wanted to crawl under a rock," Monica Smith said.

"I told him that was why he was at the university," Olsen said. "We could get him in public speaking courses and voice diction classes."

Let's get to it, Smith said. His desire to succeed, an intellect about to burst forth and the fact that he actually enjoyed going to class took over. He didn't graduate "on time" in 1982, but took classes during the NBA off seasons and returned in 1991 to don a cap and gown and proudly participate in the ceremonies.

"When I was a freshman," he told *Courier-Journal* columnist Rick Bozich in '91, "every night when I said my prayers I prayed I wouldn't flunk out. Getting my degree wasn't about money. It was about proving I could do something."

"He was a solid B-C student, and a better student, an 'A' student, in summer classes after he was in the NBA," recalled Tim Hynes, then the theatre arts department head. "He had a high level of intelligence, a sense of direction and a loyalty by promising his mother and himself to get a degree. He was among the most competitive people I'd ever met. Also one of the most gracious—but not on a ball court."

The sports information people, Joe Yates, John Crawley and Kathy Tronzo, put their media training wheels on Smith.

"He was shy at first, then when he'd start yapping he'd be going, bang, 100 miles an hour," Crawley remembered. "You'd say, 'Derek, s-l-o-w down, enunciate. It's going to help you in the long run.' And he did. He was very receptive and worked very hard at it. He knew we weren't criticizing him. By the end he was one of the most quotable guys you could ever have."

In not too long a time, Smith morphed into a persona impossible to duplicate. Olsen called him Will Rogers come back to life. There might have been slices of Garrison Keillor, Jim Carrey and Kermit the Frog in there, too.

It was as if all those wonderful, demented, perceptive sayings and observances had been locked behind Smith's frontal lobe, jumping up and down and pounding on the door to get out. Once he developed the proper elocution, they tumbled one over the other into the listening audience.

He talked of being Gilligan from the Island one minute and from Jupiter the next. He wore a pair of giant "Jupitian" glasses after one game and got a "bald-slicker" shaved head at a barber shop to "lighten the top for better rebounding."

On his expectations for a day, he said, "I don't ever wake up with a bad attitude. If one of my classes isn't going well, I won't let it get me down. Life is something to be proud of." And on recovery from homesickness in Hawaii: "Sitting around and being down is not me. I've got to have a trick in my pocket. I'm loose again. I'm thinking about my studies and thinking about winning it all."

Remembered Olsen: "Even before he became polished, once you understood Derek, he made perfect sense even if it wasn't grammatically perfect. It was so uninhibited. So natural. It was so enjoyable just to be around him. I could sit and listen to him for hours."

As could his wife, Monica.

"By the time he reached manhood," she said, "he had lived far beyond his years."

The Basketball Player

The shoulder chips were never more prevalent than when Smith hit the hardwood. He brought steel and fire to the Freedom Hall game court and meanness and nastiness to the Crawford Gym practice floor.

Poncho Wright was his protagonist and erstwhile tackling dummy for three years.

"He was so tenacious," Wright said. "He did things within the rules, and out of the rules, but I never ran into a guy who played harder. I was his main adversary—he on the white team, me on the red, us guarding each other. There were no square-offs. No need to lose your head. Just him pushing me. It helped me as a player."

Smith was off the radar screen in high school until the last minute. He had to battle for a place on the screen at U of L. The pro draft brought more headaches.

He finished No. 1 at Louisville in career field goal percentage, No. 2 in points and No. 5 in rebounds and was still an undersold commodity.

"When he came out, in most circumstances he'd have been a first-rounder," Rodney McCray said. "But he was a 6-6 small forward, and in the pros he'd have to be a two-guard. When James Worthy and Dominique (Wilkins) declared early, he got pushed back."

He was drafted in the second round, No. 35 overall, by Golden State. He played in 27 games and averaged 5.7 minutes, then was gone. "A tweener," Monica Smith said. "That's why they cut him."

He caught on with the San Diego/Los Angeles Clippers, still whittling furiously at those chips, and in 1984-85 had the most glorious of breakthroughs. Starting 80 games, he shot 54 percent from the field, 79 percent from the line, averaged 22.1 points and 5.3 rebounds, dunked on Michael Jordan and was considered one of the five best shooting guards in the NBA.

The next season, 11 games in and averaging 23.5 points, he blew out his knee. "Then the Clippers cut him, too," Monica said.

The knee was never the same, but Smith hung on for five more seasons with four other teams, averaging between 8.7 and 16 points in four of them.

"When I moved to California (in the early '90s), the Clippers were a second-rate team," Wright said. "But Derek was known in Los Angeles just like he was in Louisville."

The Person

Smith's need to be recognized dribbled off the court, too.

When Darrell Griffith graduated, Smith thought the bulk of the publicity should gravitate to him, the No. 2 scorer and No. 1 rebounder from the national champs. He was seeing the McCray name too often, particularly the younger Rodney's, a whippersnapper getting more headlines than a vet.

"Rodney got a bunch of them," sports information director Joe Yates said. "Scooter, being transitioned from position to position and still having the big high school rep, was getting plenty of ink. Derek was most paranoid about Rodney. From time to time he'd say, 'You like him better than me, so you all are working harder for him.' Which was not true. We'd take whatever we could get for anybody."

Teammates could get Smith's dander up by pretending a player he'd be checking on a given night was in line for a "player of the year" award or something. He'd also get upset when he felt the Cardinals in general also weren't getting their rightful due in the papers.

Manager Randy Bufford remembered the non-swimming Smith being tossed into the U of L pool and coming up scared and mad. And the time his Georgia "buddies" kidded him without letup about how painful a trip to the dentist was going to be—he became so frazzled the novocaine had no effect and the doctor couldn't work on him.

Derek Smith was flailing at whatever Quixote-like windmills appeared.

"He'd say, 'I'm going to prove it to . . . whomever, whatever,'" Monica Smith said. "He didn't even think about the NBA until after Griff got drafted because he had to prove so much to others. After that he couldn't do anything behind anybody. He had to be a leader.

"To know him was to love him. But if you didn't know him, you might not have liked him, because he didn't bite his tongue."

Derek and Monica arrived jointly at U of L in 1978 and never parted. Watching him grow from age 16 to 34, Monica had the best view of Smith's transcendency from a tongue-tied, "ernge (orange)"-eating, no-clue kid to the worldly traveler dispensing warmth and the king's English wherever he went.

"I run into so many people who say he had such an impact on their lives, and as I've had time to reflect on it I have to sit back and say, 'Wow,'" said Monica, now a paralegal with Washington Sports and Entertainment, owner of the NBA Wizards (formerly Bullets). "He spoke at one high school and one college graduation, and the things people said to him, that was like, 'Wow'.

"How could a person change his leopard stripes like that? Well, he did. When he left Hogansville he was one person, and when he went back, he was another."

Each summer during his NBA years when he returned to Louisville to work with kids in camps, he was more vibrant. When he came back for three full years, 1991-94, his heart reached increasingly deeper into the community.

He established basketball camps and a golf tournament to benefit Family Health Centers, an arm of which is Boys & Girls Clubs of Kentucky, "his passion," Monica said. She continues the golf tourney.

He sat on the board of the Louisville Ballet, starting a program to bring arts to kids who knew little more than dribbles. He sat on the board of the Home of the Innocents, a place for youngsters in need.

And he loved being home.

"He made it a family trip to go to 7-11s and get slurpys," she said. "We went everywhere, always as a family. He was home every night at supper-time, putting the final exclamation point on what family meant to him. Not many people came close to what he stood for as a father. He was truly my hero, too."

Bosey Thrasher, U of L's equipment man, smiled and gently shook his head.

"Derek never met a stranger," he said. "He'd come up to you point to your chest, you'd look down and he'd run his finger up your face. He seemed like one of those guys who never had a bad day, or at least wouldn't show it. And he seemed like one of those guys who never got the recognition he deserved."

Seemed like it. Smith thought so. But a personality that never made it to a billboard dug deeply into the souls of a great many people. Derek Smith reached out, ran a finger up a bunch of faces and left everlasting imprints.

A Searing, Inexplicable Loss

At first they thought Derek Smith died of respiratory arrest. He had been taking medicine for motion sickness aboard the Norwegian cruise ship Dreamward as it returned from Bermuda on August 9, 1996.

Next doctors guessed that he could have had a severe allergic reaction to something he ate.

Finally, in early September, an autopsy revealed he was lost to a fairly common—but rarely fatal—heart defect, an abnormal heart rhythm caused by the thickening of a heart valve.

No trace of seasickness medicine, alcohol or any "drug of abuse" was found in his system. "An extremely rare event," said Dr. Barry Maron, a Minneapolis cardiologist who had studied sudden death in young athletes.

Gone. At age 34. No history of trouble. No warning. The killer wasn't even a threat to the majority of the few people who had it. And it was his heart! Who had a bigger, better heart than Derek Smith? How utterly unfair.

The men from 1980 were so completely stunned.

Seven years later:

Joe Yates, the SID who had his aggravating moments with the bloke from Hogansville: "How tragic that he is not with us any more. That he had a heart attack on a ship. No way. Not this guy. His heart was as big as the world."

In the days following the shock:

Jerry Eaves: "It's a hell of a loss. A hell of a loss for the community, more importantly for his family. We're going to have to help Monica, Nolan and Sydney. We're going to have to rally, step up and do our damndest. You look at immortality, you look at Derek, so strong and full of life. That's probably the scary thing."

Darrell Griffith: "Basketball was just an added value to him."

Bill Olsen: "His loss is bigger than us. It's a loss to society."

Scooter McCray, at the funeral: "Derek touched all of us. That's why we're all here. We need to carry that love and touch somebody else."

Denny Crum, at the memorial service: "When I think about Derek, I think about what it's possible to do."

Dozens of NBA and former Louisville players attended the funeral. One was multiple all-star Charles Barkley, who would have been able to give Smith lessons in outspokenness.

"Usually when you go to a funeral, people say great things about a person who really wasn't a good person," Barkley told *Courier-Journal* columnist Rick Bozich. "With Derek it's the opposite. You can't say enough good things about him. The world is a poorer place than it was a week ago."

CHAPTER THIRTEEN

Where and Who Are They Now

Denny Crum looks as if he's busier than when he was coaching, thus bringing up the age-old cry of the retiree, "How did I ever get things done when I was really working?"

Darrell Griffith seems to be involved in as many different operations as he has fingers.

Jerry Eaves has just emerged from his first college head-coaching season, one that would drive many to Sigmund Freud's couch, with a feeling of joy apparently not unlike the one he had two decades ago.

Tony Branch has just emerged from a high school head-coaching season that he can stuff in the scrapbook next to the one from long ago, despite a rough finish.

Others run their own companies, supervise for companies, build things, fund-raise and develop things creatively, analyze portfolios, run printing teams and help Don Zimmer recover from Pedro Martinez' takedown.

And Wade Houston . . . well, we should probably call him His Wadeness whenever we can. The assistant cum prankster eventually ran his own big-time program, left basketball after being bounced off a wall or two for five years, and began to expand on fledgling businesses in the private sector he had dabbled in earlier with an old friend.

He and wife Alice (and the old friend) now seem to own a goodly portion of Louisville, earning Wade at least something close to one of the stage names his young levitating protégé named Griffith carried a quarter-century ago.

Eleven of the 13 players have college degrees, some being prodded toward that achievement years later by teammates. Poncho Wright said he would still need five to eight elective courses and Daryl Cleveland said he is about a semester and a half short.

Six of the 13 got anywhere from a sip of coffee in the National Basketball Association to a full pot. Two others played in Europe and the Middle East and one of them had two years on a National Football League roster.

A look at who and where the 1979-80 coaches, players and some support troops were as of spring, 2003:

THE COACHES

Denny Crum

After 30 seasons, all at Louisville, Denny Crum resigned in 2001. He did not receive a gold watch upon departure, but an eight-million-dollar check made for a lovely parting gift.

He had signed up in 1971 for about $20,000 and had a base salary in the high 30s when he won his first title. Now eight million dollars? Considering the physical strides the university had made and the stature it had reached, much of it in response to Crum's body of work in the first 15 years, U of L might have gotten off cheap.

His final record was 675-295. He won two national championships. His teams made six Final Fours, seven Elite Eights, six Sweet Sixteens and 23 NCAA Tournaments.

When he retired he was tied for fourth among all coaches with the six Final Fours, tied for sixth with five Final Four victories, tied for fourth with two titles, tied for fourth with 42 tournament triumphs and tied for 17th on the list of coaches with most seasons at one school.

In 1994 he was elected to the Basketball Hall of Fame. He won 20 or more games his first 13 seasons and 21 campaigns in all, the latter then good for eighth all time. His 675 victories placed him 15th on that list in 2001.

Golf, fishing and hunting used to be big-time escape mechanisms for him. He still does all three, but generally restricts golf to fund-raising events and hunting to game birds.

His charity involvement is enormous: (1) American Cancer Society's golf tournament chairman; (2) Cystic Fibrosis fund-raiser and golf tourney chair; (3) Denny Crum Scholarship Fund, awarding grants to greater Louisville area students who meet certain criteria and plan to attend area colleges (15 in 2003-04); (4) Spina Bifida golf tourney chair and fund-raiser; (5) a program where he reads books to students at Jefferson County (Louisville) schools; (6) fund-raising for the Library Fund, and (7) chair of a golf tournament for Friends For Michael, a fund established for golfer Michael Brett when he became paralyzed, proceeds going to Louisville's Frazier Rehab Institute.

He's also on a hospital board, speaks often to alumni groups in and out of town and has begun a radio call-in show with former coaching rival Joe B. Hall of Kentucky.

He is partners in a place in Idaho hard by a good-fishing lake and gets to Alaska "two or three" times a year.

Is he too busy? "I can't remember when I wasn't busy," he said.

Daughter Cindy and son Steve each have two children. Son Scott works in the music industry in Louisville. Crum is married to the former Susan Sweeney, an anchor for a television station in Louisville.

Bill Olsen

Olsen, a Louisville graduate and one-time high school head coach, assisted U of L's John Dromo and Crum for 12 seasons before being named athletic director in 1980. He stayed in the latter position seventeen years, laying the financial foundation that pushed the athletic department deeply into the black ink, before retiring January 1, 1998.

The things he is proudest of during his tenure as AD, in order: (1) Renovation of Freedom Hall; (2) achieving self-sufficiency of the athletic department after entering with a two-million-dollar subsidy from the school's general fund and exiting with its own 50-million-dollar reserve fund; (3) recruitment of football coach Howard Schnellenberger; (4) football team winning the 1991 Fiesta Bowl, and (5) building Papa John's Cardinal Stadium, the school's own football facility.

Life now includes a large amount of travel other than buses that break down and planes that don't take off. He and Sharon's three children, Lynn, Doug and David, are scattered throughout the southeast heavily involved in their own businesses.

Wade Houston

Houston played for U of L from 1963-66, coached at two Louisville high schools from 1966-76 with one year out to play in France, then assisted Denny Crum from 1976-77 through 1988-89.

He was offered the head job at Tennessee for the 1989-90 campaign, accepted and took along his immensely talented son, Allan, whom Crum graciously allowed out of the letter of intent he had signed with Louisville.

Although Allan was a Southeastern Conference superstar, the seasons were often rocky for Wade, and after the 1993-94 season he was gone.

But in 1979 Houston had linked up with fellow 1966 grad Charlie Johnson, a former U of L and pro football player who was then a supervisor at Louisville's Ford auto plant.

They tried their hand at operating three small grocery stores at different times, but the venture lasted only three years.

In 1983 they secured a contract to deliver in-bound truck parts to the Ford plant and formed Johnson-Houston Corp. In 1986 Ford offered them the chance to deliver the finished product to dealers throughout the Midwest and Southeast, and the pair formed Active Transportation with a third partner in Chicago, Jupiter Corp.

In 1994 Houston quit coaching, the principal owner of the Chicago firm died, and Johnson and Houston obtained a $54 million bank loan to buy the transportation division of Jupiter.

They instantly went from two companies to six: Dallas & Mavis (hauling steel, aluminum and heavy machinery, run by Houston); Automotive Carrier Services (handling big-rig cross-country transport, run by Wade's wife, Alice); Active Transportation (run by Johnson); ATC Leasing (leasing all equipment plus other functions, run by new minority partner Dennis Troha); Johnson-Houston Transportation (the parts delivery service), and HJI—Houston-Johnson Inc. (a warehousing, logistics and distribution center not operating until 1994).

In 2002 they got into a dry ice business used to quickly clean things like vehicle engines arriving from Europe for Ford.

"From 1994 to 2001 Charlie's and Alice's companies controlled about 80 percent of all the (delivery) traffic produced by all heavy-duty trucks built in the U.S.," Wade said. "So, after falling on our face in the grocery stores..."

The Houstons have three children—Allan, a megastar with the New York Knicks; Lynn, an industrial engineer who has developed software for Johnson-Houston, and Natalie, a resident in dermatology at U of L.

Houston, 59 in October of 2003, said he and Alice have talked about retiring to Miami, Florida, where the dry-ice company has an office, when the time comes. He didn't say how much of Miami he planned to buy.

Jerry Jones

After 1980, Jones became a "permanent part-time" coach. He wasn't allowed to recruit, and he was under a restricted earnings mandate from the athletic department.

He was mainly employed (and paid by) the school's administration, and continued to coach some through 1995. By 1996 he was working solely for Louisville's president until officially retiring the last day of 1999.

He says he plays a lot of golf and substitute teaches at an Indiana junior high school. He and Beverly have three daughters—Sherry, Nancy, and Kathy.

THE PLAYERS

Tony Branch

One of Louisville's two seniors in '79-80, Branch stayed on as a graduate assistant while picking up his degree with three more classes.

He then climbed aboard the coaching carousel—assistant jobs at Manhattan, Purdue, Tulsa and Lamar and two seasons as head coach at Division I Lamar, where he couldn't win enough games to keep his job but stayed on in administration there until 1992.

He returned to Louisville, got his master's in teaching and took a job at All Saints Academy, a Catholic elementary and middle school, as principal and fund-raiser. In 1998 he moved to Seneca High School, a public school where he taught U.S. History and African-American History and became head coach of the basketball team.

In 2003-04 Seneca won 26 of 32 games and was ranked 15th in Kentucky by the end of the season, but lost in the first round of its regional.

"I like this level," Branch said. "When my kids get older and off to college I might consider a part-time thing somewhere, but college coaching is a very insecure profession. We all like it here."

Branch and his wife, Margaret, have three children.

Wiley Brown

Brown returned for the 1980-81 season in not nearly the shape he was in for '79-80 and didn't start his last two seasons. But he had enough athletic gifts to catch on with Philadelphia of the NFL for two seasons.

Georgia's Player of the Year as a tight end-defensive end his senior year in high school played only on special teams as a tight end for the Eagles in 1982 and was hurt and released in '83.

"It took a whole year to get back in football shape," Brown said. "If I had it to do over again, I would have played one year of football at U of L."

Back to basketball. He played 1984-85 with the semi-pro Louisville Catbirds, then headed overseas for six seasons in Spain, France, Israel and Belgium.

In 1991 he came back to Louisville and went to work for a furniture company. In '92 he was hired by U of L in the strength and conditioning department, completed his degree requirements and two years later was promoted to strength and conditioning coach. He's been there ever since.

In March of 2004 he was 43 years of age, "old and broke down," he said, but he didn't look like it.

Son Caleb was born to Brown and his wife, Anne Marie, on April 1, 2003. He has two other children.

Roger Burkman

Disruptive reserve Burkman played six games with the Chicago Bulls in 1981-82, scoring five points before being released. He finished the season with a Continental Basketball Association team in Anchorage, Alaska, and was drafted the next season by the CBA's Lima, Ohio, club.

He was contemplating going overseas when Crum said he had a student assistant spot open. Burkman took it and finished the nine hours he needed for a degree.

He then worked for Pepsi-Cola from 1984-90 in sales and marketing and moved to Louisville's DeSales High School as development director from 1991-94. Since 1995 he has been the senior development director for Louisville's Trinity High School.

He is married to the former Judy McDonald, a judge in Louisville. They have a son and daughter.

Steve Clark

Clark, the non-scholarship freshman who gained a spot on the travel squad because of Scooter McCray's injury, stayed on the team for two more seasons before Wade Houston told him that playing time was going to be at best negligible in 1982-83.

He switched majors and left short of a degree in '83 to run a Pic 'N' Pay shoe store in Huntsville, Alabama.

He moved up in that corporation, learned how to build the stores and set them up, moved to the home office in Dallas and then to Charlotte, North Carolina, in 1986.

By then he was a construction manager. He left Pic 'N' Pay for a women's retail clothing company in Charlotte, then another—Goody's Family Clothing—in Knoxville, Tennessee.

In 2002 he hired on with Sun Belt General Contractors of Atlanta, but stayed in Knoxville where he opened a Sun Belt office. He is now a vice-president of a company that also builds stores and does "$50-60 million worth of business a year." He said his role is to supervise a general contractor after the contractor is hired.

Clark and wife Karen have two sons and a daughter.

Daryl Cleveland

Cleveland, the man who stirred Freedom Hall crowds whenever he left the bench, worked for Walgreen Drug Stores from 1982-90.

He then moved to Hamilton Printing Inc., which does the bulk of the University of Louisville's print work, and is now a supervisor in shipping and receiving.

He has two teenagers by a first marriage. He and his wife, Sharon, have been married 11 years.

Greg Deuser

It took backup guard Deuser five years to get out of the U of L, but he took with him an engineering degree and "probably a liberal arts education" while participating in a co-op program every other semester.

He started with a structural engineering firm, Senler-Campbell & Associates Inc., which was the primary renovator of Freedom Hall. "I can tell that now that it's still standing," Deuser said.

After two years he moved into the business world, working in money management for a capital management firm and taking a shot at his own management company.

In 2000 he joined his brother's engineering firm—Space Hardware Optimization Technology (SHOT)—as chief financial officer. "Our world headquarters was in the only office building in Galena (Indiana) that I'm aware of," Deuser said.

SHOT had a contract with NASA to provide equipment for space shuttles and space stations, and a $30 million deal in cooperation with Indiana University to design experiments for mice in space. But in early 2002, shortly after 9/11 but not because of it, NASA had to cut back several programs. That NASA contract dropped from seven million dollars of revenue to $700,000 overnight, Deuser said.

Deuser left and returned to the money management side. He is now a portfolio manager for a private client group with National City Bank. He and his wife, Annette, have one son.

Jerry Eaves

The Louisville point guard made the honorable mention All-America list his senior season and was selected in the third round of the 1982 NBA draft by the Utah Jazz.

He played in 162 of 164 games his first two years, averaging 19.4 minutes the first and 12.9 the second and making the all-rookie second team in '82-83. After that it was three games with the Atlanta Hawks in '84-85, a year in Manila, the Philippines, and three games with Sacramento in '86-87. He averaged 6.7 points and 2.5 assists in 168 NBA games, eight of them starts.

From 1987-90 he was assistant to a vice president for a life insurance company in Dallas, but found the basketball bug still firmly embedded when he scouted part time for the Jazz in '88-89. He became associate head coach at Howard University (1990-94) and then an assistant with the New Jersey Nets (1994-96), Louisville (1996-1999), the Charlotte Hornets (1999-2001) and the Cleveland Cavaliers (2002-03).

He accepted his first head-coaching job in 2003-04 at North Carolina A&T. It had won one game the previous season, and Eaves finished 3-25 after losing nine players for one reason or another.

But he said, "It would have been easy to feel sorry for myself and say, 'We don't have it . . . we need more players . . . we need to worry about next season.' But there's never been a day I've felt that way. Not one."

He and his wife, Sheila, have four children.

Darrell Griffith

Chosen No. 2 overall in the 1980 NBA draft, Griffith didn't start any games his first season with the Utah Jazz but still averaged 20.6 points, 3.6 rebounds and 35.4 minutes.

He became one of the three impact pros off the 1980 national champs, averaging over 20 points in four seasons with a high of 22.6 in 1984-85, starting for five seasons and playing 10 years, all with the Jazz, before injuries drove him out after 1990-91.

Some career numbers: 12,948 season and playoff points, a 16.2 season average, 3.3 rebound average, eight seasons averaging in double figures, 530 three-pointers, a .463 career field goal percentage not including playoffs.

He moved back to Louisville soon after retirement and in 1992 started Metro Enterprises, a warehouse distribution business with connections to Ford and General Electric. In 1994 he began the Darrell Griffith All-Star Celebrity Affair, one of many pre-Kentucky Derby parties in Louisville, which held its 11th soiree in 2004.

With funds raised from the party, he established the Darrell Griffith Foundation, a nonprofit organization that feeds over 600 homeless a year, provides scholarship aid and financially helps such groups as Center for Women and Families, House of Ruth (a home for people with AIDS), the Louisville AIDS walk, Clothe A Child and others.

Unmarried and 45 in the spring of 2004, he has four children (all in their 20s) and three grandchildren.

Rodney McCray

There are still plenty of lingering questions and disappointments as McCray pursues life after basketball.

As a 6-8 small forward and No. 3 overall draft pick, he started his first nine NBA seasons with Houston, Sacramento and Dallas, then won a championship as a reserve with the Chicago Bulls in 1992-93.

He had two hernia operations. Pain drove him out at age 31 "when I wasn't ready to retire," he said. He tried to rehab and come back twice, in 1994 and 1998, but couldn't, and now is a candidate for a hip replacement.

"It's frustrating to wonder about 'what if,'" he said. "Chicago would have been a great place for me had I been healthy."

He is the only member of the 1980 squad to add a world title to the national one. He averaged in double figures in points his first eight seasons, ranging from 10.3 to 16.6, and 9.0 his ninth. He averaged 6.6 rebounds and 3.6 assists, had a field goal percentage of .503 and seriously upgraded his free throw percentage from .647 his freshman season at U of L to an average of .761 in his 10 pro years.

He retired to Houston. In 1994 he and brother Scooter purchased a La-Z-Boy store in Louisville with a third partner, Brian Bloom, an enterprise that has since grown to three stores and a distribution center.

In 1998, needing about nine hours for his degree, he interned with a Houston television station, got back in the classroom and completed requirements.

In 1999 he and two partners started a construction company. Then he left and started his own with wife Judy, an interior decorator. He said he builds houses in all price ranges. He returned to Louisville to supervise the construction of one of the La-Z-Boys.

All this despite never coming close to an engineering curriculum in school. How? "A lot of people go study something that is not what they end up being a part of," he said.

Rodney and Judy have two daughters. Another daughter, Apryl, died of brain cancer at age six in 1987.

Carlton "Scooter" McCray

His surgical knee from 1979 good but not great, Scooter McCray started in the 1980-81 Louisville season and averaged 7.5 points and 5.6 rebounds. A severely sprained ankle early in '81-82 set him back again, but he rebounded to co-captain the '82-83 32-4 Final Four Cardinals, open all 36 games at forward and average 9.1 points and 6.4 rebounds.

He was drafted in the second NBA round of 1983 (36th overall) by Seattle.

He played in 47 games in '83-84, starting six, averaging 11 minutes and scoring 129 points but shooting just 39 percent. Six games into the next season, the SuperSonics cut him. He played the '85-86 campaign in France, then hooked on with Cleveland for '86-87 but lasted only 24 games. One more shot with Sacramento the next season ended early.

In 1988 he picked up the last three classes necessary for his degree and that fall was hired by Crum as a full-time assistant.

McCray held the job 10 seasons. In the meantime, he, brother Rodney and friend Brian Bloom had taken over the Louisville area's La-Z-Boy franchise. He moved into management of that operation and there are now three regional stores plus a distribution center.

He and his wife, Terryl, have two sons and a daughter.

Marty Pulliam

The fabled Snowman graduated in four years with a bachelor's of science in commerce. By the fall of 1982 he had his master's.

Pulliam's goal was not to become a tycoon for a Fortune 500 company. He wanted a job with the Kentucky Fish and Wildlife service.

"There was a hiring freeze on," he said, "but they told me if I could get on with the state in any other job they'd eventually transfer me over."

Pulliam hooked on as a guard with the department of corrections at two separate prisons over a 26-month period. The man who mentioned the transfer possibility then left.

He married another prison employee, Mary Ann, who already had two sons, then left the lockup business for R.R. Donnelly & Sons printing company in 1984. He's been with the firm ever since and is the lead man on a six-man crew.

The family lives in Stanford, Kentucky.

Derek Smith

It was testament to Smith's uniquely incessant drive to better himself that he managed to survive the NBA's political and unforgiving landscape.

After setting a Louisville field goal percentage record, finishing in the top five in three other categories and eventually having his jersey retired, he was knocked around for two pro seasons before bursting into a starring role for the Los Angeles Clippers in 1984-85.

He averaged 22.1 points and was off to an even better season in '85-86 when knee ligaments tore, canceling the rest of the year.

Somehow he recovered to play five more years, three of them in mostly starting roles although more injuries limited his number of games. He averaged in double figures for four campaigns, finishing with a career mark of 12.8 points, while playing for Golden State, the San Diego Clippers, the L.A. Clippers, Sacramento, Philadelphia and Boston.

He shot .499 from the field for his nine-year career, scored 5,232 points and grabbed 1,300 rebounds.

He returned to Louisville to complete his degree in communications in 1991 and stayed in town until 1994.

The Washington Bullets asked him to be an assistant coach then. He was in his second season and on a cruise with team personnel when he died of a heart ailment in 1996 at age 34.

His widow, Monica, has a daughter and a son.

David "Poncho" Wright

Wright was drafted in the sixth round in 1982 by the then-Kansas City Kings and survived until the final cut.

He played a few games with Detroit of the Continental Basketball Association, then left for Europe and two years in Sweden and one in France. He tore an Achilles' tendon on a 1986 Swedish team that also included former Louisville center Ricky Gallon.

He went back to his native Indianapolis in 1987 and worked concrete jobs for four years. There he began dating a former high school classmate. He and Wonna then went to California together in 1991, marrying in 1992.

Poncho took a job with the UCLA Medical Center, stocking hospital storage areas and arranging surgical equipment for operations. Wonna is a medical records director in demand across the country by facilities undergoing reorganization. "She's probably the best in the nation," Wright said.

He returned to Indianapolis in 2000 to work at the Indiana Surgery Center. He's also employed by a mortgage company with an eye on becoming a loan closer. "My mind changes like the wind," he said.

He has one son.

SELECTED MEMBERS OF
THE SUPPORT TEAM

Randy Bufford, Head Manager

Bufford graduated with a bachelor of science degree in commerce in 1981. He worked for an accounting firm for two years, then switched to a nursing home business to become chief financial officer at age 24. He then bought the owner out with investment help in 1992 and renamed the company Transitional Health Services. That merged with another firm and was taken public in 1997.

He returned to Louisville in 1999 and started his own nursing home business, Trilogy Health Services LLC, of which he's president and chief executive officer. The company has 17 campuses in Indiana and one in Kentucky.

Jerry May, Trainer

From 1977-85 he and Jim McGhee were "co-head trainers," with one student helper handling all non-revenue sports. In 1985 he moved to basketball only when new football coach Howard Schnellenberger brought in his own trainer, but was still responsible for some other sports. In 2001 he was moved to strictly baseball when Rick Pitino replaced Crum. In late 2001 he was asked to pick up some other sports, but decided to retire instead.

Robert "Bosey" Thrasher, Equipment Coordinator

He left in 1980 to become baseball and women's basketball coach at Lindsey Wilson, then a junior college, and stayed two years. From 1982-95 he trained thoroughbred horses.

He turned the stable over to his sister in '95 and worked from '96 to 2001 as a food broker for deli and grocery stores in Louisville area. He returned to school in '01, got his master's, and is working on a doctorate. He is now a substitute teacher (Spanish) at the high school he graduated from, Valley, in the Louisville area, Thrasher is coaching Valley's girls softball team.

Joe Yates, Sports Information Director

SID at Louisville from 1978-83 and SID at Louisiana State from 1983-88, then Yates was athletic director at St. Louis U. from 1988-90. He began Yates Management in 1991, promoting primarily NBA preseason games. He was vice-president of operations for indoor football, indoor soccer and minor league basketball teams from 1999-02. Yates is still in St. Louis, still has Yates Management and helps wife Kelly run field hockey camps in 12 cities.

CHAPTER FOURTEEN

The 1979-80 Louisville Cardinals' Season

GAME BY GAME

Day	Date	Opponent	Site	UL	Opp.
Sat.	Dec. 1	South Alabama	Home	75	73
Wed.	Dec. 5	Tennessee-Chattanooga	Home	87	63
Sat.	Dec. 8	Tennessee	Away	77	75

Louisville Holiday Classic

Day	Date	Opponent	Site	UL	Opp.
Thurs.	Dec. 13	North Carolina Charlotte	Home	93	76
Fri.	Dec. 14	Western Kentucky	Home	96	74

Day	Date	Opponent	Site	UL	Opp.
Wed.	Dec. 19	Ohio State	Home	75	65
Sat.	Dec. 22	Utah	Away	69	71

Hawaii Rainbow Classic

Day	Date	Opponent	Site	UL	Opp.
Fri.	Dec. 28	Princeton	Neutral	64	53
Sat.	Dec. 29	Illinois	Neutral	64	77
Sun.	Dec. 30	Nebraska	Neutral	65	58

Day	Date	Opponent	Site	UL	Opp.
Thurs.	Jan. 3	Tulsa	Home	78	58
Sat.	Jan. 5	Kansas State	Home	85	73
Tues.	Jan. 8	St. Louis	Home	94	65
Sat.	Jan. 12	Memphis State	Away	69	48
Sat.	Jan. 19	Tulane	Away	76	59

Day	Date	Opponent	Site	UL	Opp.
Tues.	Jan. 22	Marquette	Home	76	63
Fri.	Jan. 25	St. Louis	Away	99	74
Sun.	Jan. 27	Florida State	Home	79	73
Thurs.	Jan. 31	Tulane	Home	64	60
Sun.	Feb. 3	St. John's	Away	76	71
Mon.	Feb. 4	Memphis State	Home	88	60
Wed.	Feb. 6	Cincinnati	Home	88	73
Sat.	Feb. 9	Providence	Away	79	73
Mon.	Feb. 11	Virginia Tech	Away	56	54 (OT)
Thurs.	Feb. 14	West Virginia	Away	90	78
Sat.	Feb. 16	Cincinnati	Away	61	57
Mon.	Feb. 18	Virginia Tech	Home	77	72
Thurs.	Feb. 21	Iona	Away	60	77
Sun.	Feb. 24	Florida State	Away	83	75

Metro Conference Tournament

Fri.	Feb. 29	Memphis State	Home	84	65
Sat.	Mar. 1	Florida State	Home	81	72

NCAA Tournament Midwest Regional
At Lincoln, Nebraska

Sat.	Mar. 8	Kansas State	Neutral	71	69 (OT)

NCAA Tournament Midwest Regional
At Houston, Texas

Fri.	Mar. 14	Texas A&M	Neutral	66	55 (OT)
Sun.	Mar. 16	Louisiana State	Neutral	86	66

NCAA Tournament Final Four
At Indianapolis, Indiana
Semifinal

Sat.	Mar. 22	Iowa	Neutral	80	72

Championship

Mon.	Mar. 24	UCLA	Neutral	59	54

1979-80 SEASON STATISTICS

Player	G-S	Min.-Avg.	FG	FGA	Pct.	FT	FTA	Pct.	Reb.	Avg.	A	PF	Pts.	Avg.
Darrell Griffith	36-36	1246-34.6	349	631	.553	127	178	.713	174	4.8	138	99	825	22.9
Derek Smith	36-36	1222-33.9	213	372	.573	105	150	.700	299	8.3	73	105	531	14.8
Wiley Brown	36-36	1094-30.4	151	291	.519	72	118	.610	201	5.6	45	83	374	10.4
Rodney McCray	36-33	1178-32.7	107	197	.543	66	102	.647	269	7.5	72	100	280	7.8
Jerry Eaves	34-34	878-25.8	92	179	.514	78	117	.667	61	1.8	82	53	262	7.7
Poncho Wright	36-0	589-15.4	99	220	.450	35	48	.729	89	2.5	30	62	233	6.5
Scooter McCray	3-3	58-19.3	5	11	.454	4	6	.667	11	3.7	15	6	14	4.7
Roger Burkman	36-0	636-17.7	38	93	.409	66	94	.702	60	1.7	113	98	142	3.9
Daryl Cleveland	14-0	55-3.9	7	21	.333	13	19	.684	12	0.9	0	11	27	1.9
Tony Branch	25-2	109-4.4	11	29	.379	19	21	.905	3	0.1	10	6	41	1.6
Greg Deuser	22-0	161-7.3	9	25	.360	15	22	.682	11	0.5	21	19	33	1.5
Marty Pulliam	12-0	28-2.3	1	4	.250	4	4	1.000	4	0.3	0	8	6	0.5
Steve Clark	6-0	11-1.8	1	5	.200	0	1	.000	3	0.5	1	1	2	0.3
Totals	36	1455-40.4	1083	2078	.521	604	880	.686	1367	38.0	600	651	2770	76.9
Opponents	36	1455-40.4	967	2092	.462	467	658	.710	1220	33.9	508	755	2401	66.7

NCAA TOURNAMENT STATISTICS

Player	G-S	Min.-Avg.	FG	FGA	Pct.	FT	FTA	Pct.	Reb.	Avg.	A	PF	Pts.	Avg.
Griffith	5-5	178-35.6	47	93	.505	22	31	.710	27	5.4	26	15	116	23.2
Smith	5-5	189-37.8	21	45	.467	19	25	.760	40	8.0	11	14	61	12.2
Brown	5-5	164-32.8	22	40	.550	6	13	.461	30	6.0	8	10	50	10.0
R. McCray	5-5	185-37.0	15	29	.517	15	22	.682	43	8.6	12	11	45	9.0
Eaves	5-5	127-25.4	13	24	.542	7	12	.583	12	2.4	10	7	33	6.6
Wright	5-0	75-15.0	10	22	.454	6	6	1.000	12	2.4	4	7	26	5.2
Burkman	5-0	108-21.6	6	9	.667	9	12	.750	9	1.8	11	17	21	4.2
Branch	5-0	17-3.4	2	4	.500	6	8	.750	0	0.0	1	1	10	2.0
Cleveland	2-0	2-1.0	0	0	.000	0	0	.000	0	0.0	0	0	0	0.0
Deuser	2-0	2-1.0	0	0	.000	0	0	.000	0	0.0	0	0	0	0.0
Pulliam	2-0	2-1.0	0	0	.000	0	0	.000	0	0.0	0	0	0	0.0
Clark	1-0	1-1.0	0	0	.000	0	1	.000	1	0.0	0	0	0	0.0
Totals	5	210-40.2	136	266	.511	90	130	.692	182	36.4	83	82	362	72.4
Opponents	5	210-40.2	129	304	.424	58	69	.840	164	32.8	81	113	316	63.2

NCAA TOURNAMENT BOX SCORES

Midwest Regional Second Round

KANSAS STATE 69

Player	Min.	FG	FGA	FT	FTA	Reb.	A	TO	BLK	S	PF	TP
Ed Nealy, F	45	3	12	3	3	11	1	3	0	2	3	9
Jari Wills, F	33	3	5	3	4	6	2	2	0	3	3	9
Les Craft, C	24	3	4	0	0	5	1	2	0	0	2	6
Glenn Marshall, G	45	8	14	7	8	1	8	5	0	3	3	16
Rolando Blackman, G	45	6	18	0	0	4	7	1	0	1	2	19
Tyrone Adams	33	5	9	0	0	2	2	1	0	0	2	10
Team	-	0	0	0	0	4	0	0	0	0	0	0
Totals	**225**	**28**	**62**	**13**	**15**	**33**	**21**	**14**	**0**	**9**	**15**	**69**

(continued on next page)

LOUISVILLE 71

Player	Min.	FG	FGA	FT	FTA	Reb.	A	TO	BLK	S	PF	TP
Wiley Brown, F	34	4	5	1	2	6	1	3	0	0	1	9
Derek Smith, F	45	9	14	2	2	7	0	2	0	0	2	20
Rodney McCray, C	40	4	6	0	0	5	2	7	1	1	2	8
Jerry Eaves, G	18	0	3	0	0	0	1	0	0	1	0	0
Darrell Griffith, G	43	8	20	2	3	6	8	4	0	0	5	18
Roger Burkman	27	1	1	2	2	3	3	3	1	1	3	4
Poncho Wright	15	4	6	2	2	1	2	0	1	1	2	10
Tony Branch	3	1	1	0	0	0	0	0	0	0	0	2
Team	-	0	0	0	0	1	0	0	0	0	0	0
Totals	**225**	**31**	**56**	**9**	**11**	**29**	**17**	**19**	**3**	**4**	**15**	**71**

Halftime Louisville 39-37. End of regulation: 67-67.

Field goal percentages: Kansas State .451, Louisville .553. Free throw percentages: Kansas State .866, Louisville .818.

Midwest Regional Semifinals

TEXAS A&M 55

Player	Min.	FG	FGA	FT	FTA	Reb.	A	TO	BLK	S	PF	TP
Vernon Smith, F	40	6	13	0	0	8	0	4	1	0	4	12
Rynn Wright, F	43	4	8	3	4	8	2	1	1	2	5	11
Rudy Woods, C	24	4	7	0	0	9	0	1	3	0	4	8
DavidGoff, G	43	0	3	2	2	2	6	1	0	1	2	2
David Britton, G	44	7	15	2	2	3	7	10	2	1	4	16
Tyrone Ladson	5	0	0	0	0	0	0	2	0	0	1	0
Claude Riley	15	2	7	0	0	2	1	2	0	0	3	4
Steve Sylestine	11	1	3	0	0	0	0	1	0	1	1	2
Team	-	0	0	0	0	4	0	0	0	0	0	0
Totals	**225**	**24**	**56**	**7**	**8**	**36**	**16**	**22**	**7**	**5**	**24**	**55**

(continued on next page)

LOUISVILLE 66

Player	Min.	FG	FGA	FT	FTA	Reb.	A	TO	BLK	S	PF	TP
Wiley Brown, F	36	5	10	5	6	6	1	3	0	2	0	15
Derek Smith, F	38	2	6	2	2	10	5	3	1	1	4	6
Rodney McCray, C	35	0	4	4	8	8	3	2	1	1	2	4
Jerry Eaves, G	26	4	7	0	0	3	3	2	0	1	2	8
Darrell Griffith, G	43	9	24	6	8	6	2	5	0	1	2	24
Roger Burkman	23	1	2	0	1	3	0	0	0	1	4	2
Poncho Wright	20	2	5	0	0	0	1	1	0	0	2	4
Tony Branch	4	0	0	3	4	0	1	0	0	1	0	3
Team	-	0	0	0	0	3	0	0	0	0	0	0
Totals	225	23	58	20	29	39	16	16	2	8	16	66

Halftime: Louisville 35-33. End of regulation: 53-53.
Field goal percentages: Texas A&M .446, Louisville .397. Free throw percentages: Texas A&M .875, Louisville .690.

Midwest Regional Final

LOUISVILLE 86

Player	Min.	FG	FGA	FT	FTA	Reb.	A	TO	BLK	S	PF	TP
Wiley Brown, F	31	8	10	0	1	5	1	1	0	2	2	16
Derek Smith, F	33	4	9	5	9	10	3	4	0	1	4	13
Rodney McCray, C	38	4	8	4	6	10	2	6	3	0	1	12
Jerry Eaves, G	31	3	3	3	5	2	2	0	0	1	1	9
Darrell Griffith, G	18	7	12	3	4	8	7	4	1	1	4	17
Roger Burkman	26	2	2	4	5	0	7	1	0	1	3	8
Poncho Wright	13	1	5	4	4	4	0	0	1	0	1	6
Tony Branch	6	1	3	3	4	0	0	0	0	0	1	5
Greg Deuser	1	0	0	0	0	0	0	0	0	0	0	0
Daryl Cleveland	1	0	0	0	0	0	0	0	0	0	0	0
Marty Pulliam	1	0	0	0	1	0	0	0	0	0	0	0
Steve Clark	1	0	0	0	0	1	0	0	0	0	0	0
Team	-	0	0	0	0	2	0	0	0	0	0	0
Totals	**200**	**30**	**52**	**26**	**39**	**42**	**22**	**16**	**5**	**6**	**17**	**86**

(continued on next page)

LOUISIANA STATE 66

Player	Min.	FG	FGA	FT	FTA	Reb.	A	TO	BLK	S	PF	TP
DeWayne Scales, F	27	5	11	2	2	6	0	2	0	0	5	12
Durand Macklin, F	34	4	7	1	2	8	1	2	0	0	4	9
Greg Cook, C	25	2	4	0	1	7	5	2	0	1	5	4
Ethan Martin, G	31	1	11	0	0	2	8	5	0	1	4	2
Howard Carter, G	29	5	14	2	3	7	0	0	0	0	5	12
Willie Sims	22	4	8	2	2	1	1	3	0	0	5	10
Jordy Hultberg	20	8	10	1	3	1	1	2	0	2	2	17
Joe Costello	6	0	1	0	0	0	0	0	0	1	0	0
Mark Alcorn	1	0	0	0	0	0	0	0	0	0	0	0
Brian Bergeron	1	0	1	0	0	0	0	0	0	0	0	0
Tyrone Black	1	0	0	0	0	0	0	1	0	0	0	0
Duane DeArmond	1	0	0	0	0	0	0	0	0	0	0	0
Andy Campbell	1	0	1	0	0	1	0	0	1	0	0	0
Gus Randolph	1	0	0	0	0	2	0	0	0	0	1	0
Team	-											
Totals	200	29	68	8	13	35	16	17	1	5	31	66

Halftime: Louisville 31-29.
Field goal percentages: Louisville .577, Louisiana State .427. Free throw percentages: Louisville .667, Louisiana State .615.

National Semifinals

IOWA 72

Player	Min.	FG	FGA	FT	FTA	Reb.	A	TO	BLK	S	PF	TP
Vince Brookins, F	32½	6	18	2	2	6	2	2	0	1	5	14
Kevin Boyle, F	38	0	8	0	0	7	5	4	0	2	2	0
Steve Krafcisin, C	31½	4	5	4	4	3	0	1	1	0	5	12
Kenny Arnold, G	39	9	17	2	2	3	5	1	0	1	1	20
Ronnie Lester, G	12	4	4	2	2	1	1	0	0	0	2	10
Steve Waite	29	4	6	1	1	2	0	3	0	2	5	9
Bob Hansen	17	2	8	3	4	4	4	0	0	1	2	7
Mark Gannon	½	0	0	0	0	0	0	0	0	0	0	0
Mike Henry	½	0	0	0	0	0	0	0	0	0	1	0
Totals	**200**	**29**	**66**	**14**	**15**	**26**	**17**	**11**	**1**	**7**	**23**	**72**

(continued on next page)

LOUISVILLE 80

Player	Min.	FG	FGA	FT	FTA	Reb.	A	TO	BLK	S	PF	TP
Wiley Brown, F	29	1	3	0	2	5	2	4	0	0	4	2
Derek Smith, F	36½	3	7	7	8	8	2	1	0	0	2	13
Rodney McCray, C	36½	5	7	4	4	9	3	2	2	2	2	14
Jerry Eaves, G	22	2	4	4	5	4	1	1	0	0	1	8
Darrell Griffith, G	36	14	21	6	8	5	6	4	2	3	1	34
Roger Burkman	22	2	3	3	4	2	0	5	0	1	3	7
Poncho Wright	15	1	2	0	0	3	1	1	0	0	1	2
Tony Branch	1½	0	0	0	0	0	0	0	0	0	0	0
Greg Deuser	½	0	0	0	0	0	0	0	0	0	0	0
Daryl Cleveland	½	0	0	0	0	0	0	0	0	0	0	0
Marty Pulliam	½	0	0	0	0	0	0	0	0	0	0	0
Totals	**200**	**28**	**47**	**24**	**31**	**36**	**15**	**18**	**4**	**6**	**14**	**80**

Halftime: Louisville 34-29.

Field goal percentages: Iowa .439; Louisville .596. Free throw percentages: Iowa .933, Louisville .774.

National Championship

UCLA 54

Player	Min.	FG	FGA	FT	FTA	Reb.	A	TO	BLK	S	PF	TP
James Wilkes, F	24½	1	4	0	0	6	0	5	1	0	3	2
Kiki Vandeweghe, F	36½	4	9	6	6	7	0	1	0	1	3	14
Mike Sanders, C	34	4	10	2	4	6	0	0	0	1	4	10
Rod Foster, G	38	6	15	4	4	1	5	2	0	6	3	16
Michael Holton, G	29	1	3	2	2	2	3	2	0	1	2	4
Cliff Pruitt	16	2	8	2	2	6	1	3	2	1	2	6
Darren Daye	13	1	3	0	0	1	2	2	0	0	1	2
Tony Anderson	5	0	0	0	0	0	0	0	0	0	0	0
Darrell Allums	4	0	0	0	0	2	0	1	0	0	0	0
Team	-	0	0	0	0	3	0	0	0	0	0	0
Totals	**200**	**19**	**52**	**16**	**18**	**34**	**11**	**16**	**3**	**10**	**18**	**54**

(continued on next page)

LOUISVILLE 59

Player	Min.	FG	FGA	FT	FTA	Reb.	A	TO	BLK	S	PF	TP
Wiley Brown, F	34	4	12	0	2	7	3	3	1	1	3	8
Derek Smith, F	36	3	9	3	4	5	1	3	0	2	2	9
Rodney McCray, C	36	2	4	3	4	11	2	1	3	0	4	7
Jerry Eaves, G	30	4	7	0	2	3	3	3	0	1	3	8
Darrell Griffith, G	38	9	16	5	8	2	3	4	1	1	3	23
Poncho Wright	12	2	4	0	0	4	0	1	0	2	1	4
Roger Burkman	11	0	1	0	0	1	1	2	0	1	4	0
Tony Branch	3	0	0	0	0	0	0	0	0	0	0	0
Team	-	0	0	0	0	3	0	0	0	0	0	0
Totals	200	24	53	11	20	36	13	17	5	8	20	59

Halftime: UCLA 28-26.
Field goal percentages: UCLA .365, Louisville .453. Free throw percentages: UCLA .889, Louisville .550.

FINAL 1980 METRO
CONFERENCE STANDINGS

Team	Conference W	L	Overall W	L
Louisville	12	0	33	3
Virginia Tech	8	4	21	8
Florida State	7	5	22	9
Memphis State	5	7	13	14
St. Louis	4	8	12	15
Cincinnati	3	9	13	15
Tulane	3	9	10	17

FINAL ASSOCIATED PRESS POLL

March 4, 1980

Pos.	Team (1st-place votes)	Record	Points
1.	DePaul (54)	26-1	1,173
2.	Louisville (2)	28-3	1,030
3.	Louisiana State (1)	24-5	1,018
4.	Kentucky (2)	28-5	956
5.	Oregon State	26-3	872
6.	Syracuse	25-3	785
7.	Indiana	20-7	746
8.	Maryland	23-6	722
9.	Notre Dame	22-5	594
10.	Ohio State	20-7	586
11.	Georgetown, D.C.	24-5	564
12.	Brigham Young	24-4	485
13.	St. John's, N.Y.	24-4	479
14.	Duke	22-8	450
15.	North Carolina	21-7	322
16.	Missouri	23-5	278
17.	Weber State	26-2	240
18.	Arizona State	21-6	156
19.	Iona	28-4	142
20.	Purdue	18-9	120

Epilogue

Scooter McCray sat in his office at the La-Z-Boy distribution center he owns with brother Rodney and a friend, Brian Bloom. He leaned back in his cushioned chair and flipped the pages of his mind backwards through 23 years.

None of Louisville's 1979-80 boyz-to-men got to where they are today strolling automatically down a yellow brick road.

Not even Darrell Griffith and Rodney McCray, who started a combined 14 of 20 NBA seasons and wound up with more than a couple zeros at the end of a number on their paychecks. Griffith was forced to yield his pro career prematurely to a broken foot and never got to an NBA championship series. McCray still wonders if a hernia operation was done properly when he had to step aside after 10 pro seasons, not ready to retire at age 31.

Others bounced off a wall or two, unable to sustain an NBA (or in Wiley Brown's case, NFL) career, playing a bit in Europe, coming home, trying construction or insurance or life as a prison guard before finding their niche.

None, however, had to endure the what-might-have-been anguish of Scooter McCray.

He arrived at U of L ticketed to be perhaps the most versatile player in its history, an astonishing passer and deft dribbler, so knife-like he was almost impossible for enemy rebounders to block out, a 6-8 point guard, point forward and point center. If you couldn't quite say "Hello, Magic," you wanted to.

Then he tore up his knee in December, 1979. Furiously rehabbing after surgery, he was back on the court weeks ahead of schedule. He made the smart decision to redshirt, ending up with 58 minutes of playing time for the national champions, turning the second squad into an even nastier practice force than it had been and becoming a pseudo coach and cheerleader on the bench. He was as much a celebrant of the crown as anyone, but he was mostly an onlooker whose internal joy had to be muted.

His knee never returned to its previous pristine condition. He was a major contributor to the next three Louisville teams, all of them superb, but the gnawing feeling of a lesser athlete remained.

He hooked on with the Seattle Supersonics for a little over a year, played a year in France, made the Cleveland Cavaliers for not quite a season, then failed in a tryout with Sacramento.

He came back to Louisville, finished the last three classes needed for his degree and was hired by Denny Crum as an assistant coach, replacing Bobby Dotson. He was on staff for 10 years, departing when a newspaper investigation turned up discrepancies with a player and the player's father Scooter was connected to, leading to probation by the NCAA.

"Like my injury, that was part of life, you deal with it and move on," he said.

Does he miss coaching?

"I would have liked to have had the head coaching experience," he said. "I don't think you can be an assistant that long and never call your own shots."

But he's calling his own shots now. He, Rodney and Bloom operate a four-store La-Z-Boy franchise in the Louisville area, mostly under the jurisdiction of Scooter.

It's not a surprise, considering the journeys of the other '79-80 Cardinals and support people. There are CEOs and coaches, contractors and entrepreneurs, portfolio managers and major league trainers.

As Scooter returned to the glory days of yesteryear, his chest swelled with a sense of attainment. Not just from the title, but from the work and character of the men who sought it. No bad knee or workplace trouble could dispel that.

"Coach Crum told me this: 'You can coach 50 years and never have a group of guys that dedicated to a common goal like we were,'" Scooter said. "You look at these guys 20 years later and they're still conducting themselves as champions. That's what they believe. That's what's in their heart. That's why, when you look back, that's how amazing that group of guys was."

Scooter sighed deeply and leaned forward.

"It shows that Coach Crum was right," he said. "You can be around a long time and never come across people like that. I think a lot of individual pride had been instilled in them as youngsters, had carried over into team pride, and after they had a taste of success it carried over into personal pride.

"When I see these guys nowadays I'm so proud. None of them is obese. They are going to represent themselves as well as your team and school in the proper manner. They carry themselves as gentlemen. They carry themselves as winners in every walk of life."

The kind of protest seen in the Museum garden does not in any way resemble the summoning of spiritual force in the face of the technical age that Bergson had demanded. And most significantly, the negative quality attributed here to the machine contrasts sharply with the germane and constructive role it played in the work of the four great masters we are honoring in these cycles.

It is quite evident that the climate of thought today does not entirely share the optimism of the first machine age. Since the bomb, the idea of a progressive humanism siding with the machine has become difficult to maintain without serious qualification.

The second machine age, the age of nuclear power, electronics, automation, of new control and communication devices, differs in important aspects from the first. It shows a characteristic physiognomy of its own. The technical apparatus of the now obsolete preceding phase is exchanged for a radically different one. Yet our organizational concepts remain geared to the old patterns. They are thus ineffectual against the new forces that are now shaping our lives.

Present day technical potential has far outstripped our ability and our willingness to formulate new objectives. The technical ability so necessary to the survival of a population which is dangerously on the increase is squandered on trivial tasks, giving performance without value instead of rendering much-needed service.

We are exploring outer space whilst we have lost control three blocks from here. Machines, the tools for our survival, have assumed all the aspects of a scourge by their misuse for short-term gain. Like locusts, we are devouring our resources of land, material, and human beings. There is an overwhelming need to reestablish the ecological balance between human beings and environment in the new terms of a mechanized society.

267

The second machine age, in contrast to the first, lacks in confidence and in conviction. It lacks in a sense of the future and a will to live. It lacks, therefore, in objectives and commitment to a program. Are we then, in the words of Mumford, "demoralized passengers in a runaway car, without driver, steering wheel, or brakes, hurtling towards destruction"?

Cast adrift from any tradition to guide us, our confusion is further compounded by the fact that the machines themselves on which we had relied are beginning to assume new and puzzling aspects of behavior. As a scientist who is involved in the new "zoology of machines" has said, "the fact that we have built them does not necessarily mean that we know all about their behavior." These new machines of the second machine age are no longer the simple extensions of our muscle power, the superathletes of the first machine age, but subtle and cunning "servo-mechanisms" which, responding to environment, can redirect themselves by means of feed-back networks. The new machines are no longer blindly set on a path of repetitive performance. They react and are self-steering to an as yet unpredictable degree. Thus, they begin to throw a glaring light on our own inadequacies of programming and the lack of purpose of our actions. They suggest that, with advantage, they may short-circuit our intervention in their performance.

As confirmed a believer in technology as Dr. Gropius has recently begun to talk of "robotism." But a danger of this exists only where we fail to show a will to action. Without the will to existence, the man of the second machine age may indeed be replaced by automatons. Karl Anders, a German writer, in his book The Outdatedness of Man, suggests that "man sees himself as an inferior tool, a morphologically limited model, inferior ballast in the ascendancy of equipment." To this, he largely ascribes the tragic loss of identity from which modern man suffers.

The re-establishment of human identity in the technical world is a main point in our program for action. To achieve a new equilibrium between the individual and the group, the mechanized and the natural environment, is the program for the architect in the restructuring of environment.

268

Yet to achieve this, the architect appears to be singularly badly placed, both by his attitude and his training. His orientation towards machine technology is ambivalent and hesitant. He alternates between passivity, submission to environmental control techniques, and contemptuous ignorance of them. He shows his ambivalence often by over-reacting and, of late, even engages in deliberate and picturesque primitivism in building. Or else he is simply involved in working compliantly on limited briefs for private, rather than common, advantage. He is easily satisfied with narcissistic performance and self-expression. He is lost in neohistoric reveries or exploits for the sake of sensation the new technical facility.

The architect, therefore, lays himself wide open to the kind of criticism that the mordant English critic, Reyner Banham, the author of Theory and Design in the First Machine Age, has levelled against him. In this book Banham proposes that the architect either "get with it," this is to say, jump on the technological and human engineering bandwagon, or become extinct as a species. This, it is suggested, he may be anyway, whether he follows this advice or not.

In the face of this provocation, Mr. Philip Johnson in an article for The Architectural Review shows a surprising willingness to abdicate in what we regard generally as the most important area of architecture, namely the Human Habitat. He grandly advocates that, as far as he is concerned, architects could be content to design the tombs and monuments of our society and leave the dwelling to Mr. Buckminster Fuller's Dymaxion technique.

Those of us who know Mr. Johnson know, of course, that he does not always say what he really means, nor mean what he actually says. But there is enough seriousness in the argument for us to be concerned and to find both alternatives equally preposterous.

269

If we still hang on to the idea of building for life rather than the necropolis, we may take comfort in the work of Le Corbusier, who builds both the acropolis and the poorest peons' houses at Chandigarh; a man of such scope that he can build the monumental monastery at La Tourette at the same time as sitting down with the engineers of the Renault Company to discuss his long-cherished plans for an industrially produced dwelling.

In a recent broadcast over the British Broadcasting Company, Le Corbusier stated both as a message of hope and order of command: "The First Industrial Era began one hundred years ago, and it was an Age of Chaos. The Second Industrial Era will be the Era of Harmony, and it is only just beginning. The whole world is ready to open the eyes and ears, and all things are fluid now. This is true because the human scale is being considered afresh."

The first machine age may have started and may even have ended in chaos, but at one state in the nineteen-twenties there existed a vision of a possible order for the machine age -- a first imaginative sketch for an age of harmony. All the four great masters we are honoring in one way or another laid the foundations of this order and designed their prototypes for it. It was particularly the Bauhaus group, under the leadership of Walter Gropius, that, in a very specific sense, identified itself with the establishment of a new order in a radically changing society.

Deliberately uninvolved in the egocentric problem of the self-expression of the individual genius, the Bauhaus aimed at a universal language for design in action, and sought to arrive at a methodology for it. In doing so, it produced for the twentieth century principles of design education which by virtue of their authority and aptness replaced the obsolete tradition of the academies.

The interest which the youngest generation in architecture today shows in the period of the twenties has nothing to do with that pilfering of the historical larder which comes up with a bit

270

of Soane, art nouveau, or De Stijl for a fashionable neohistorian.
Nor is it motivated by the psychoanalytical fervor with which Mr.
Banham digs back to the so-called "zone of silence" in the childhood of modern architecture. The youngest generation's interest
is rather the interest in a period much like our own, which made
courageous attempts to solve problems which, in an intensified
form, are ours also. It is an interest in rediscovering working
methods which may hold important clues for us today.

Though the second machine age differs from the first, it
has more in common with that programmatic phase of the twenties
than with later periods of diffusion of issues. Common to our
period and theirs is the awareness of a fateful threshold of social
and technical change. This in particular makes our younger
generations regard themselves once more as "primitives of a
new age" (in the futurist Boccioni's term). The Bauhaus was
committed to the machine as a cardinal factor of the new civilization, though it did not worship the machine as, say, the futurists
did. It recognized not only its potential but also the discipline
that mass production and standardization would impose as a price
to be paid for the enormous benefit it would bring to general living
standards.

The Bauhaus was aware of the evolutionary change that technology represented, and it consciously attempted, with a great
heave, to bring men's environment into the orbit of the machine
age. It joined the twentieth century; it did not feel displaced in
it. The zest of this enterprise is contagious even when viewed
at a great distance in time, in our day. It was the Bauhaus's
missionary belief in a total metamorphosis of environment which
attracted so many diverse and gifted artists to its school and to
the ranks of its admirers. Preoccupied, as we are today, with
superficial formal adventures, with vacuous decorated shells
rather than buildings, with spurious items in a deteriorating
matrix of the cities, the Bauhaus effort shines like a beacon,
promethean and responsible, inspired and realistic. To look at
its effort just as another handsome style is missing the important
aspects of the Bauhaus altogether.

271

Like Le Corbusier, the Bauhaus made the Home of Man
its palace and the humblest piece of equipment its splendor and
adornment. Just as the Bauhaus sought to break down the bar-
riers between the arts and sciences, the individual and the group,
it began to break down the barrier between inside and outside
space. Each item of the Bauhaus workshop became an element
of a total environment. It was designed in terms of mass production, developed towards a universal type form, in order to
become the molecule of the technical landscape surrounding
man.

The new identity of man in the technical world did not have
the nightmarish quality of contemporary German expressionistic
films such as the famous Cabinet of Dr. Caligari, but the lyrical
glow which can be felt in the figures ascending the famous "Bauhaus Stairs"of Oscar Schlemmer's painting. For Walter Gropius's
visions did not isolate the individual in a cocoon of the individual
and autonomous shelter, but, through the mediating images of
architecture, he underlined the individual's role as a social
being in the twentieth century. He established an elastic frame-
work within which both individual and community could communicate
without being destructive of each other's domain.

Thus, instead of exhibiting la Cellule Humaine (in which
he was interested quite as much as Le Corbusier) at the Paris
Werkbund Exhibition of 1930 and at the Berlin Building Exhibition
of the following year, Gropius showed the collective rather than
the individual spaces of an apartment house of the future. One
space is a lounge, the other a kind of physical regeneration
plant for workouts and a pool. It reminds us of Le Corbusier's
enthusiasm for the idea of a running track on the roof of apartment blocks, both eminently sane ideas for the reestablishment
of balance in the life of sedentary work which is increasingly
that of the city dweller.

It was Gropius, also, who suggested in another apartment
house project for Wannsee (1931) that a floor at mid-height should
be dedicated to recreational purposes. Gropius actually had no

272

opportunity to build any of these apartments of the future until thirty years later when, returning to the Berlin Exhibition of the Interbau (1957), he built a tautly curved slab building.

Behind these demonstrations lay profound social aspirations: the liberation of modern man from the suffocating tenements of the nineteenth-century industrial and urban slums, the establishment of the rights to light and air, the view of the sky, and a tree. The objective, to make, by means of industrial production, a higher quality of environment available to all, triggered the enthusiasm and deliberate experiment with the new materials and machine processes.

To regard the Bauhaus products and interiors as individual stylish items means disregarding the role they were intended to play in the total reconstruction and refurbishing of environment. Gropius made a continuous effort not to let Bauhaus production be sidetracked into stylistic cul-de-sacs. There were many phases of stylistic influences and emphases, such as elementarist, constructivist, neoplastic directions. But throughout Gropius's sense of discipline kept going a kind of formal ethic, which demanded that visions should be sharpened on the touchstone of function, material, and process. The objective was not sensation or originality, but, by elimination of the extraneous, it was to achieve an objective universal language of types and norms, to be produced by machine process and to be communicable to the eye and sense of touch with unmistakable clarity.

In his own studies and in those of his architectural collaborators, Gropius produced a range of prototypes for the larger urban environment. In the studies of land use, sun angles, densities, and orientation, as well as in the optical studies that occupied Gropius's mind, he engaged in those processes of verification without which all exploration becomes idle speculation.

We may regard these parallel rows today as only one of many possible ways of urban grouping and find the tall isolated apartment-type block, per se, a very obvious proposition. But

273

at that time they were radical departures and, indeed, laid the foundation for most of the work that was built in the thirties, forties, and fifties. These efforts at a new urban typology were not confined to Gropius and the Bauhaus. Through CIAM, of which both Gropius and Le Corbusier were prominent leaders, they were in general communication with other European colleagues seeking a common basis of agreement on principles. Le Corbusier, Gropius, Mies van der Rohe, Stam, and others exhibited jointly and were well acquainted with each other's thinking, and the homogeneity of their efforts no doubt helped the spread of their ideas.

Though the Bauhaus speculated in larger urban terms, its essentially pragmatic attitude kept it short of such absolutes as Le Corbusier's Ville Radieuse. It was too early also for the period to become involved in problems which occupied later phases, such as the problems of the city core or the interrelatedness of city space.

At Bauhaus city visions one can only guess. There is a project by Breuer and Yorke, shown in the London Mars Exhibition of 1936, for a City of the Future, an agglomeration of rather self-centered and fantastic structures, and a film set by Moholy-Nagy for an H. G. Wells movie in futuristic terms. Closer, perhaps, to Bauhaus intentions would be the later studies by Hilberseimer of the linear city. And, in a sense, Mies van der Rohe's Detroit Gratiot Quarter of the nineteen-fifties can perhaps be regarded as characteristic of Bauhaus aspirations of the earlier period, more so than the present work of the Gropius group, T. A. C. , which, in a new phase, has incorporated deliberately regional aspects into their architecture.

Since the Bauhaus was committed to the technical civilization, its attitude towards building technology is of particular significance. It must be remembered, however, that architecture at the Bauhaus school was never developed into a full curriculum. It was subject rather of a master workshop, and consisted largely of work on Gropius's own commissions, and the

274

projects of his collaborators. Most important as demonstrations of architectural thinking were the famous Bauhaus school buildings themselves, the school itself (1926), a germinal building in modern architecture, and the master houses (1925).

In general, Bauhaus architectural construction must be regarded as experiment for future constructural possibilities. The new program demanded new materials and techniques. Particularly for the larger span projects, construction precedents only existed in the work of nineteenth-century engineers such as Eiffel and Cottancin, and in the early twentieth-century concrete technology of Perret, Freyssinet, and Maillart.

In the Stadtkrone-Halle Project (1927) with its open latticed towers from which the great hall is suspended, Gropius reminds us of nineteenth-century construction as well as of work by Russian contemporaries, and at the same time, anticipating future space structures evolved in the fifties.

In his Total Theater (1927), Gropius not only revolutionized the fundamental program of the theater to a degree not yet realized in our own time, but also indicated geodesic structuring of a much later technical era. The frank and bold juxtaposition of hall and circulation elements in its exterior development is of particular significance to us at the present moment.

The structural means which the Bauhaus visions anticipated became available only at a much later date when the constructors of the fifties, Le Ricolais, Füller, Wachsmann, developed the spacial networks to make constructivist dreams reality; and when Nervi, Torroja, Candela, Catalano, Salvadori, made a general breakthrough into warped and curved surfaces. These developments finally provided constructural possibility for the biotechnical forms speculated in Moholy-Nagy's New Vision. However limited the Bauhaus know-how appears in retrospect, the architectural achievement was masterful. Never just functionally or technically determinist, their buildings are always in that realm of spaces which is architectonic fusion. It is particularly in our present phase,

275

when we are about to emerge from a period of relentless and
alienated exhibition of structure per se, that the more complex
construction images of the Bauhaus work can claim our particular attention. In the interlocking cubes of the master houses,
in the frank dispositions of openings in the outside walls related
to functional process within, we can recognize a preoccupation
similar to ours with a synthesis of space and function. Construction is as much an emanation of the human process enclosed as
of gravitational forces without.

The limitations which we see now in certain aspects of the
Bauhaus idiom reflect only on the technical know-how and the
deliberately restrained esthetic range of the period. They do
not reflect on the validity of their objectives or methods. The
accelerated pace of our expanding technology and the extension
of our patterns of perception may lead us in many ways beyond
the vocabulary of the twenties. This does not make our adoption
of a pragmatic and elastic discipline similar to that of the Bauhaus in any way superfluous.

To give an accurate account of Bauhaus methods is extremely
difficult. "The Bauhaus," said Mies van der Rohe, "was not an
institution with a clear program; it was an idea, and Gropius form-
ulated this idea with great precision." Gropius and his collaborators
elaborated and changed this idea from the early days at Weimar
(1919-1925) and throughout the Dessau period to the end of Gropius's
own tenure in 1928. During these short ten years, "the Bauhaus
idea" was shaped and declared in a series of statements. Of
these, Gropius' Idee and Aufbau (1923) and Moholy-Nagy's Vom
Material zur Architektur (1928) are the most significant. There
were many other contributory statements such as Paul Klee's
Pedagogical Sketchbook (1924) and Kandinsky's From Point and
Line to Plane. The famous Foundation Course, which, in one form
or another, has become a somewhat academic operation in many
of our architecture schools, underwent significant and continuous
change. It was wrapped in mystic and expressionistic overtones
during its inception under Klee's and Kandinsky's influence, and
finally it acquired somewhat tougher and realistic contours under
Albers and Moholy-Nagy.

276

Throughout all these mutations, the Bauhaus believed in learning by doing; in exploring by doing. It believed in the inductive method instead of teaching from an authoritative academic platform. Gropius believed in three stages of the design process: first that of observation, then of involvement, and finally of "getting into the inventive mood"; it will be noticed that all three encourage an attitude of openness as to result.

Gropius wanted to merge the phenomena of art and science, and he joined these literally in the Bauhaus workshop, where Form and Werklehre were taught concurrently. Formal and technical training were combined; so that form was always linked with function, material, and process. The form and technique men who emerged from the workshop (such as the gifted Breuer and Albers) became the new "ambidextrous" Bauhaus masters. Moholy-Nagy was that kind of man, a painter, expert photographer, and light enthusiast. They represented the ideal which underlies all Bauhaus production, which Paul Klee called "precision winged with intuition." In essence, the Bauhaus was an experimental workshop, staffed with a faculty and with students of a high order of dedication and ability. A course like that of the Bauhaus can only function on a highly selective and demanding level. For this was an advanced experimental station of design and education "which dared to make the discovery and renewal of life's innate forms into a curriculum."

The program was always to build. The school was called the House of Building. It was therefore never academic. The Bauhaus carried speculation into action, and from action redirected speculation. Idea and image were joined in a circle of renewal, and somewhere on that circle occurred the images of the splendid Bauhaus projects.

For us today, as we become increasingly aware of accelerated change, when finite goals become obsolete on our drawing boards, the Bauhaus's experimental and pragmatic procedures appear increasingly significant.

277

We find remarkable confirmation of their effectiveness in
tha fact that such methods are now being employed in advanced
fields of the experimental sciences, where a methodology of
exploration of possibilities witnout quite foreseeable results
is being developed. Methods like those of the Bauhaus employing
provisional codes of action, probing, feedback, and redirection
are now explored in the piloting science of cybernetics and
applied to the new control of communication devices and computers.

Walter Gropius's idea of teamwork, at first sight an idealis-
tic and moral but highly improbable working method in our com-
petitively organized society, has proven on the coolly rational
level to be an increasingly applicable method for our present day
condition. Since the correlation of environmental data on a quite
unprecedented level has become one of our problems, teamwork
becomes a major working method. It of course does not replace
altogether the non-method of creative genius. But let us not
forget that this is always an exceptional case. There are many
useful architects operating on all kinds of levels. On them, in
fact, falls the heavy responsibility of structuring the new environment in a way that is precise and authoritative, if it is to be
effectual.

If we thus can find many instances in which Bauhaus aims
and methods apply to our own period, we must also note the significant differences between our situation and that of the first machine age. These differences require an extension or redirection
of this first age into new channels.

Mr. Kallmann, writer, critic, and practitioner, was trained at
the Architectural Association in London. He is an adjunct
associate professor of architecture at the School of Architecture,
Columbia University. With two associates, he is currently
preparing drawings for the Boston City Hall, a commission won
in a competition in 1962.

278

NEW PERSPECTIVES FOR THE SECOND MACHINE AGE

Gerhardt M. Kallmann

Recently there has been a significant change in general out-
look which tends away from such concepts as Carnaps's Logical
Build of the World and Theories of Verification which were influ-
ential in the 1920's. Today's speculation would be more likely
in terms of Husserl's Phenomenology. Wholeist rather than ana-
lytical thought processes have put emphasis on concepts such as
connectedness, interrelationship, or Gestalt configuration, rather
than type absolutes, elements, and systems. Thus, for example,
our interest is no longer and unqualifiedly for the breakdown of
the city into the "four functions" of CIAM, and their clear demonstration which was axiomatic in the early programmatic phase.
Instead we are moving into areas of more complex configurations
which dissolve the former house cubes, slabs, and point blocks
into pile-ups, conglomerates, clusters, enchainments, and gal-
axies, all of them reflecting more energetic patterns of population
grouping and intensified mobility.

With the increasing demand to put space under cover for our
growing mass society and the new dimensions of space blocks with
artificial climate, man's relationship to natural environment has
been radically altered. An increasing remoteness during the hours
of work from the stimuli of the natural world (with as yet unfore-
seeable results to the psyche) necessitates a new contact relationship with growing things and the cycle of life on the private scale
of the dwelling.

Furthermore, large-scale flexible spaces of universal structure have added new problems of expression. The impassive coun-
tenance, the uncommunicative aspect of our buildings causes a
loss of individual reference to environment. The functionally

expressive articulation of the first machine phase has been largely replaced by overall sameness, whereas the ascendancy of circulatory systems and equipment has not only affected size but has also added important new declarative elements to our architectural volume.

Other changes have occurred in our space envelopes. These are no longer dogmatically transparent as in the earlier phase. They are now often realized in terms of a heightened sense of enclosure, to the point where, in late Corbusian work, the window wall has become a fourth "solid" wall in the physical sense of the word. In terms of the space itself and its new ambivalence, we may say that the rational Euclidian space of clearly defined volumes, the crystalline bodies of the twenties, are now joined by another -- Le Corbusier's espace inédicible, a non-analyzable, poetic, but still mathematically disciplined space, or by Kahn's phenomenological space and structure intertwined.

Equal'y, the idea of a monological system of structure, a regularly spaced grid scanning all urban space, foreshadowed by Kiesler's Cité dans L'Espace (1925) and realized in the general trend of the 1950's, is, in today's most advanced work, evolving into a multiplicity of superimposed networks in which random, spontaneous-seeming, chance patterns can occur at the level at which they may be appropriate.

The very different nature of environmental relationship that occurs at the level of the individual and the family, as against the level of the community, is beginning to be expressed. Kenzo Tange, a member of the younger generation in architecture, attempts to show this difference between individual human scale and mass human scale. He also introduces new aspects of scale by means of a differentiated technology, dependent on differing time cycles of obsolescence; he distinguishes between that which is to be replaceable at relatively short intervals, and that which has to be more massively constructed and is therefore more permanent.

280

Visual distinction is therefore made between, for instance, the individual shelter which can be lightweight and flexible, almost improvised; and the community structure of places of rest and mobility, of public places and networks of communication, which are built on a larger scale by means of a massive technology. In his new proposals for community structure, the main carrying structure of large concrete arches, and the circulatory system belongs to the more permanent mass scale and is likened to the organization of a tree trunk, whereas the dwelling units attached are of a more ephemeral nature and are likened to the replaceable foliage. In this manner, the individual dwelling unit within such a large concentration of dwellings is declared as an architecturally distinct structural image.

The human scale is further being considered anew in recent thinking about structure. There is now a departure from the idea of the relentless demonstration of structure as a system per se, characteristic of the forties and fifties, towards a more specific relatedness towards the space served and the human presence. Louis Kahn, in particular, has rejoined space with structure and space with function in an archetypal manner and in a highly developed hierarchy.

Among the younger generation there are deliberate attempts to depart from platonic absolutes and abstractness of architectural space towards a new vitalism. In the work of these architects, we have no attempt at idealization as in Mies van der Rohe's architecture, but a more physical, functionally immediate, and authentic space and structure. In the work of the so-called New Brutalists, the gesture of construction is aimed at the heart of the human process within.

In thus pursuing a kind of functionalism in depth, we find ourselves returning to sources of strength and discipline which also nourished the nineteen-twenties. Neither period engages in a low level functional or technological determinism, as formalist polemics will have us believe. The difference between this and the earlier phase lies in the fact that we have to include a much greater body of fact, of environmental and perceptual data. It is a difference of method rather than of objective.

Thus, once more we have to undertake the arduous tasks of verification to back up our new explorations. The density studies and optical research of the Bauhaus have to be extended, redirected, deepened on our own level of experience and in our own studies of the human sciences. These sciences now extend, said Reyner Banham in a recent broadcast over the B.B.C., "from world environment to the chromosomes." In view of the fact that our atomic tests are beginning to affect both, including even the genes of future generations, this statement is in no way an exaggeration. The architectural schools already begin to reflect this kind of thinking. Two prominent schools in London have just appointed heads from among environmentalist architects, and a congress there in the summer of 1961 made these problems its main topic. At Columbia's School of Architecture, we have Professor Henry Wright, prominent in this area, and Professor J. M. Fitch, who has made these aspects his special interest for many years.

Mr. Banham, however, has recently qualified his environmental enthusiasm in one major respect. In the same talk he states that "the human sciences will not become architecture, unless formal or visual means are found to express them...." and that "even though the motive power will come from the outside, the formal convictions will have to come from the inside."

Walter Gropius was much concerned with this problem of "the missing visual language." Although the esthetic potential of machine form had been extolled even before Bauhaus days, in such polemic as van de Velde's "the good form," a communicable language capable of phrasing the larger extension of urban space had still to be developed.

Though it was deliberate Bauhaus policy to develop form mainly from within function and the processes of machine production, it was found already then necessary to employ compositional techniques outside of them. These varied, but generally consisted, as in the case of most work of the period, of simple mathematics, Euclidean geometry, and, specifically, the

Phileban solids, now reorganized in the careful unsymmetrical balances of the neoplasticists. Generally avoiding the pyramidal compositions of the classical tradition, there was nevertheless in these equilibrations a trend towards the classical.

The Bauhaus has been criticized for these classicizing restraints. It has been pointed out that neither Gropius nor Le Corbusier have produced the genuine machine à habiter, the machine to live in, but that this was truly accomplished by Buckminster Fuller in his Dymaxion dwelling of the same period, 1927-1930. The Bauhaus has been criticized for moving away from the futurist dynamics of the machine age towards classical abstraction. (This complaint should actually and more justifiedly be levelled against the "soft" period of the accomodating fifties.)

It should be noted that Gropius regarded the architectural language as a metaphor of the machine age, not its literal transcription. He aimed at creating "symbols for the machine age" by a fusion of human requirement, human purpose, and the technical world, through the mediating images of his architecture. It so happened that his preference for a purist discipline at the time made it possible to accomplish much larger ordering patterns than those envisaged by Fuller or the purely technical forms of the period.

At a later stage, Moholy-Nagy, the "new wave" at the Bauhaus, enlarged the vocabulary to include so-called "biotechnic" elements, and his New Vision begins to include the new world of form opening up in microcosmos and macrocosmos. His disciple Gyorgy Kepes, in our own period, has further increased the range of this "panopticum" and has organized this material in the light of new perceptual theory, in The Language of Vision (1944) and The New Landscape (1956).

Today we are not so much concerned with a dearth of visual material as with limitations in compositional technique to organize such diversity of stimuli. The traditional compositional technique of classical arrangements and the dynamic equilibrations developed during the nineteen-twenties are now joined by our own experimental methods of configuration.

Esthetic communication of spatial events is achieved today on a much vaster keyboard which contains the new signals of our complex machine technology. Communication modes have to be transcribed into the terms of these signals. Myriads of combinations are now possible which in no way resemble the primitive repetitive patterns which a low-level use of our technology in commercial building employs today. Rather it constitutes a compositionally intricate and serious game within new rules. It is beginning to yield new assemblies which resemble more the mathematics of chance and probability than Euclidian geometry.

Tapping out mysterious messages, these may appear like the imaginative gibberish of a pre-speech child. But, not so different from the unfamiliar combinations of sound that occur in the tone rows of serial composition, a new language may be in the making. It is, moreover, a language that is in key with contemporary visual phenomena such as the city viewed from the air at night, bejeweled ribbons and clustering lights of the skyscrapers with their dancing patterns of light, random yet played within a perceivable allover network.

The problem of the second machine age for the architect is the difficult problem of re-entry into the verities of the age of technology which changes our lives and not only on the physical level. Technology, if not misused for ignoble purpose, is neither servile nor robot, but a phenomenon of our intellect, an extension of human expression on a significant scale. Gropius was aware that the age of technology has brought new social objectives into the realm of possibility. He demonstrated a new way of living. He used the new technology to instrument a renewal of life. Since then, we have largely been content to employ technical potential for very limited and largely formal objectives. And this contentment occurs at a time when technological and population pressures are hitting our cities with the ruthlessness of a nature force, knocking any mandarin illusions of grandezza into shambles.

284

The lessons of the Bauhaus for us today are that we can no longer afford to ignore the formulation of human programs bold enough to be worthy of our technical ability. True homage to the Bauhaus demands a redirection of architectural effort towards the synthesis between art and life in terms of the second machine age, and with the same seriousness of purpose that imbued the masters of the Bauhaus.

For a biography of Mr. Kallmann see page 278.

285

INDEX

Adler, Dankmar 29, 93
Afro (Basaldella) 255
Albers, Anni 235
Albers, Joseph 236, 238, 239,
   242, 254, 276, 277
Anders, Karl
   The Outdatedness of Man 268
Aristotle
   Metaphysics 3
art nouveau 88, 250, 271
Arnheim, Rudolf
   Art and Visual Perception 198
Arp, Hans 254
Ashbee, C. R. 31, 32, 36
automobile 2, 60, 66, 71, 73, 189,
   194, 195, 262, 264

Baker, Ray Stannard
   Adventures in Contentment 75
Banham, Reyner 252, 269, 282
   Theory and Design in the First
      Machine Age 269
Bauhaus School of Design 22, 131,
   275
   Gropius, Walter 22, 131, 224,
      230-243, 244, 247-248,
      253, 257-258, 266, 270-273,
      274, 275, 276-277, 282-283,
      285
   Meyer, Hannes 115, 131, 240
   Mies van der Rohe, Ludwig 115,
      131, 133, 154

Bayer, Herbert 235, 238, 239, 243,
   254
Beaux Arts 118, 173, 175, 196, 234,
   270
Beehive Department Store 256
Behrens, Peter 14, 109, 113, 129,
   131, 135, 158, 159, 211, 252
Bellamy, Edward 68, 69
   Equality 69
Bemis, F.
   The Evolving House 203
Bergson, Henri 3, 267
Berlage, Hendrik Petrus 95, 130
Boccioni, Umberto 252, 271
Bock, Richard 30, 31
Borsodi, Ralph 70
Breuer, Marcel 238, 239, 253, 255,
   274, 277
Brownell, Baker 67, 70, 72
Burnham, Daniel 65
Burton, James 21, 22
Butler, Samuel
   Erewhon 70

Calder, Alexander 256
Canaday, John 238
Carnap, Rudolf
   Logical Build of the World 279
   Theories of Verification 279
Casson, Sir Hugh 44
Carlyle, Thomas 29, 77, 79

Comey, Arthur C. 60, 63, 73
constructivism 102, 119, 121,
    122, 275
Cooper Union 244-246
Cottage industries 70, 259-260
Crystal Palace 21, 200
cubism 11, 14, 22, 88, 181,
    182, 250, 252

decentralization 55, 57, 69
Deutsche Werkbund 113, 141,
    252, 272
Dobson, John 21, 22
Duchamp, Marcel 11, 252

Eiffel, Gustave 9, 275
Emerson, Ralph Waldo 28, 29,
    32, 33, 34, 37, 68, 70, 79
    "Art" 28, 36, 246
expressionism 252

Feininger, Lyonel (Lux) 234, 235,
    242, 252, 253
Fibonacci see Pisa, Leonardo da
Fitch, James Marston 282
"form follows function" 22, 44,
    149, 282
Fourier, Charles 69-70
Friedell, Egon 231
Froebel, Friedrich 25, 29, 33,
    238

Fuller, Buckminster 269, 275, 283
functionalism 250, 252, 266, 271

Gabo, Naum 256
garden cities 46, 50, 68
Garnier, Tony 22, 66
Gaudi, Antonio 22
Geddes, Patrick 13, 261
George, Henry 57, 69, 73
    Progress and Poverty 69
Gesell, Silvio 69
    Natural Economic Order 69
Ghyka, Matila 201, 202
Giedion, Sigfried 251, 252, 253
Gropius, Walter 14, 18, 20, 22, 41,
    45, 48, 51, 109, 110, 113, 114,
    118, 129, 131, 146, 151, 154, 211,
    216-285
Buildings
    Bauhaus at Dessau 237
    Berlin villa 240
    Fagus Works 247, 252
    Grand Central-Pan American
        Building 53, 253
    theater in Jena 239
    The Architects' Collaborative
        247, 253, 254, 274
    Baghdad University 254
    Harvard Graduate Center
        254
    Littleton School 254
    Needham School 254
    UNESCO Headquarters 255

Gropius, Walter continued

Buildings continued

Projects and experimental
designs
experimental building,
Bauhaus exhibition,
1923 239-240
slab building for the
Berlin Exhibition of
the Interbau 273
Stadtkronehalle project
275
Wannsee apartment house
272

Writings and books
Idee und Aufbau 276

see also Bauhaus
Grosz, George 113

Haussmann, Georges 46, 186
high rise buildings 38-43,
44-54, 124, 191, 260
Hilberseimer, Ludwig 105, 114,
115, 143, 274
Hoffman, Josef 33
Horta, Victor 22
Howard, Ebenezer 44, 53
Husserl, Edmund
Phenomenology 279
Huxley, Julian 220

International Congress of Modern
Architecture 68, 259, 260, 274,
279
The Social Basis for Minimal
Dwelling: Flat, Middle, or
High? 260
International Style 14, 41, 109, 253
impressionism 17
Itten, Johannes 235, 238, 251

Jefferson, Thomas 48, 68, 84, 90, 91
Johnson, Philip 101, 127, 269
church in New Harmony, Indiana
241
Jones, Owen
A Grammar of Ornament 179

Kahn, Louis 122, 280, 281
Kandinsky, Wassily 214, 235, 242, 253
From Point and Line to Plane
276
Karnap, Rudolf see Carnap, Rudolf
Kepes, Gyorgy
The Language of Vision 283
The New Landscape 283
Kerr, Alfred 233
Kiesler, Frederick 250
Cite dans l'Espace 280
Klee, Paul 232, 235, 242, 253, 277
Pedagogical Sketchbook 276
Klimt, Gustave 34
Kropotkin, Peter Alexeivich
Fields, Factories and Workshops 70

Le Corbusier (Charles-Edouard
    Jeanneret) 14, 18, 20, 22,
    41, 46, 47, 48, 50, 51, 52
    53, 68, 74, 88, 98, 99, 109,
    110, 111, 113, 114, 118, 121,
    129, 131, 146, 151, 154, 158,
    164-215, 247, 249, 259, 260,
    274
Buildings
    Brasilia 46, 187, 192
    Brazilian Pavilion, Cite
        Universitaire 176, 181
    Chandigarh 46, 98, 182,
        187, 191, 192, 203,
        270
    Chapel at Ronchamp (Notre
        Dame du Haut) 111,
        112, 176, 177, 181,
        182, 187
    Maison Domino 208, 209,
        213
    Maison a Garches 210
    Maison Jaoul 212
    Maison aux Mathes 210
    Maison la Roche 210
    Maison Sarabhai 213
    Maison a Stuttgart 210
    Ministry of Education and
        Health, Rio de Janeiro
        187
    Nantes apartments 168-169,
        192
    Saint Mary's Convent at La
        Tourette 176, 187, 270
    Swiss Pavilion, Cite Univer-
        sitaire 181, 187

Le Corbusier (Charles-Edouard
    Jeanneret) continued
    Unite d'Habitation, Marseille
        46, 47, 49, 176, 181, 188,
        201, 203, 213, 214
    Villa Savoie 115, 182, 210
Projects and experimental designs
    Citade dos Motores 187
    Lima and Bogota 187
    Pavillon de l'Esprit Nouveau
        208, 209
    radioconcentric city 64,
        164 - 165, 169, 170, 171
    Rio de Janeiro and Algiers
        187, 203, 214
    Saint Die 46, 187
    Ville Contemporaine, Salon
        d'Automne, 1922 185-186,
        187, 189, 190, 195
    Ville Radieuse 45, 46, 186,
        211, 214, 274
    Voisin Plan for Paris 45,
        46, 186, 209, 214

Writings and books
    Creation is a Patient Search:
        a Self-Portrait 179
    "Five Points of a New Archi-
        tecture" 209
    Modulor 196
    Une Petite Maison 175
    Vers une Architecture 183
    When the Cathedrals Were
        White 45

"Civilization Machiniste" 174
Modulor 169, 196-204, 214
new brutalism 98, 250, 269, 281

Ledoux, Claude-Nicholas 20-21,
    66-67
Leger, Fernand 180, 181
Lehmbruck, Wilhelm 119, 156
L'Eplattenier, Louis 172, 179
linear city 60, 64, 68, 165, 169,
    170
Lippold, Richard 254
Lynes, Russell 31

Mahler, Alma 251
Malevich, Kasimir 102
Marcks, Gerhardt 235, 251
Meyer, Adolf 235, 253
Meyer, Hannes see Bauhaus
Mies van der Rohe, Ludwig 14, 18,
    20, 22, 23, 41, 48, 49, 51, 52,
    53, 93-163, 247, 249, 250,
    252, 257, 260, 274, 281

    Armour Institute of Design 261
      see also Illinois Institute
        of Technology
    "G" magazine 113
    "less is more" 53, 118-123,
      127, 129, 159
    Buildings
      Barcelona Pavilion 95, 100,
        105, 109, 119, 133-135,
        155-156, 159, 161-162
      Detroit Gratiot Quarter
        (Lafayette Park) 143, 274
      860 Lake Shore Drive 125-
        128, 142-143
      Esters house 133

Mies van der Rohe, Ludwig
  continued
  Buildings continued
      Federal Center 142, 144
      Illinois Institute of Techno-
        logy 95, 101, 102, 103,
        105-108, 115, 116, 139,
        141-142, 144, 159, 160
      Kroller house 129, 132
      Lange house 133
      Lemcke house 137
      McCormick house 139-140
      Newark apartments 125
      Promontory apartments 125
      Seagram Building 52, 78,
        111, 121-122, 125
      Tugendhat house 115, 130,
        136-137, 154, 156-157,
        158
      Wolf house 133

  Projects and experimental designs
      Alexanderplatz project 141
      Berlin Building Exposition
        demonstration house 135,
        136
      brick country house 114, 132,
        133
      Chicago Convention Hall 144
      concrete country house 114,
        133
      concrete office building 114
      curved glass skyscraper 114
      prismatic glass skyscraper
        111, 114
      Resor house 138-139

  see also Bauhaus

291

Milan Cathedral 198
Miro, Joan 254
mobility 8, 262, 264
modernism 14
Moholy-Nagy, Lazlo 235, 238,
    253, 261, 274, 277, 283
    New Vision 275
    Vom Material zur Architektur
    276
Mondrian, Piet 101, 119, 159,
    250, 266
Montessori, Maria 238
Morris, William 21, 22, 29, 33,
    70, 95, 259
    A Factory As It Might Be 70
Müche, George 235
Mumford, Lewis 268
Museum of Modern Art 67

neoplasticism 250
Neutra, Richard 260
Newcastle Station 21
New Towns 5, 46, 50

O'Keeffe, Georgia 34
Olmsted, Frederick Law 65, 66
order and chaos 2-5, 96, 150-
    151, 216-217, 220-221,
    234, 258, 270
Oud, J. J. P. 109
Ozenfant, Amedee 179, 181

Panofsky, Erwin 159
Paris World's Fair of 1889 9
Paris World's Fair of 1925 180
Parthenon 5, 52, 183
Paxton, Joseph 21, 22, 200, 203
Pentagon building 190
Perret, Auguste 10, 13, 14, 179, 184
    234, 275
Peterhans, Walter 105
Pevsner, Nikolaus
    The Masters of the Modern
    Movement 259
Piazza San Marco 144, 228
Piazza San Pietro 229
Picasso, Pablo 17, 18, 48, 88, 172,
    180, 234, 255
Pisa, Leonardo da (Fibonacci)
    200, 202, 204
Pittsburgh's Golden Triangle 187
Plato 161, 163, 169, 198
population explosion 2, 146-147, 262,
    267, 284
post-impressionism 17
Pugin, Augustus 21, 29

railway terminals 9, 21
Richardson, Henry Hobson 65, 95
Richter, Hans 113
Rivera, José de 256
Rudolph, Paul 152
Ruskin, John 21, 29, 33, 68, 77
    Seven Lamps of Architecture
    177

Sant' Elia, Antonio 22
Schaper, Hinnert 251
Schawinsky, Xanti 235
Scheerbart, Paul
    Glasarchitektur 252
Schinkel, Karl Friedrich
    94, 130-131
Schlemmer, Oscar 235, 238,
    253, 254, 272
Scott, Geoffrey
    The Architecture of Humanism
    245
Sert, José Luis 252
Sezession 33
Stein, Clarence 44, 53, 143
Stijl, De 60, 101, 182, 250, 252,
    271
Sturm, Der, magazine and gallery
    251
Sullivan, Louis 10, 14, 22, 25,
    29, 31, 36, 39, 43, 48, 65,
    66, 88, 93, 154
    Auditorium building 29, 30
    Schiller Theater 30
    Schlesinger Building 154
    Transportation Building 10, 31
Summerson, John 177, 181

Tange, Kenzo 280
teamwork 33, 110, 182, 226-228,
    240-241, 248, 258, 278
Tennesee Valley Authority 64
Trans World Airlines Building 78
Tzara, Tristan 113

Unwin, Sir Raymond 44
utopia 5, 22, 74, 163, 190, 205,
    212-215

van Doesburg, Theo 101, 156, 250,
    252
van de Velde, Henry 282
Vignola, Giocomo da 166-167
Viollet-le-Duc, Eugène
    Essays 29, 31
Vitruvius (Marcus Vitruvius
    Pollio) 199, 201, 245

Wagner, Otto 33
Whitman, Walt 65, 68, 70
Worlds Fair (A Century of Progress)
    Chicago, 1933 66
World's Fair (Columbian Exposition)
    Chicago, 1893
    10, 30, 66, 89
Wotton, Sir Henry 245
Wright, Frank Lloyd 14, 18, 20, 22,
    24-92, 95, 100, 101, 106, 110,
    114, 118, 131-132, 133, 138,
    146, 147, 158, 247, 249, 257, 260
    Organic architecture 57, 59
    pre-Columbian architecture 29,
        88, 89
    Taliesin 32, 34, 35, 38, 67, 90, 91
    Buildings
        Barnsdall house (Olive Hill) 34
        Browne's Bookstore 32
        Coonley house 32, 73, 90

293

Wright, Frank Lloyd
  continued
  Buildings continued
    Coonley playhouse 33
    Dana house 32
    Ennis house 88
    Fallingwater (Kaufmann
      house) 35, 41, 90
    Guggenheim Museum 15,
      27, 89
    Heller house 31
    Imperial Hotel 33
    Johnson Wax tower 40, 41
    Larkin Building (destroyed
      1950) 101
    Martin house 32
    Midway Gardens (destroyed
      1923) 32-33, 36
    Millard house 34, 88
    Price tower 40, 41, 50, 51
    Robie house 101, 115
    Thurber Art Gallery 32
    Unity Temple 32
    Usonia houses, Ardmore, Pa.
      60
    windmill 39, 40
    Winslow house 30

  Projects and experimental
    designs
    Broadacre City (Broadacres)
      46, 48, 49, 50, 55-75,
      79, 82

Wright, Frank Lloyd
  continued
  Projected and experimental designs
    continued
    Chicago City Club Residential
      Development 60, 61, 65
    Crystal Heights Hotel 50
    Illinois Building (Mile-High
      Skyscraper) 41-43, 48,
      51, 79
    Luxfer Prism Building 43
    National Life Insurance
      Company tower 48
    Quadruple Block 81
    San Francisco Call Building
      39, 48
    St. Mark's in-the-Bouwerie
      Apartments 40, 49, 50, 60

  Writings and books
    An Autobiography 35, 77
    An Organic Architecture 72
    Architecture and Modern Life
      72
    The Disappearing City 65, 67
    The Living City 67
    When Democracy Builds 49, 67

Wright, Henry 282
Zeising, Adolf
  Neue Lehre von dem Proportionem
    des Menschlichen Korpers 200

LIST OF CONTRIBUTORS

Anthony, Harry A.   Potentials of the Skyscraper-Studded Park
Anthony, Harry A.   The Influence of Le Corbusier

Barzun, Jacques   The Architect and the Aspirations of His Day
Blake, Peter   A Conversation with Mies
                          (edited by Gerhardt M. Kallmann)
Blake, Peter   People, Mass Production, and the Miesian
                          Universal
Brenner, Daniel   Mies, the Educator
Brownson, Jacques   The Urban Space Concepts of Mies van
                          der Rohe

Chermayeff, Serge   Let Us Not Make Shapes: Let Us Solve
                          Problems
Churchill, Henry S.   The Social Implications of the Skyscraper
Colbert, Charles R.   Conformity, Chaos, and Continuity
Collins, George R.   Broadacre City: Wright's Utopia Reconsidered
Creighton, Thomas H.   Walter Gropius and the Arts

Dearstyne, Howard   Miesian Space Concept in Domestic
                          Architecture
Dow, Alden B.   The Continuity of Idea and Form

Fitch, James Marston   Architecture and the Avant Garde
Fitch, James Marston   Mies van der Rohe and the Platonic
                          Verities
Fitch, James Marston   Wright and the Spirit of Democracy

Genther, Charles   Habitats for American Cosmopolites
Gropius, Walter   Unity in Diversity

295

LIST OF CONTRIBUTORS
(continued)

Heald, Henry T.   Mies van der Rohe at I. I. T.

Johnson, Philip   A Personal Testament

Kallmann, Gerhardt M. Lessons of the Bauhaus for the Second
            Machine Age
Kallmann, Gerhardt M. New Perspectives for the Second
            Machine Age
Kaufmann, Edgar, Jr.   The Fine Arts and Frank Lloyd Wright

Le Corbusier   A Talk to Students
            (translated by Charles Rieger)
Le Corbusier   Convocation Address
            (translated by Richard Arndt)

Manson, Grant   Frank Lloyd Wright and the Tall Building
Moholy-Nagy, Sybil   Has "Less Is More" Become "Less
            Is Nothing"?

Rogers, Ernesto   Villa, Townhouse, and Unité: the
            Utopian Spectrum

Sert, Jose Luis   Le Corbusier and the Image of Man
Shaw, Esmond   The Influence of the Bauhaus
Smith, Norris   The Domestic Architecture of Frank
            Lloyd Wright
Sweeney, James J.   The Corbusian Trinity

von Eckardt, Wolf   The Bauhaus in Weimar

Wittkower, Rudolf   Le Corbusier's Modulor

296